THE BIGGER PICTURE SERIES-VOL.1

THE NEW
5D HUMAN

*A MULTIDIMENSIONAL
PERSPECTIVE ON THE RISE OF
HUMAN CONSCIOUSNESS AND OUR
KARMIC JOURNEY THROUGH THE
SHADOW OF THE CURRENT
3D WORLD!*

Andie SantoPietro

Andie SantoPietro / 5DHU Press
www.andiesantopietro.com

Cover design by Andie SantoPietro and
Patsy Balacchi, Zenotica
Front cover photo and "swan" photos on pages 157–8
© Andie SantoPietro
"Lemuria" back cover painting © Greer Jonas. Used by permission.

Library of Congress Control Number 2022917745

The New 5D HUman / Andie SantoPietro – 1st ed.
ISBN 979-8-9866647-0-5

Diane of Aveidon
For Lifetimes of Camaraderie,
Crazy Life Missions, and
Unwavering Love & Support...
I Love You, My Dear Friend.

Jonathan III of Aveidon

CONTENTS

NOTICE:
5D Upgrades in Process!

This Book Contains High Frequency Words and Source Code Light and Love.

Do not Drive or Operate Heavy Machinery While Reading. ;-)

FOREWORD
STEVE ROTHER

I first met Andie during a private session. After just a few minutes, I realized that there was a deeper connection than most and the communication between us was wide open. I guess you could call it being kindred spirits, but it was deeper somehow, as if our spirits were remembering each other. The group I channel calls this a *reunion of spiritual family*. There is a lot of it going on during these transformative times on Earth. Each time one of these reunions takes place, it helps to reset everyone involved to remember what they came here to do. It puts them back on track so to speak. Such was the case with my introduction to Andie SantoPietro.

Humanity is experiencing a slow, sometimes painful dimensional shift. Of course, from a larger perspective it is all happening in the blink of a cosmic eye. Change is everywhere as the norms that hold your world together are slowly dissolving. The word *unprecedented* is being used unprecedentedly. Change is no longer at hand, but fully underway. This is the dimensional shift from the third to the fifth dimension. Unfortunately, no one said it was going to be easy and easy it is not, especially for those leading the way. It seems that HUmans often leave deep scratch marks on the things they finally let go of when faced with change. But in the midst of all the chaos, there is good news.

There are expert spirits that have incarnated to help others walk through these transformative times. Even when the light is split into light and shadow, there are spirits who can walk that path and span the gap to assist others in the ultimate journey. This dawns a new light. Andie SantoPietro is one of these people. Carrying the ability to walk between the worlds as a TransDimensional Healer can be difficult. But our struggles often bring forth our highest gifts. In Andie's case, it is the gift of a hand to hold as we HUmans take this big step up. When you can see both sides of duality, you can clearly see the *Bigger Picture*.

What you hold in your hands is a guidebook to what is ahead and how you can prepare. It offers an empowering perspective of the changes we all face right *now*. It offers a vision of hope for our time. No, you're not going crazy, you're just evolving—and by the way, it's not just *you*. All of HUmanity is moving as well. That is, unless they get scared and hang on too tight.

Well done, Andie. We all win when one of us steps up into the light. It is with the pride of a father that I *now* say to you: *Espavo* (A Lemurian term meaning "Thank you for taking your power").

Steve Rother
Author, Spiritual Teacher, Channeler, Proud Father
www.espavo.org

Steve Rother *has been channeling the Group for over twenty-five years. He has been a beacon of light and a bellwether of Earth's current paradigm shift. Author of seven books translated into eighteen languages, including* Re-member *and* Spiritual Psychology. *Five-time presenter at the United Nations. Creator of Espavo TV. His 5D Ascension/LightWorker Seminars have been held in twelve countries around the world.*

INTRODUCTION

Back in 2015, shortly after my students graduated from *"The Golden Bridge,"* my *5D Consultant Training Program*, I found myself slowly pivoting away from teaching and mentoring work. Although I still very much enjoyed working with clients individually, I no longer had the same desire to lecture or hold classes anymore. I wasn't downloading any new information or receiving any new *marching orders* that I felt inspired by.

Part of me accepted the work change but another part of me felt a little lost. For the first time in decades, my career's GPS didn't indicate the next turn to take, and my guides weren't giving me any higher *directions*. With nothing clearly showing itself on the horizon, I assumed that my professional life as an *Earth-based LightWorker* was beginning to wrap up.

A few years later, while I was putting the final touches on my plans to move out of New York City to a beautiful island in the Caribbean, my life came to a *screeching halt*. The world around me was beginning to explode as scattered COVID outbreaks were quickly turning into a global pandemic.

As we all waited in isolation at home—*which felt like it would last forever*—nothing seemed to be making much sense anymore. Riveted to our TV sets, we watched surreal political dramas unfold. We witnessed a society unraveling due to misinformation, violence, and panic. Sharp social views compounded the chaos further. Everything was rapidly spinning out of control and fear was spreading much faster than the virus itself.

Like everyone else, I struggled through many crying jags because I felt confused, scared, and, at times, angry. After all these decades of working towards 5D Ascension, countless hours of self-introspection, healing, and pursuing spiritual growth: *"What the hell just happened? What was the friggin' point of it all?!"* At times, I felt betrayed by HUmanity, but even more so by some of my own beliefs about what could be possible for our *now* devolving, out-of-control world.

The situation on the planet was so dire that although almost three years had passed since I had taught my last class, I felt *called* to reach out to my *peeps* and offer an online class about the coronavirus so we could look at it through the lens of a broader *spiritual* perspective. What started out in March 2020 as just *one* online class had by February 2021 turned into a *thirteen*-class series titled *"The Bigger Picture."*

Once a month, for over a year, these classes covered the most pressing issues of the period, from the ongoing pandemic and the crazy world of USA politics to social unrest, systemic racism, and more. We were covering the headlines as they occurred and working with a variety of approaches on how to best cope with it all personally.

INTRODUCTION

For me, what was very different about these classes was that I was not only addressing very serious, real-life HUman events, but I was also doing it from the much broader *spiritual* perspective. As I began to align other, more spiritually based components to my teachings to provide a backdrop for what was happening, things that seemed random and senseless in the mundane world began to fall into place and make a *little* more sense to me and my students.

Although, the world was undergoing a massive shakeup, contrary to how everything *appeared,* HUman consciousness was actually *evolving.* At an unprecedented rate, more people than ever were waking up from eons of living with their consciousness on *dim* and their dreams, desires, rights, and happiness held captive.

The rise in consciousness, and the subsequent *paradigm shift* that occurred, were actually *triggering* the disruption and chaos that were exploding all around us. As HUmanity was *waking up, collectively* they also brought with them a multitude of old *Karmic circumstances* that also needed transmuting. And if they *chose,* they could use these events as a conduit for evolving any remaining miscreations left over from their eons of lifetimes spent in 3D *(un)*consciousness.

I have come to understand that, as reflected in these pages, *if used well*, many of the players on our current world stage, all the unfathomable events occurring around us, as well as *your* own *personal life's challenges* can serve as a *poultice* that's drawing to the surface all that no longer supports your highest good or the *new 5D HUman* vibration into which your *soul* has grown.

As you will discover, many of these *seemingly* unrelated events, actually tie perfectly into the unprecedented rise that is currently unfolding in the *collective consciousness* on Earth.

We are in a profound time on the planet *not* just because of all the horrible, out-of-control things that have happened and are still happening, but because of all the equally amazing *capabilities* that we *now* have access to as advanced *5D Earth HUmans*. Never before were Earth HUmans able to carry as much God-Light in their physical bodies as we are *now* able to do because of our new HUman vibrational makeup.

Our upgraded HUman is able to move back and forth through several dimensions of consciousness while remaining grounded in the same body and lifetime! This is a *miraculous* period in time, and I know that many of my readers have chosen to incarnate *now* to finally experience this evolutionary leap after working towards this milestone for so long.

As part of this *post-12/12/12* 5D Ascension period, we are once again being *"called"* into higher service and asked to *"hold the space"* so that the *Shadow side of HUmanity* can also surface, as it too is trying to make its way back to the Light.

In 5D, it's the *"heart"* that *now* leads the way. Your willingness to be present, awake, and embrace *"The Bigger Picture,"* including the Shadow part of life as well as the Lighted side, will allow for the vibration of **Love** to enter and our Earth's HUmanity to evolve. But *most* importantly, it will allow *you* to compassionately birth your own *new 5D HUman.*

My classes and the chaos, along with the worldwide 5D HUman *"birthing crisis"* that we are all going through became both the foundation and inspiration for this book. I humbly found myself a scribe, channel, and guide for a *moment in time* where current events directly crossed *timelines* with our past spiritual history. The Karmic meeting of the two turned out to provide some key pieces to the *back story* of LightWorkers, as well as my personal journey from the fall of Lemuria and Atlantis until *now*. Some of these past-life stories I will share with you in this book.

I *now* know why *(for me)* the international airports all shut down just two weeks before I was scheduled to leave the country back in 2020. It was my destiny to write *The new 5D HUman*. If it were not for the fallout from the global pandemic I might never have penned it. I would have probably been living on a Caribbean Island and taking in the sun's rays every morning while *reading* a really good book instead of *writing* a very important one.

You too, *yes,* **YOU,** are a very important and integral part of this 5D Ascension mosaic. Some of my readers have come to this planet disguised as LightWorkers, others as ShadowWorkers, but more often in less conspicuous roles, such as Mom, Dad, Nurse, Neighbor, Bus Driver, Waitress, Cashier, and others, to be here *now* for what most of us waited thousands and thousands of years for, to assist Earth's HUmanity in our epic evolutionary transition out of 3D consciousness and into a 5D world.

As you read through this book, you will be taken on a journey. Please note it is specifically from *my* point of view as it was presented to me throughout the many years of my work. It's a compilation of real-time events and people, decades of being a 5D Ascension guide for HUmans, and how it all dovetailed into my memories of my past life in Lemuria. It's about the story of LightWorkers here on Planet Earth and the emerging consciousness of the new 5D HUman. But woven throughout it all is a *guidebook* that will help validate and support your experiences, assist you in managing Earth life, and *remind* you to nurture this very significant incarnation that is occurring during one of the most tumultuous times on the planet. If you are still a little bit *asleep*, the information will help wake you up; and if you are already *up,* the information will help to keep you awake. Like an alarm clock, you and your guides have set the teachings to *remind* you only when *you* are ready to stretch and rise.

As you read further, you will often find yourself connecting your own, *personal* dots. Service contracts, *soul* assignments, maybe even some past-life memories from *Lemuria or Atlantis* might begin to fall into place for you and you will see how they relate to your current life here on Earth. Each written passage is coded with the vibration of LOVE to gently assist you in growing into more of your amazing, incredible 5D HUman self.

I am honored to lend my support and Love, if only through the frequency of my written words. May this information help you make some sense during all these crazy times, head shaking twists, and mindblowing turns that come with the challenge of being a *"5D HUman Living in a 3D World."*

We are *now* all forever part of the same beautiful
mosaic of God's 5D Ascending Light.
We have been waiting for you.
Welcome back.
Espavo!

Andie, aka *Jonathan III of Aveidon, Lemuria*

A CHANNELED MESSAGE TO
THE READER

*"Earth to HUmans . . . Earth to 5D HUmans . . .
Come in 5D HUmans."*

We will start off our reunion by reminding you of this: There will be nothing bigger in your lifetime than what has been unfolding over the past few years on the planet. We lovingly say to you that this is not a fire drill. This is the real thing.

Everything that has culminated, leading up to 2012 and beyond, into 2021, is what you came to this planet to do. If you have found your way to this book, somehow you played a very important part in what unfolded on the planet between those two benchmarks of time here on Planet Earth. But even more importantly, your *soul's* contract to incarnate on this planet created the possibility for all those who *choose* to Ascend to the higher level of 5D consciousness to do so.

You incarnated with an intention to create a global miracle, a 5D Ascension on Gaia. Though you are all on this same mission, you have been veiled from each other and prevented from remembering the *bigger picture* truth. Just a couple years ago, 5D Ascension was just a possibility. Nobody knew how it was going to turn out or if you would even be able to accomplish your goal. Until it happened, even the higher powers that be didn't have the inside intel regarding the outcome. In 5D, the only real time that exists is the *"Now."*

To arrive at a successful 5D Ascension was considered a cosmic miracle because you basically had to create it from the inside out. Energetically speaking, you first had to build a new, higher frequency grid while still being plugged into a grid of a lesser frequency. The challenge of having to raise your individual frequency to a higher vibrational level while you were functioning and living your life in a 3D world was nothing short of *superHUman!* Up until this point on Earth, the *soul* had to be out of its "physical body" to make a vibrational shift that was of dimensional proportion.

This was a big deal. Individually you did this.
Collectively, you did this.

As challenging as it is for a single individual to Ascend while in physicality, to accomplish this feat with a mass collective of *souls* who were still embodied during the transition had the awe, admiration, and deepest gratitude from all the higher powers of the Multiverse. Galaxies of Lighted Beings throughout time and space have watched your every action, heard your every prayer, witnessed your every struggle, and caught your every teardrop with their great abiding Love for you. All sentient and nonsentient Beings are so humbled by all that you contributed to making the 5D Ascension possible.

Many of you readers have come from the past, while many others have come from hundreds of years in the future to be here for this period of time on Earth. Yes, you have joined us from the future—for in 5D, time is circular, not linear as you experienced it in 3D. You have come back with advanced skills and mastery honed from lifetimes and way beyond your limited 3D world's toolbox.

You have agreed to come back to live in a very challenging, much lower density field primarily to help stabilize the *vibrational rudders* of the Earth's grid and its HUmans as HUmanity moves through the final stages of its roughly 27,000-year journey towards the closing of the doors on your *now-expired* 3D lives. The second part of your assignment was to use your own life and all your personal experiences, both those of the Light and of the Shadow, to help HUmanity transmute polarity and Ascend into 5D consciousness.

Every single one of you, both those from the past and those from the future who were assigned as Earth-based volunteers, came in not only to raise the level of your individual consciousness but, ultimately, to elevate the collective consciousness. And through that process, you have inadvertently contributed your own raised frequency and Lightbody allowing for the evolution of consciousness for others to be easier and quicker. Your heartfelt efforts have made their *soul's* journey more accessible.

At the start of 2020, HUmanity was at a crucial fork in the road. It needed to wake up *quickly,* often to what felt like very inconvenient, even harsh realities and truths. This awakening was not only critical for Earth Humans' individual and collective *soul* growth, but for all the Planets, Galaxies, and Universes throughout existence. If it was not successful, the 5D attempt at Ascension could have signaled that Earth's HUmanity was too far into a descension; that somehow turning the dimensional "airplane" around was not even a possibility. The long-awaited "liftoff" associated with December 12, 2012 (or 12/12/12), was the official beginning of your 5D Ascended life. It also marked the end of your 3D world and life as you knew it.

As ominous as it sounds, for approximately the past 100,000 years or so, the mission of elevating the frequency of HUman consciousness to 5D has been your main Karmic calling, your *soul's* honored responsibility. Lifetime after lifetime, challenge after challenge, this mission is what you and Andie both came here to do. Period. Your 5D heart might not only start remembering some of this as you read these pages, but it will also come to understand that a miracle had taken place. And you—yes, YOU—were a big part in that miracle occurring.

Perhaps some of this information and dimensional jargon doesn't make too much sense to you yet, but as you continue to read it will. Know that right *now* we are not just addressing your HUman self; we are speaking to your Higher Self as well. YOU are part of a larger *soul* group that has assembled on Planet Earth. Many of you are being called to read these *bigger picture* transcripts and rejoin your *"5D family of Light"* here on Earth. As your HUman frequencies are being raised, activated, and expanded, you are also being *reminded* simultaneously of why you are here and what you incarnated to do. You are the first settlers, the pioneers of 5D consciousness on Earth.

A CHANNELED MESSAGE TO THE READER

There are an infinite number of *souls* on and off the planet (in and out of bodies) who are working on your behalf as members of your personal guide team. Many aspects of these *souls,* which include many aspects of your expanded Self, are not encased in a physical body that would severely limit their ability to accomplish their work. Whether embodied or disembodied, they are nonetheless working tirelessly on behalf of the Earth and all its resident HUmans for the *Soul* Assignments they were given.

Some of the Light Beings working on the planet's behalf will be introduced to you by name at different points throughout this book. The many that will remain unnamed are already speaking to you through the frequency of the TransDimensional scribe's HUman vibration, writings, and some of the specific words that will be used.

Information on these pages is coming from a Higher Source and its words and messages are vibrationally coded. You might encounter a specific passage and energetically connect with what you need to remember, release, or vibrationally tweak at that very juncture in your life. Someone else might read the same passage and experience something else. At those moments feel free to reread the passage as many times as needed, until you feel a Lightness, release, or completion of its download. It's very important that you pay attention to those signals, for in those moments we are speaking directly to YOU.

You are an elite member of the Multiverse's amazing group of LightWorkers, LoveWorkers, and ShadowWorkers. You planned this journey eons ago . . . and your current incarnation was always meant to be nothing short of the *trip of all your lifetimes!* You were needed here and specifically "chosen" for this 5D Ascension mission during this exact portal in time. You not only had the perfect "spiritual resume" for the job but most likely, have been on the front lines of massive evolutionary change time and time again and deserved to be here for this profound, unprecedented, Earth-based 3D–5D Ascension.

Claim your coveted seat at the table.
No Humility Required.
Welcome Back.

The *Bigger Picture* Multidimensional Guide Team

CHAPTER ONE

LIVING IN A MULTIDIMENSIONAL REALITY

What Is a Dimension?

A vast number of dimensions exist throughout Universal time and space, some already known to us, but many still unknown. Of the "twelve *main* dimensions" that currently exist, this book will be focusing specifically on 3D, 4D, and 5D. These three dimensions are currently impacting and directly shaping your everyday life as a HUman being on Planet Earth.

A dimension is not a *place*. When spiritually referenced, dimensions represent different levels or aspects of *consciousness*. When a large enough group of *energies* or *individuals* collectively vibrate to a similar frequency throughout time and space, a dimension is created. By reflecting the *totality* of a "collective consciousness," a dimension then *mirrors* what this group experiences as a *reality*.

The *frequency* of the energy of which each dimension is comprised includes all the *coding* that embodies thoughts, beliefs, emotions, actions, inactions, Karmic lessons, life experiences, *soul* experiences, and service contracts of every individual or entity who is a part of that overall collective. A dimension then takes on identifiable characteristics, such as shape, depth, time, space, and so forth. Sometimes it "resides" on one or more planets or in a star; other times, it resonates as part of a galaxy, constellation, or Universe. Based on its collective level of consciousness, each dimension will *hold* different percentages of collective Light and Shadow energy. At the higher rungs on the dimensional ladder, there is a greater concentration of God-Light/Source-Light and less of Shadow energy. Shadow energy consists of anything that is not 100 percent pure *Light or Love*. On the lower rungs, there is less God-Light/Source-Light and more Shadow energy. Each dimension represents another level of consciousness, a different combined frequency of the collective that it is mirroring. None is necessarily *good or bad*.

Your beautiful *soul* exists *simultaneously* in many dimensions of time and space, sometimes in the form of spirit and sometimes as an incarnated being with a physical body. The 3rd through 6th dimensions of consciousness are the only levels of consciousness that can sustain life in a *physical* body. No matter which realities your *soul* moves in and out of, or whether these are physical or nonphysical, each expression of your being always comes with experiences to grow, opportunities to evolve, and *assignments* that serve the greater whole. Access to the various embodied and spirit-based planes of existence allows each *soul* to *evolve* or *devolve* as it alters its own personal vibrational quotient of Light and Shadow.

Earth HUmans Are Some of the Highest Vibrational *Souls* in Service

Souls who have spent much of their existence in dimensions that require a "physical" body are not any less evolved than *souls* who have never served in a HUman incarnation. Quite the contrary. In fact, those who have had many lifetimes in HUman form are some of the most revered and honored *souls* throughout the Multiverse. The *Multiverse* is the ultimate *collective consciousness* as it reflects a combination of all known and unknown Universes, dimensions and infinite realms of potential, possibilities, and realities throughout time and space.

Taking on a HUman incarnation and committing to a *service-based lifetime* in which you assist in creating more God-Light/Source-Light throughout all the dimensions of consciousness is one of the most challenging of all *Love-based contracts*. To use your own life experiences, struggles, relationships, childhood, and the difficult array of HUman emotions you feel as a springboard for serving the highest good is nothing short of divine providence.

Each level of consciousness offers the *soul* a moment-to-moment choice to evolve into a more complete source of its own "God-Light/Source-Light." As we transmute pieces of our personal Shadow into Light, inadvertently we serve the higher good for we are all a part of the mosaic that makes up the dimension that we are "residing" in. This is how we reduce the amount of Shadow energy and all that's associated with it in that collective's particular dimension and concomitant reality. In addition, your 3D and 4D experiences also included intense *soul* work that immersed you *intentionally* in specific circumstances, some that were not just "your" Karmic creations but instead the Karmic miscreations on a *societal and ancestral level.* Experiencing these situations allowed your *soul* to be in vibrational resonance with many of life's very painful collective experiences. Taking on those issues as an individual was often part of your purpose here, as this allowed you the perfect vantage point to help transmute them from their lower Shadow state into a higher frequency of transmuted Light.

When enough of the balance of Light and Shadow has shifted in a given dimension, the consciousness of all the HUmans of that reality is also raised. The new elevated vibration creates an accelerated path for all others to walk once their *souls* are ready to evolve and carry a higher vibration of Light and consciousness. In addition, those whose vibration was already at the top end of their current dimensional realm, were able to rise to the next dimensional level, thus *Ascend*. This was the case in the massive *soul* exodus of 12/12/12, our long awaited *5D Ascension*.

None of your experiences was for naught. Every time you did your personal work or faced harrowing situations, you created the possibility for others, *if they choose,* to also evolve. This incarnation has been one of the most emotionally trying, physically exhausting and mentally confusing, even for the most evolved *souls* on the planet.

Multidimensionality: 3D, 4D, and 5D

The realities of 3D, 4D, and 5D are the crux of what is currently playing out in our lives and in the *cray-cray* world today. With each level of consciousness having its own very strong, distinctive perspective, their individual purposes have often collided. The friction between three dimensions at cross purposes has created a ripple of unbridled chaos throughout the consciousness of HUmanity, while at the same time acting as an unprecedented catalyst for some of the most profound awakenings, truths, and evolutionary opportunities that our world has ever experienced.

Living in a multidimensional world is not just about different groups of people residing in different dimensions and experiencing clear lines of delineation that define who they are and what they believe in. For those of us who are more conscious and awake, multidimensionality at times can feel like a bad, convoluted dream that we can't make sense of no matter how hard we try. Our expanded level of awareness combined with our *soul's* desire to experience everything as Love can make life on our planet feel pointless and, at times, hopeless and depressing.

And no, you are not *crazy, unevolved, or alone* in your experience. What we are witnessing *(as much as any reality is actually real)* are indeed certain realities that unfortunately *do* exist. And yes, at times our current world is both insane and horrible!

As beings of Light who are both *purposely veiled and vibrationally dialed down,* it is often difficult to make sense of it all, as our *soul's* work requires us also to live amid the chaos.

The ongoing confusion lies in the fact that you are a highly sensitive HUman, far away from home, who doesn't fully remember all the *spiritual logistics* of what your Earth visit is all about. Your *soul's* challenge here is not just to raise your vibration beyond the lower level of the world's consciousness, but to learn how to become a *multidimensional being* and simultaneously navigate life within the 3D, 4D, and 5D realities that coexist on Earth.

The 3rd dimension has been around for hundreds of thousands of years. It reflects both the most populated and visible level of Earth's mass consciousness today. Because it holds more Shadow energy than 4D and dimensions above it,

3D is where a lot of the pain, struggles, and injustices are born that we see being played out in our everyday lives and in the lives of others. This dimension is one of several very *real perspectives* that exist in our world today. It's comprised of the Light and Shadow components derived from *belief systems* that collectively reflect what is referred to as *3D duality consciousness.*

The 4th dimension is the level of consciousness that has the shortest stay on the planet, although it is the most significant in advancing our spiritual evolution. It serves as a temporary *bridge* reality, a place where 3D HUmans can deprogram from their first incarnation here, release old storylines, complete original contracts, transmute Karma, and raise their vibration gradually while also exploring new thoughts, beliefs, and feelings associated with their, soon to be, 5D HUman consciousness. Because of all the shifting, navigating, and conflicting ideologies, 4D can be a highly emotional weigh station for *souls* on the move, inadvertently, creating a lot of stress and chaos for *all* the other dimensions on the planet because of its chronic state of *4D polarity consciousness.*

The 5th dimension is the highest level of "collective" consciousness available on the planet today. Although 5D exists throughout many levels of the Multiverse, it wasn't a viable frequency for Earth HUmans to *physically* acclimate to until this past decade.

The long-anticipated planetary alignment on December 12, 2012 (12/12/12), became the target date for our world's modern-day 5D Ascension. This level of Ascension has been attempted before throughout existence, specifically on planet Earth, but without much success. Many, many variables, including massive assistance from the heavens, our solar system's astrological positioning and a large enough group of 3D/4D HUmanity had to be vibrationally *ready* to evolve into this higher dimension of God-Light/Source-Light. The feat of attaining this tier of spiritual evolution while still living in the same physical body we were born in was nothing short of a miracle for incarnated HUmans! Prior to the last twenty-five years or so, most 3D Earth HUmans did not have the physical, emotional, or spiritual capacity to sustain and carry a frequency of Light at such a high level. Although you might not identify with the 5D aspect of yourself yet, if you haven't tossed this book to the side by *now,* most likely you are *already* vibrating as a 5D HUman.

3D *Duality* Consciousness

The 3rd dimension has been on our planet for hundreds of thousands of years or more. Although 3D reality has encompassed varying levels of consciousness, from Neanderthals and up, the core characteristic throughout the levels has remained the same. *Each level of 3D consciousness is based on duality, a system of thinking and perception that is formulated by opposites.*

This system is easily identified through subjective definitions of experiences and feelings as either good or bad, right or wrong, healthy or sick, rich or poor, black or white, and eventually me versus you. Male or female, masculine or feminine, were complementary concepts that defined HUman sexuality and gender identity, as well as the "roles and rules" that 3D societies upheld. Night or day, happy or unhappy, and more, were the types of concepts that shaped and created our 3D world. Hardwired into this template of perceiving, it became the backbone of how we led our everyday lives and the primary measuring system for how we saw and experienced our world.

Contrary to much of our evolved thinking, 3D is *not* bad. Nor was any part of it ever wrong. As a matter of fact, 3D was a major evolutionary leap from the lower dimension of 2D towards restoring HUmanity's oneness. Like all dimensions, 3D only reflects the principles, tenets, and Light/Shadow quotient of the collective consciousness that creates and subsequently sustains it. No matter how spiritually advanced any of us might be *now,* the majority of us were born into a 3D life here and will have to, at some point, pass through aspects of 3D as we evolve into other, higher levels of consciousness.

All of us, at one time or another, have signed off on a *soul contract* to recreate, address, then transmute our *Shadow* creations from our prior 3D incarnations back into 100 percent pure Light. It is very possible, even common, for some HUmans to evolve very rapidly through various tiers of a 3D existence; but skipping it altogether, prior to the Ascension was highly unlikely. For it was through all the difficult and challenging lifetimes spent as a HUman in a physical body that we were able to transmute some of our *soul's* division of its own Light and in turn, HUmanity's separation from God. Without that process of transmutation, *as excessively long as it took,* we wouldn't have been able to Ascend consciousness to where it is today, with all Earth-based HUmans having access to 5D thinking, perspectives, frequencies, and world.

4D *Polarity* Consciousness

Think of a rubber band. When it's just sitting on a desk or table, there's no visible tension in it. If you begin pulling the band in two opposite directions, you will create tension just through the act of stretching it. Similarly, when you have two issues or strong perspectives that are based in opposition, the energy fields around them engage in an intense game of tug of war and they inadvertently become *polarized*. What we are experiencing on the planet today is like the act of pulling a rubber band in two opposing directions—the ends being representative of 3D and 5D mass consciousnesses—overstretched to a point of extreme tension and creating unprecedented chaos as they grow farther and farther apart.

The last decade in USA politics and elsewhere is a great example of the vast distance in consciousness between different groups of HUmans and their perceptions and beliefs. The tensions, uprisings, and breaking down of many of our longstanding systems, including our once iron-clad *"rule of law"* are both palpable and evident reflections of the paradigm shift that is underway from 3D to 5D.

Both 3D and 5D realities, although currently coexisting on Earth have overlapped and crossed over one another, eclipsing into what we are all experiencing as a 4D reality and level of consciousness. Often, seemingly volatile, this is the dimension which has become the chosen intermediate ground where a real-life epic resembling the plot of *Star Wars* is playing out.

Contrary to how our world often appears, 3D consciousness is taking its *final* lap on the planet. After tens of thousands of years existing as the main frequency of consciousness, Earth HUmans have finally outgrown it *vibrationally*. But just like third grade isn't any less important than fifth grade to a child's education, both grades have an important place on the Ascending ladder of the child's growth and advancement. Third grade is appropriate for eight-year-olds, and fifth grade is appropriate for ten-year-olds. Likewise, 3D is appropriate for *souls* whose vibration and consciousness are at a certain level and 5D is appropriate for *souls* whose vibration and consciousness are at another level.

At first, it's hard not to judge or even look down on 3D consciousness and a lot of their HUman members. But as you come to understand the challenges of multidimensional living, you will quickly realize that evolved or not, you too also move in and out of 3D consciousness, and you will for a while.

Consciousness is an alive entity. If a level of consciousness, personal or dimensional, senses its demise, it will make great efforts to fight for its life. That is what 3D consciousness is doing *now,* as it is starting to dissolve.

Simultaneously with this fight for survival, 5D is beginning to rise as the planet's new, higher-level template for consciousness. Back in 2020, all the shifts of frequency and the upheaval that followed created such vibrational discordance that the stretch placed HUmanity under tremendous pressure. Without having any real leadership, moral compass, or spiritual direction available to stabilize the process, both the world and many of us energetically *blew a fuse!*

On a mundane 3D-4D level, the world was creating often horrific levels of chaos, panic, hate, and fear, through experiences like the emergence of a novel deadly virus, global pandemic, and political discord, to name a few. At the same time, the same out of control set of experiences were also streaming elsewhere but on a different channel on a 5D level. The mindblowing aspects of what we experienced in our everyday lives on the *3D channel, as horrible as they were,* became an *opportunity* for the Universe to utilize those unexplainable events and reveal yet another possibility for why these were unfolding on the *5D channel.* Each very real situation that we were facing in the 3D world was being utilized and repurposed in a very significant way to consciously serve the highest good of planet Earth and all its precious HUmans. Unbeknown to us, the chaos and breakdown of our lives as we knew them was all a part of the *bigger picture* plan.

5D *Triality* Consciousness

As you transition from a 3D to a 5D vibration, the total experience at first can feel very disconcerting. Things that you once believed to be ensconced in hardcore truth are often first shaken, then afterwards blown to smithereens! This is the first time *ever* on Planet Earth that we have been able to make a quantum leap from 3D consciousness to 5D consciousness while still alive in the same physical body into which we were born. This is what makes the process we are undergoing both evolutionary and very profound. While still alive, the vibration or person you once were had to be released and *die off* so that you can transition into your higher-vibrational 5D self.

Throughout each lifetime, culminating in the current one, we've released eons of programming, storylines, and Karma from our emotional bodies, in turn gradually activating dormant aspects of our DNA. We repeatedly outgrew copious

26

old versions of who we *were* until we stripped down to a more accurate version of our "real" selves–spiritual beings beyond just our physical bodies and their perceived limited abilities.

The 5D Ascension journey that most of us have traveled has been lengthy, arduous, and taken a very big toll on most of us, especially in our physical and emotional bodies. Many of us have morphed our belief systems, thought patterns, and life experiences at warp speed, often at the expense of our nervous system, mental and emotional health, and overall well-being. Without a *bigger picture* understanding of what was unfolding, we weathered intense and continual waves of vibrational shifting. Our immune system was weakened, and often our self-worth mangled. An evolution of this magnitude did come with a price at times because we were pulling off something that had never been done before.

As we were raising the vibrational frequency of our own consciousness, by osmosis we also were raising the collective consciousness of HUmanity as each individual is ultimately a microcosm of the consciousness reflected in the greater whole of that dimension.

You Jump, *I Jump!*

You *cannot* shift any aspect of yourself without indirectly impacting other individuals or groups that vibrate to the same frequency. We *belong to* or are *in resonance* with numerous individuals, groups, clans, families, societies, and dimensional beings. The totality of your "consciousness" is therefore not limited to your spiritual reality. It is comprised of information related to your physical, emotional, and etheric bodies–of which there are several. As your thinking, perceptions, sexuality, likes, dislikes, and chromosomes (DNA molecules) go through radical shifts and changes, you will inadvertently raise or lower the collective level of those in resonance with you, as you are also impacted when other similar frequencies shift. Furthermore, when aspects of our *rising* frequencies are vibrationally met by similar *pings* from any source, the meeting makes higher frequency thought and Light more accessible to others who are also trying to raise their consciousness. By both holding and maintaining a higher vibration, we make it easier for people everywhere—*even those who live far away from us*—to rise and embody that higher frequency themselves.

Our spiritual energy travels through the etheric realms on a dimensionally structured vibrational grid. It doesn't require proximity or direct HUman to HUman contact to be received. It is as instantaneous as the speed of LOVE. The more we release and transmute our Shadow energies, the higher a frequency we hold, the more God-Light our *souls* expand into and are able to physically carry while on Earth.

This is the crux of the Ascension process. When we Ascend, we are energetically transplanting our HUman body into a more viable 5D container that is capable of holding more God-Light than our prior 3D HUman container could hold. The term *God-Light* is a way of describing the all-encompassing *soul* Light emanating from our existence's original blueprint. Prior to incarnating and being limited by compressing and squeezing into a physical finite form, we were all expansive, whole beings of one Light.

According to *Steve Rother and the Group,* those of us on the planet who have Ascended into a 5D HUman form are *now* comprised of *approximately* 20 percent God-Light (*spirit*) and

80 percent (*physical*) matter.[1] The physical self is our tangible HUman self, and the spiritual self inhabits the intangible, intuitive, and creative dimensions of our *soul's* expression. Contrary to how small this ratio of spiritual being to physical being might sound, it is the highest level *ever* of God-Light that a HUman on Earth has been able to retain.

Each of us has chosen to do our *soul's* work this time around as an Earth-based HUman being. Assigned to a *"boots on the ground"* platoon, as a HUman on our planet, you still require a physical body to contain and give the etheric aspects of your *soul grounding*. Physically, you can only contain so much of your high-frequency God-Light without imploding. And yes, there are some avatars and evolved Beings walking the Earth who are of 6D who carry more Source-Light than others, but it is rare to encounter these individuals, who are few and far between.

Ascending into a 5D frequency is much easier to do *after* you leave the body (post-incarnation) or *before* you enter the body (preincarnation) than it is to do while in the body. And even when the *soul* is unencumbered by a physical body, evolving into a higher frequency of Light or *soul* consciousness isn't automatic *just* because the *soul* is in spirit form. Even when in spirit, expanding into a higher frequency or consciousness level, *the definition of soul growth,* generally requires the *soul* to also move through several, incremental levels of out-of-body consciousness, whatever that might reflect for them. The *soul* evolves by transmuting its Shadow aspects (mostly our unconscious and conscious 3D miscreations) into Light. Achieving God-Light/Source-Light wholeness, *even outside of a constricting physical body,* always depends on the *soul's* state of consciousness.

When the *soul* is outside a body, it has experiences, assignments, and even lifetimes on other planets and galaxies besides Earth. Those are its evolutionary work. Although the *soul's* spurts of growth will happen at a different pace, on different levels and timelines, no matter where it is whether or not it is veiled and incarnated, every *soul* in existence has the same impetus to move towards God and Oneness which is our original state.

Year 2020 Was Our Tipping Point

What happened that contributed to the massive chaos on our planet over the past few years is that the planet's *exiting* 3D consciousness came head-to-head with its new *entering* 5D reality. While intensely moving in opposite directions, the two very different levels of thought found themselves overlapping, and at significant odds with each other. Stretched energetically, these two levels of consciousness put a tremendous amount of pressure on HUmanity, mainly because 3D consciousness was coming to its end. The monumental period of the old structure leaving while a *new order* was being formed has been both emotionally traumatic and disorienting for most of the Earth HUmans. Those who identify as LightWorkers or have extremely *sensitive personal vibrations* probably felt like they were losing touch with their *sanity* at one point or another.

What was different about what you experienced in the five years or so leading up to the year 2020? Whatever it was, it wasn't just *personal* anymore. The entire world responded to the "paradigm shift" by having a "collective meltdown" as many things simultaneously appeared out of control. The planet hit a vibrational tipping point that made the 5D Ascension of 2012 a tangible truth. A virus caused a pandemic that brought the world to its knees. Our familiar 3D reality and lifestyle were dissolving before our very eyes. The changes were an epic shock to our 3D HUman selves but, to our higher 5D *bigger picture"* selves, we intuitively knew something more profound was unfolding.

4D: Our Transitional Bridge to Higher Consciousness

The consciousness level of 4D acts as a bridge between 3D and 5D. This allows us a safe passage while we are evolving both individually and collectively. It's not intended to be a permanent destination for our consciousness. In Universal time the "stay" in 4D is considered a blink of an eye. In Earth time, the stay can last from several months to one hundred years or more.

The 1960s were a major turning point for 4D consciousness in much of the world, as many people began to expand how they perceived life, Love, sex, and the 3D status quo. It was then that a segment of the collective consciousness broke free, pivoted, and released some of the belief systems and subsequent restrictions of the 3D HUman. This was the first quantum leap of consciousness away from the monochromatic 3D thought culminating with the 1950s.

The level of consciousness in 4D provides *grist for the mill* for 3D HUmans who are expanding into broader emotional and spiritual aspects of themselves. This transitional consciousness is a safe space where HUmans on Earth can start to evolve beyond their 3D limitations and test new experiences. It allows them the time needed to catalog new emotional patterns, thinking, perceptions, beliefs, and frequency changes to their rapidly morphing 5D physical bodies. It is here where we begin to develop a new understanding of the HUmans, places, and things in our everyday lives and learn to view them from a higher, broader perspective.

The 4D consciousness of recent decades brought us the gifts of intuition, meditation, guides, past lives, therapy, healings, spirituality, alternative medicines, and *choice*. It also enabled us to connect to our *souls'* purposes so we could more easily interface with the Laws of the Universe and its *bigger picture* plans. 4D is also a safe place where you get to connect with a likeminded community of friends.

As we collectively began to both emotionally and spiritually wake from our 3D slumber, the newly evolved 4D consciousness of the heart and spirit found itself in an ongoing battle with the more dominant consciousness of the 3D world. Those with 4D resonance shook up the previously stable and unchallenged status quo of 3D reality, for the rise in consciousness produced a new generation of more *enLightened,* evolved HUmans who no longer vibrated to the constructs and rules of 3D.

Often appearing to be at cross purposes, 4D houses both those with a large part of themselves still identified with their 3D reality and those evolving out of it. This is the reason for the intensity and polarized reality that we have seen playing out in our world since 2015. Ironically, the higher 4D vibration (as opposed to 3D) on the planet is at present the main energetic reason why a lot of chaos unfolded in 2020. We have and will continue to witness 4D polarity for a while as it is reflected in politics, violence, social unrest, mental health issues, and medical emergencies like the COVID pandemic. All those areas of our *old life* are being upheaved as we bear witness to the energetic fallout from the world's 3D growing pains.

Although Earth-based HUmans have successfully experienced 4D consciousness in other historical periods, they have never collectively moved from it into a 5D level of consciousness. Prior to having a viable 4D steppingstone in place to help with the vibrational transition, there was no sustaining means for HUmans to ground themselves as their *souls* evolved into a higher composition of God-Light. HUmans back then were not able to transition into a 5D life at a frequency that was emotionally, spiritually, and physically safe and doable while still in an Earth body.

The most *challenging* dimension to navigate on the planet today is 4D. It poses a constant dilemma because it is here that we evolve through our choices, experiences, realities, perspectives, and ways of seeing life. Everything we once accepted at face value in 3D, such as marriage, sexuality, and gender roles, race, religion, privilege, HUman rights, and the *rule of law,* will come into question. You will find yourself going in and out of feeling challenged, specifically as you begin to *wake up.*

With each veil that lifts, a new level of truth will emerge and your newly awakened 4D *heart* will officially no longer allow you to be a passive bystander to life. This level of consciousness is where your HUman self begins to reach for a more authentic life. It gets harder and harder to suppress or ignore your wants and desires as they become the spiritual catalysts that lead you to move out of a life centered around *basic survival* in the limited and conditioned 3D comfort zone. You will become freer, more able to feel, Love, and advocate for your happiness on a much deeper level. It is also . . . *very scary* at times to have to face change of that magnitude.

Your 3D self, by becoming more aware of the *bigger picture* in play, expands into the knowing of a Universal higher power and a spiritually guided higher self. Uncovering this new level of truth from a more evolved place emotionally and spiritually creates a higher frequency of embodied Light and automatically moves you into a 4D resonance. This crucial stage of 4D development plays an integral role in supporting you through the evolutionary journey of your 5D Ascension.

The 5D Ascension:
Our Intergalactic Miracle and Then . . . *Fzzz*

Although our 5D Ascension culminated back on December 12, 2012, many of us thought that the most difficult parts of our 27,000-year journey to get there were behind us. It was an exciting passage in the spiritual community as we met our astrological launch date goal of 12/12/12 and successfully created a 5D Ascension on planet Earth. All our lifetimes of intense personal work and treacherous *soul* assignments had paid off. The 5D Ascension finally had happened . . . *for the most part.*

In the year 2015, everything began to unravel on the planet very quickly. The *faster timeline* of 5D began to take shape and move into position, seriously bumping the prior timeline sequencing from our old 3D lives. We didn't take notice at first, but over time nothing seemed to make much sense anymore. Aspects of daily reality started to feel surreal, as we were only just a few years past our "5D Ascension *miracle*." Could the afterglow have faded that quickly? Life on the planet was supposed to become really great, *not* horribly worse. Our collective consciousness Ascended and there was supposed to be a lot more Love, more God-Light and a higher caliber of HUmankind, right? *So, what the hell happened?!*

In part, when a dimensional plane goes through a steep upward incline or *Ascension,* after the progress levels off, it will go through a similar cycle of *descension.* What goes up, must come down. In retrospect, perhaps we just failed to contemplate the possibility of what *now* seems like an obvious trajectory? But more likely, most of the LightWorkers, including key players of the original 5D Ascension plan were veiled from anticipating the second act of this laborious mission. The impending descension was shielded from our foresight, intuition, and perception. In retrospect, it was a monumental blessing. If we all knew what was up ahead, it would have been mindblowing, devastating, and inconceivable to process the magnitude of the changes. It would have made no sense to us because the actual backbone of these past few years was to live out the reality before us, awake, conscious, and with the 3D emotional element of shock and disbelief so we could finally *release* it.

In addition, our post-5D Ascension period required all the *higher frequency* HUmans who had already Ascended into 5D consciousness, to come in for a landing, ground their new, higher vibration, and reintegrate their 5D selves into the still existent 3D world on the planet.

By 2015, a very palpable vibrational *polarization* began to take shape as we watched it visibly rise from a deep-seated core only to explode around us as the years and dramas progressed. *The higher frequency of Light and Love on the planet was actually the catalyst for all the subsequent chaos that was unfolding.* The frequencies of Light and Love always brings up anything unlike themselves. The higher vibrational energy of 5D consciousness acted like a poultice for HUmankind, drawing Shadow energy, circumstances, beliefs, and emotions to the surface where they could be seen, felt, and experienced.

Given the impact that all of the higher frequency, turbo-charged God-Light was having on the remaining 3D world, we were basically navigating in the dark, trying to make sense of what continually felt nonsensical. Even though we were on an extended journey to get here, by the time we arrived at the 12/12/12 launch mark, we had an exceedingly small window of time to move Earth's collective consciousness past the finish line of our spiritual goal, a 5D Ascension. It took millions of incremental, synchronized actions and shifts both on Earth and throughout the Multiverse to create the "perfect" moment in time that would allow for this new portal of 5D consciousness to fully open to the masses. Even with the level of perfection that only something greater than us could oversee and orchestrate, we still came very close to missing our Karmic opportunity once again.

On 12/12/12, we *technically* reached our 5D collective "altitude." Although airborne, we had no clue if we would be able to sustain, integrate, or maintain our elevated frequency without causing a significant amount of disruption in the coexisting 3D and 4D worlds.

CHAPTER TWO

FROM LEMURIA TO ATLANTIS

Spiritual *Law* and Divine *Order*

As more and more HUmans crossed over from 4D into 5D, in turn, it allowed a very large group of people who were occupying the *upper rungs* of 3D to also Ascend and move into a 4D level of consciousness. In fact, this multilevel paradigm shift created a domino effect throughout all the other tiers of the dimensional ladder.

Along with all those shifts of consciousness that the 5D Ascension process set in motion, it also bumped many lingering Shadow aspects left over from the Karmic history of our 3D past to the surface of 4D reality. These unresolved pieces of Earth's social Karma moved into our world's consciousness and eventually materialized in our day-to-day lives. Following the same channels that our personal Karma does when it is ready to be faced and addressed, it erupted all around us, reflected throughout everything from the world's political climate to our most intimate relationships.

Previously, 4D was often used as a short-term stopover while HUmans transitioned from 3D to 5D. Although *mass consciousness* didn't make its final *"group"* shift until 2012, many individuals led the way for the historic passage of 5D consciousness long before the portal opened. 4D is known to be an extremely *polarized* dimension. But prior to our recent Ascension, the multiple levels of beliefs it held were not occupied by a lot of *souls* at the same time so, even though it had a lot of space, it didn't pose too much risk of creating conflict.

Specific aspects of *social Karma* can only manifest when enough of a collective is present at the same time who have at one time been impacted, either directly or indirectly, by the circumstances that created the Karma during its original go-around. Residual Karmic storylines from our 3D timeline vibrationally seeded the world's current tumult and descension, including the political narrative of Donald Trump's Presidency starting in 2015 and the disassembling of many of the 3D democracies around the world.

Spiritual law is based on the premise of *like attracts like* and dictates that, if you want to alter or transmute any prior programming, event, or Karma, you first must be in resonance with at least an aspect of its frequency. Being in a more evolved place in your consciousness than where you were when all was first created, allows for the vibrational foundation and perspective needed to resolve it versus just repeating it. One of the main tenets of 3D is the existence of the Karmic law of *cause and effect.* As we began to enter the final stages of our process of Ascension from 3D to 5D, we needed to *recreate* the unfinished business of our 3D lives, both personally and socially, in order to transmute any remaining connected Karma.

A Karmic situation is *not* something that can be willed, forced, or summoned into play. It takes an alignment of millions of moving parts both in the seen world and the unseen world to manifest simultaneously in a single moment in time.

Before we could arrive at a successful 5D Ascension on Planet Earth, HUmanity, *particularly those in service,* had to have lined up people, the planet, and the Universe at the perfect coordinates to vibrationally overlap enough of the same *aspects* from original Karmic experiences that needed to be transmuted. Aligned, these individuals had to vibrate at a high enough level to contain a percentage of Source Light that would enable them to weather and eventually transmute the 3D/4D Karma that had been stirred up.

For thousands of years, 3D HUmanity has been working its way towards the time when HUman Lightbodies, consciousness levels, and all-around circumstances were in an alignment that would allow us to safely circle back, *Karmically speaking,* to a current reality mirroring our last attempt at a 5D Earth Ascension. Like a homeopathic dose of our 3D prior reality, reentering these circumstances allowed the planet a Karmic opportunity to recreate, experience, act, and then, hopefully, move past the last failed outcome and complete the healing of the old, unresolved circumstances and trauma.

During this incarnation, for most of us, our subconscious goals and *soul's* work has been to arrive at this place and time to transmute the current circumstances and ensure a successful evolutionary 5D Ascension this time around. Up until the moment it happened, we never knew for sure if we were going to be able to have a successful 5D Ascension.

If there was a *sLight* possibility that we were going to make our "connecting *fLight*" this time around, we had to marshal all the forces in the seen and unseen world to align with divine timing and then act swiftly and with laser precision. And even with all that higher assistance, still being a planet of *free will,* Earth could have only Ascended via the collective readiness and receiving a *green Light* from all its people.

Many of us who incarnated in this generation made the ultimate sacrifice to be here in HUman form during what was going to be an often emotionally taxing and turbulent set of circumstances. As part of our 5D Ascension *soul contracts,* we agreed to be the group to go first, like canaries in a vibrational coal mine. Long before we arrived, we agreed to do most of the "heavy lifting" to complete an Earth Ascension, which meant that we also were taking greater risks and addressing and facing massive amounts of "clean-up" Karma.

We had spent eons of lifetimes working towards this goal and did not want to repeat the errors and trauma that unfolded in the period leading up to the disastrous failure of our last attempt at 5D Ascension on our planet. This time around, we knew we had to be better prepared, more consciously awake, and program ourselves with *"source codes"* that were strong enough to help us survive the confusing upheaval that was going to come during an Ascension process of epic proportion.

What Are Source Codes?

Very similar to the way a bar code helps inventory managers and cashiers identify products, HUmans also are vibrationally coded with identifying markers or *source codes.* On a physical level, these source codes are found in our DNA and RNA. On an emotional level, they are reflected in our feelings, moods, temperament, reactions, and range of sensitivity. On a spiritual level, they connect us to our intuition, higher selves, and spirit-guide teams. Collectively using our navigational abilities as multidimensional beings, we are networked into the matrix of not only "our" game plan but also the *"bigger picture"* plan. Our source codes on all these levels are alive, active, and fluid.

They alter, change, shift, and get modified during and between incarnations, when we are both in and out of a body.

Source codes that are from our *soul's* original blueprint are very different. They are not fluid and are mainly constant. They record and store all our events, actions, deeds, thoughts, experiences, lifetimes, and so forth, for cataloging in the Multidimensional Library of the Akashic Records. HUman *soul* source codes rarely ever change during major Ascension or dimensional shifts, which, in and of themselves, are HUman anomalies.

None of us here who have worked on the frontlines for lifetimes was ever duped. We all knew the magnitude of what we were signing up for. Our *souls'* service contracts, long before we incarnated, clearly outlined the kinds of discomfort and pain that were potentially in store for each of us if we were to meet all our deadlines, timetables, and relay points in route to a successful 5D launch. LightWorkers assigned to the 5D Earth Ascension project were aware that coming down to Earth meant we would be entering into a lifetime of very intense experiences, childhoods, extreme highs and lows, massive changes, trauma, fears, confusion, and feelings of being lost, alone, and, at times, hopeless.

All these potential emotional challenges were byproducts of living in a physical body as a HUman. Emotions are not experienced the same way, if at all, when the *soul* is out of body. Although not *consciously* after we were born, we did know, to a certain degree well ahead of time (before we signed off on these contracts and reincarnated) of all the mindblowing twists that would come with life while on Planet Earth. We anticipated that the process of allowing our 3D spiritual and genetic source codes to morph into new 5D codes while remaining in the same physical body that had held the predecessor codes was going to pose an unprecedented challenge.

As a part of our service here, we agreed to condense into one crazy, accelerated incarnation all our remaining personal 3D Karmic lessons—many of which would otherwise have been distributed over *many* different lifetimes. In addition, many *souls* in very high positions took on double and triple assignments picking up ancestry, family, and societal Karmas to transmute. Those of us who have had some of the hardest and difficult lifetimes are some of the most Universally revered LightWorkers on the planet today. In order for us to have accomplished a successful 5D Ascension in 2012, many of us had to quadruple down and process more Shadow energy than the average HUman and carry some complexing realities that were going to manifest in the form of our daily trials, tribulations, traumas, pains, and dramas.

R U a HU from MU?

The last time we attempted a 5D Ascension on Planet Earth was 27,000 years ago. At the time, we were living on the lost continents of Lemuria and Atlantis. Lemuria, which is also affectionately known to many of us as *MU,* is *now* believed by some to be in many locations throughout the Pacific Ocean and Atlantis throughout the Atlantic Ocean. Just as we have *now,* the LightWorkers living back then had spent thousands of years and many, many lifetimes working to build an energetic portal, or *Light bridge,* so Earth HUmans could evolve more easily from a 3D to a 5D level of consciousness.

THE NEW 5D HUMAN

Everyone alive today is a genetic and energetic descendent—at least in part—of the people who lived in Lemuria and Atlantis and the surrounding territories. Both time and evolution in the Multiverse are not linear, so although we hadn't yet reached a 5D Ascension, many of our HUmans back then were already largely inhabiting a 5D reality on Earth. The planet and specifically those continents, were deep in the throes of its upcoming Ascension.

Although oceans apart and very different in some ways, the people of Atlantis and Lemuria shared many attributes that from a multidimensional perspective left very little difference between the two populations. Both civilizations were highly evolved and utopian, each possessing advanced skills, creative brilliance, and the ability to communicate with one another and beings living on other worlds telepathically. Their respective lands were lush and abundant, their economies thrived, and their societies excelled.

The Lemurians were spiritually evolved, multidimensional beings assigned the sacred responsibility of being the record keepers of the Earth and its HUmans by the Universe. They carried many of the secrets of creation and transcendence and some the highest teachings from the *ancient ones,* gods, and various entities of the unseen world. Their ancestors were indigenous to this planet; however, their *soul* energy was hybrid. Some coming from other, distant solar systems.

Lemurians were said to be direct descendants of inhabitants of planets in the solar system of Arcturus, the brightest star in the night sky of our northern hemisphere. Throughout the cosmos, Arcturians were known to be extremely advanced and prolific healers, as were the Lemurians residing on Earth.

They were masters in the use of crystals and semiprecious stones for healing, transmuting, and storing ancient texts, teachings, and source codes. By vibrationally aligning the codex (sacred manuscripts) with the frequency codes of specific quartz crystals, they preserved this sacred information to transfer to the Light Ascendents of the future. Hidden in visibly undetectable swirls and etchings within these crystals, they also protected the data from being misused for nefarious purposes by those not operating in the Light.

All the actions of the Lemurians were heart-based and filtered through values such as HUman unity, unconditional Love for all people and creatures, and the core foundational principle of a harmonious comMUnity. They had a very strong connection to the spirit of life and advocated for the nurturance and empowerment of all beings. They celebrated each individual's unique life path and never engaged in power struggles with other teachings and beliefs or participated in any form of competition. Respecting one another and the Earth was their basic tenet. Due to this profound commitment, they mainly experienced *one* emotion: **LOVE.** The Lemurians knew that whatever they thought and did and how they reacted to anything would be imprinted in Universal time as a *creation*. Highly telepathic and empathic, they also knew that *any* exchange embodying less than the frequency of Light or Love, would only be eventually absorbed and experienced through their own being.

Responsibility and accountability were the cornerstones of their principles. Without rigid, punitive consequences or judgments, they also thoroughly understood and embraced the HUman condition and welcomed any transgressions that occurred as opportunities for those who experienced them to grow from. Elected individuals, groups, and committees were assigned to hold energetic constructs of great Love, Light, and Compassion for those who chose to transmute their HUman foibles out of their lower Shadow frequencies. Advanced alchemical knowledge gave them the ability to change anything that HUmans were personally facing almost instantly through the direct application of *focused* Love and Source Light.

The Atlanteans were also highly advanced, multi-dimensional beings but in a different manner. They were skilled with local and interstellar technology. For example, they had tools that made it possible for them to communicate effortlessly with beings from other planets, even those in galaxies beyond the Milky Way. Their intellectual abilities created everything necessary for corresponding on wireless frequencies similar to how we currently do with our computers, smartphones, and 5G technology. Their astronautics exceeded our present-day, spacefaring vehicles. Using propulsive principles akin to those we use to make our airplanes and rockets fly, they successfully explored interdimensional travel. This exposed them to beings from other planets (aka, *extraterrestrials)* and inspired them to experiment with some of the ideas, concepts, and thinking of these other "species."

The Atlanteans were extremely gifted mathematicians and developed algorithms, computer programs, and a variety of applications for their inventions. They were brilliant engineers, designers, and builders of homes, landscapes, and urban environments. They built the equivalent of our current cars for accelerated Earth-based transportation but without emitting harmful fumes or electromagnetic radiation.

They exalted the use of the HUman mind and intelligence capabilities. As premiere scientists and doctors, they had a well-developed acumen for treating HUman physiology and developed sophisticated techniques akin to, but more advanced than, our medical equipment, tests, scans of today. They diagnosed issues within the body through advanced means such as topography and treated all physical, chemical, and emotional issues that we currently refer to as ailments or diseases as primarily *energetic* imbalances. Because of their extensive level of knowledge of the physical body, they often experienced long lifespans, sometimes living for as many as 400–500 years per incarnation.

Like the Lemurians, who had mastered the use of crystals from the Earth and energy from the sun as tools for healing, the Atlanteans excelled in using many of these same natural resources, but for other important purposes. Their scientists discovered that many quartz crystals have piezoelectric properties. They had found that when you apply pressure and heat to certain minerals, they will emit an electric current. They also noticed when the process was reversed and an outside electric current or mechanical force was applied to the mineral, this force moved around the atomic structure of the mineral, forcing it to both contract and expand.

Minerals such as clear quartz, tourmaline, and topaz were in abundant supply in Atlantis, so they were extensively researched and used in engineering and technological applications like computer hardware, precision watches, microphones, radar and sonar systems, and various intergalactic communication systems. When quartz chips were found to be programable, with wide frequency ranges and expansive amplification capability, these discoveries produced advancements in their fields of science, medicine, space travel, and fuel.

With such a broad range of practical applications, piezo-electricity became the backbone of Atlantis's prosperous and thriving economy. Although, it has been documented in our historical records that piezoelectricity was discovered in the late 1800s by Jacques and Pierre Curie, there is a very good chance that most likely they were former Atlanteans "remembering" their original discoveries from their life's work back then.

Almost 27,000 years later, looking back, we could have never anticipated how the discovery of piezoelectricity could have led to our failed first attempt at a 5D Earth Ascension and the Karmic ties that it was going to have in our current world's dismantling of 3D duality.

Many Things Went *Amazingly Well*

Lemuria was one of the main continents in the southern Pacific Ocean, roughly located between North America and parts of contemporary Asia and Australia. There has been considerable continental drift over the millennia, so the current placement of the continents does not exactly resemble the configuration of that era. Lemuria was considered a motherland to a group of many small islands immediately surrounding it. Back then it had approximately thirteen outer colonies located throughout the Pacific Ocean, as well as in the Atlantic Ocean.

Atlantis was one of Lemuria's colonies. But the core of the Atlanteans *soul* energy (and their ancestry) was sourced from planets in the cluster of stars that ancient Greeks named the Pleiades. Six can still be seen today with the naked eye but there are actually 500-plus stars in that area of our night sky.

Although the populace of Atlantis followed the same Universal laws of *free will* and were technically independent from Lemurian governance like many of the other Earth colonies of that age, Atlantis still fell under Lemuria's *Karmic jurisdiction*. The Lemurians oversaw most *"bigger picture" soul* contracts regarding the spiritual evolution of Earth's Indigenous HUmans and potential 5D Ascension.

The people of both continents and throughout all the various colonies worked very well together, for each had different strengths and made a different overall contribution to sustain and grow the planet. Because Lemuria's neighbors and colleagues in Atlantis excelled with technology, medicine, and science, and continually made profound advances and breakthroughs, Lemuria chose to collaborate with this colony in experimental research programs addressing different areas of HUman evolution. Some of these programs focused on the development of new forms of energy and others on HUman genetic coding, specifically the modification of HUman DNA for the creation of new highly advanced people and societies.

Lemurians mainly created through the intelligence of the *heart* and their feelings and Atlanteans created mostly through the intelligence of the *mind* and their intellects. Even though the main industries and skill sets on these two continents were different, the consciousness levels of both groups were equally matched. Energetically speaking, their complementary processes made for a well-fitted collaboration.

All the Lemurian elders concurred that a blending of those two types of intelligence would not only benefit HUman evolution, but ultimately was part of the *bigger picture* plan that was unfolding even back then. The *heart and mind* merger had to include laying down first a foundation of spiritual beliefs and Universal teachings for all involved, specifically the Atlanteans and people living in other outside surrounding colonies. If the sharing of venerable sacred information was going to commence, then spiritually based schools had to be established that properly taught ancient Lemurian and Universal knowledge, such as transcendental secrets, cures, and remedies.

Instructions and guidance from Lemuria's trusted master teachers would explain how to utilize color, sound, aroma, vibration, and frequency for healing, creating, and evolving consciousness. This would constitute the backbone of the curriculum. All the alternative medicines available at the time, including those that employed the properties of Earth's natural resources, particularly the stones that we consider "semiprecious" today and quartz crystals, had to be presented with the ultimate sense of trust and respect for all those who were called to study at these institutes of higher learning.

A Shared Interest in the Power of Crystals

The landscapes of both Lemuria and Atlantis were abundant in precious and semiprecious stones and home to megalithic-sized quartz crystals. Although they employed the stones and crystals differently, both societies understood their importance and value beyond transactional value, such as would occur in a monetary exchange. Although often used to make jewelry, adorning ornaments, and artwork, the Lemurians mainly used their crystalline resources for transmitting spiritual energy as well as for HUman, animal, and Earth rebalancing. *Rebalancing* is a term they used that is equivalent to our current term *healing*. The stones were used for vibrational rebalancing of energy, color and sound therapies, the manufacture of medicinal elixirs, and the power-charging of water, food, animals, chakras, and Mother Earth.

Temples, study halls, houses, and intergalactic communication centers were all designed with crystalline elements in them, ranging from crystal beds, realignment chairs, and healing tools, to salt baths, vibrational antennae and more. Most importantly, they were incorporated into the floors, ceilings, windows, and walls. Perfectly aligned and shaped with coordinates of sacred geometry and astrological positioning, these structures captured magnificent rays of Light and cosmic energy that emanated from the sun, moon, and distant stars. Their precise placement in designs and sacred spaces allowed the color and energy from the crystals to be directed onto the structure and surrounding landscape, where it could be absorbed by all who inhabited the various dwellings.

Each temple had its own energetic objective. Individuals as well as groups would enter these holy creations to experience and adjust their vibrations. *Temple Beautiful, Temple Peace,* and *Temple Love* were the names of a few of the temples that were located on key points in Lemuria. There are no words to describe how magnificent these structures were to behold.

HUmans who had past incarnations as Lemurians—many of the LightWorkers of today—who frequented these sacred places and experienced their architecture would say it was the closest they ever got to directly experiencing the Divine while alive in a physical body. Of course, we know many memories of Lemuria are veiled for most of us. I personally remember, however, and therefore can attest, that the effect of the architecture was truly humbling.

In Atlantis, crystals were appreciated both for their aesthetic beauty and for their piezoelectric properties. Quartz crystals in the form of tiny pieces carved into chips were used in devices similar to our modern-day timepieces, computers, smartphones, pacemakers, magnetic resonance imaging (MRI) technology, and NASA-type equipment for space vehicles because of their amplification and metronomic properties. Large quartz crystals were erected to supply power to Atlantis, its surrounding islands, and many parts of Lemuria. These huge, pillar-shaped crystals were used as electrical generators, with the potential force equivalent to the intensity of our atomic power plants of today.

Of the natural resources that were available on Atlantis, clear quartz was the most abundant mineral. They were not only embedded throughout the Earth and ground in various shapes and sizes but were also found above ground in *ginormous natural Crystal structures.*

Most of the supersized mega-crystals that the Lemurian colonists found when they arrived in Atlantis were too large to be moved; nor should they have been, for the Atlanteans, especially the astronomers and mathematicians, assumed their specific location on the continent was related to their intergalactic coordinates—a form of sacred geometry. The seers and ancient ones of both Lemuria and Atlantis understood these massive Atlantean crystal monuments had been divinely seeded to grow in these specific locations. They functioned like "acupuncture needles" placed into sacred points on the surface of the Earth to circulate energy, frequencies and transmit coded *"bigger plan"* messages.

The size of the largest quartz structures in Lemuria paled in comparison to the ones in Atlantis, which were often several stories high. Although the Lemurian landscape had many large and medium-sized crystals in it, many of the crystals they harvested were smaller ones that could be held, carved, and physically able to transport or program. These were used for energetic rebalancing and spiritual purposes. Larger ones were used for architecture and their breathtaking Temples.

Because the smaller crystals were in ample supply in Lemuria, they were made available to all residents and visitors alike at no cost. The Lemurian crystals were very much sought after for they carried very unique frequencies and were highly in demand.

Although it is getting more difficult to find *genuine* Lemurian crystals today, when discovered they are recognizable because they look and feel distinctly different from similar-sized crystals that originated in Atlantis. Often, they are less "pretty" than the Atlantean, clear and sparkling ones. They have an odd, finger-like shape, with one end wider than the other. Atlantean crystals are mostly six-sided with more consistent shapes. (For more information on Lemurian crystals and prints of the back cover artwork visit www.andie santopietro.com.)

Many Things Went *Inconceivably Awry*

Lemurians and Atlanteans carried more advanced skills, knowledge, and multidimensional capabilities than any other Indigenous HUmans living elsewhere during the same time period in our prehistory. The combination of large groups of people having access to powerful Universal knowledge and living under the law of *free will,* created the *potential* for a serious misuse of the knowledge to occur. All sacred information shared was meant to empower all HUmans so that they could spiritually evolve and collectively Ascend.

Lemurians went into this Universal experiment wide awake, consciously knowing they were taking an unprecedented risk and vibrational leap of faith. Disaster, miscreation, and failing were always a real possibility.

During the attempted 5D Ascension, it was the *soul* work of the Lemurian teachers and avatars to disseminate previously concealed Universal knowledge to all the people. Transparency and full disclosure of all these teachings was a *spiritual right* that all *soul*s possessed. Withholding and controlling teachings from either an individual or collective, for fear of a Karmic backlash, would have been out of alignment with *bigger picture* integrity, beliefs, and the service contracts of the Lemurians and Atlanteans to spiritually evolve HUman life on Planet Earth.

At all times, *then and now,* on a planet governed by the principles of *free will,* each person is responsible for the choices they make *moment to moment* of how to act, think, feel, respond, and utilize everything that is placed before them through the cornucopia of opportunities, gifts and *mishaps* given generously and continuously by the Universe.

Atlanteans were the chosen society—along with their beautiful and abundant quartz-rich land—as the premiere test group and Earth location for Lemurians to bring their sacred teachings to. Information more spiritual in nature would include ways of using quartz crystals to heal, shift and reprogram realities and lives. Over time, the Universal secrets of working with the alchemy of energy and quantum physics as well as interacting with the powers and magic existing in the invisible realms, would also be shared. Dogma, Karma, multidimensionality, and timelines were included in the intended *spiritual teachings* and curriculum to name a few.

Lemurians and the Universal powers that be saw Atlantis as the quintessential choice for their evolution project despite it being a society that prided itself on leading life with the mind, intellect, and ego. Although Atlanteans were mental body dominant, they also had a sincere desire to learn about spiritual energy and the intelligence of the evolved heart. Although *many* Atlanteans were very spiritually evolved, many were still ensconced in a 3D level of consciousness. This unique combination of attributes made Atlantis the clear and definitive choice of location for the heart-based, dominant Lemurians to extend their Earth-based 5D Ascension plan.

This powerful, exciting, and Universally watched exchange between these two civilizations ended both *dramatically* and *traumatically* for many of us who did some of our most treasured *soul work* living there. Aspects of the project went so terribly off course that it culminated in the complete des-truction of life and land on many of the islands, continents, and colonies of our beloved homelands. Many of our hearts were broken . . . and coming into this lifetime—*still were.*

The Seers of *MU* Long Ago Knew

Four hundred to 500 years before the final demise of these two ancient civilizations, prophets predicted that years into the future HUmans living in these lands would have the option to seed several potentially consequential timelines, trajectories, realities, and *planetary outcomes.* Based on the individual choices they would make regarding their HUman evolutionary direction, collective consciousness, and energy-based creations, their focus could net radically different outcomes.

Throughout many lifetimes in the final 500 years of the Lemurian and Atlantean civilization, the Universe sent many avatars, teachers, and LightWorkers to these two continents to assist and guide the 5D Ascension process. Their presence and counsel provided direction for the HUmans during all those prior years to help choose more Light-based actions, identify right/wrong behaviors, and assist them in the raising of their individual consciousness. All this support was offered without grasping for any control, trying to sway their decisions, or interfering with the much-honored Universal law of *free will.* There were years of oversight, patience, and unconditional Love freely given from the elders and HUman guides, as incrementally, over time, HUman consciousness grew. It wasn't until almost 500 years and several lifetimes had passed that Lemurians were ready to implement the second part of their 5D Ascension plan: to bring the sacred teachings of the Universe to the masses.

FROM LEMURIA TO ATLANTIS

For the most part, the merger of the Lemurian and Atlantean HUmans with all their strengths was seen as a hand and *"gLove"* fit. This evolutionary moment was not launched haphazardly or impulsively. That's why in part, it was particularly devastating to many of us. Strong personal, professional, peer, and family bonds were forged for lifetimes leading up to the initiation of the project. Most of the inhabitants of these continents shared a Love for the planet, respect for each other's gifts, a desire to grow spiritually and share in their respective abundance. The priests, guides, and Ascension Project Managers from Lemuria were making incredible progress. They were accomplishing all that they had set out to do through their plan of bringing the Universal ancient teachings to the people of Earth, specifically the Atlanteans. But after several lifetimes, it became apparent that a few of those who were originally aligned with the new teachings and higher laws were breaking away and forming various rogue factions.

Most of these errant groups and their leaders were of Atlantean descent, but *some* Lemurians, although significantly fewer, also joined them. Members of these factions began to align with others in Atlantis *(and the surrounding areas)* who had not expressed interest at any prior time in the teaching of the various Lemurian schools of Universal thought. Although many of these HUmans weren't outwardly opposed to the Atlantean Ascension project or to the spiritual teachings, behind the scenes they were often discussing ways that they could exploit the higher information for their own gain.

Some of the genetic modification experiments and programs on Atlantis, which were designed to extend life and advance HUman capabilities, were being egregiously coopted.

Originally born from the Light, these GMO HUmans were modified for nefarious purposes. Horrifically, HUmans were being cloned for personal gain, slavery, and sex-related purposes.

Several other well-intended experiments were also dragged across ethical lines. HUman DNA was merged with the DNA of other species for similar misuses and despicable purposes.

Greed, competition, and elitism became very tempting to those who were inadvertently beginning to choose HUman competition, status, and prosperity as a way of gaining dominance, power, and control over others. Presented with both Light and Shadow options, HUmans were given copious opportunities to choose harmony, peace, and Love and to reach higher.

HUman division and the Light/Dark struggles for power grabs were not completely unknown to our forebearers. These *Shadow-based* issues existed not only on our planet but throughout all prior incarnations, dimensions, and realities. During most of HUman greed's past existence, people often were driven by their covetous instincts and choices for many of their needs were based on *scarcity and survival* purposes.

What is hard for many of our hearts to grasp is that in Atlantis there was *no* scarcity, lack, or survival-based disadvantage that could have justified their decision to resort to dominance. During what turned out to be a very dark period in our planet's history, a segment of what once was a highly evolved and abundant society chose to intentionally misuse the teachings of the Light for its own personal gain. Those Humans, as well as all of us, were entrusted with the very high blessing and the *gift of free will* by the Universe. Without any spiritual constraints, some of the HUmans elected to desecrate, betray, and entirely reject some of the key spiritual laws of Earth-based life. Established by a benevolent Universe, their disregard eventually brought an end to the 5D Ascension project that was originally meant to create a HUmanity of the highest order.

Throughout eons, the Lemurians were often given many pivotal intergalactic roles as "Ambassadors of the Light." They were often called on, both before and after their time in Lemuria, to serve on the frontlines of evolutionary change. Lemurian *souls* were among the ancient Aboriginal healers in Australia, the apostles of Jesus, disciples of Buddha, and devotees of all the spiritual avatars from the higher dimensions that have ever walked the Earth in the name of the Light.

Lemurians and Atlanteans were and still continue to be architects for the unseen world, our planet's record keepers and scribes, the Universe's secret holders, tasked with the passing of sacred teachings from one generation to the next. These individuals, *many of you who are reading this*, were the *chosen* conduits for very significant *bigger picture* energy transmissions from the vast number of transcendental realms. You've worked with *Light-Magic* and were the gatekeepers for the higher dimensional realities and Light Forces. For lifetimes, in your *beLoved* earthly home, you modeled creatorship, HUman evolution, and Light-based consciousness for all beings throughout the galaxies, residing on the various planets circling their twinkling stars. You deeply embodied the vibration of Love. To many primitive HUmans and *souls* throughout the Universe, your *Light, Love, and Soul's* commitment to stay the course appears Godlike.

Many of Us Here Today Were There Back Then

While deep into the advanced stages of our attempt at Ascension, the key *Light Commanders (I was one of them)* stationed in Aveidon,[1] Lemuria began to receive higher, *bigger picture* intel conveyed from the *ancient ones,* the LightWorker elders. Information received at the time indicated that our 5D Ascension Project appeared to be off course and it's trajectory, if followed, could take it into a direction that could lead to great chaos, flooding, and potentially ending our civilization with several of the main continents sinking.

The juxtaposition of our potentially game-changing 5D Ascension Project alongside the devastating reality of the end of our beloved homelands was nothing short of *surreal.* By the time we got that news that the worst had happened, we had already forged deep trust and heart-based bonds with the majority of the Atlantean people, most of whom had envisioned another outcome, grown, and walked alongside us. They became our friends, our partners, our comrades in arms, and our *soul* sisters and brothers. By then, we were all deeply connected through a common thread of our Love and Light.

Although we knew from the inception that failure was a possibility, when the reality of it arrived, we were *devastated.* Many of the 5D Ascension project managers were emotionally stunned, although they were not caught totally unprepared. Many of these frontline prophets and Ambassadors of the Light came back from the future to spearhead this profound 5D Earthly assignment. They had been chosen to lead this unprecedented evolutionary process because they already had the experience of working with the darker energies from other lifetimes in different dimensions. They bore witness to how quickly *Shadow energy* can erupt, duplicate, and multiply itself, often without much warning or notice.

Prior experience in doing LightWork when active Shadow was in play taught them always to have an exit plan in place in case a time came when they had to either abort or concede a crucial planetary mission. The ancient ones in spirit knew for hundreds of 3D years in advance that an exit plan might be necessary. They began downloading coded information and programming it into the minerals and quartz crystals and embedding them in the Earth's core for future retrieval. These seeded crystals held important data, instructions, and 5D Ascension contracts. They were also *vibrationally set* to the exact frequencies of those who would be working on Planet Earth years in the future. The vibrational resonance of a HUman with an assigned crystal would create a clear signal that would magnetically draw them together to unlock Plan B.

When *Plan B* Becomes *Plan A*

A specific group of Lemurians were chosen by their peers to manage, design, and oversee the *bigger picture* fallout plan that was known to many of us as Plan B. Our planetary LightWorkers, both in spirit and in flesh, knew that if our 5D Ascension project in Lemuria and Atlantis failed, it would be a *very long time* before the planet would be at a place in its evolution where HUmanity would be able to attempt another 5D Ascension.

Over a period of hundreds of years, this committee, which included several generations of LightWorkers in rotation, built safe and efficient underground shelters for comMUnities from MU, where future generations in charge of the Ascension project could take safe refuge, rebuild our civilization, and reseed all of the secret teachings and information necessary without any of it getting coopted for another purpose or destroyed.

The LightWorkers in both Lemuria and Atlantis also oversaw the recording of all the sacred teachings through etchings and Light languages inscribed into specific "teacher" crystals. Vibrational codes were energetically embedded into the matrix of different mineral compositions. Some of these crystals were alchemized into a liquid state for imprinting purposes, then transmuted back to a solid form for preservation. These high-frequency elixirs held copious amounts of Universal knowledge that could only be deciphered when a specific sequencing of individual HUman DNA became available. In order for these codes to be *activated,* the collective at the time they were discovered would have to be also vibrating to a more advanced level of HUman consciousness than what was required during the prior failed Ascension attempt in Atlantis and Lemuria.

The committee assigned other highly trusted LightWorkers to be responsible for many of the treasured artifacts, scrolls, sacred objects, transcendental information, and coded Lemurian and Atlantean "seed," "teacher," and "recorder" crystals. Many of these same LightWorkers were also in charge of personally transporting these doctrines and items off the island to secret locations around the world if the need arose.

The whereabouts of these items, transportation instructions, and regularly changing access codes were to be passed down in the sacred tradition of *oral transmission* to consecrated holders of the Light, verbally shared from one assigned LightWorker to a successor. Generation after generation, if needed, each Earth steward of this kind was prepared to evacuate and leave the continent within a moment's notice with *their assigned objects and responsibilities, upon command.*

Wow, Did We Miscalculate?

The majority of the Atlantean people grew into amazing, brilliant, and advanced HUmans who applied the intelligence of both their minds and their hearts to all their Earth-based creations. But over the years, their work and relationship with some of their other peers and collectives began to dissolve. Although there were several groups whose beliefs and ideologies were very different from the *bigger picture* plan, they all peacefully coexisted for many lifetimes. The Atlanteans developed an egalitarian society where most were very accepting and open to a lot of the spirituality that the Lemurians were teaching.

As time went on many attitudes morphed, value systems changed, and HUman competition began to grow. It was palpable, as if a cancer was beginning to silently spread on the planet. The vast abundance and prosperity of Atlantis and Lemuria added to the metastasizing of this mentality and created an even worse HUman disease: *apathy.*

Many of the once evolved HUmans on both the continents were becoming complacent. Some were so overidentified with their newfound spiritual lives that they became arrogant. They felt protected, untouchable, and often above the fray. Others felt that their personal wants and desires were more important than the needs and best interest of the collective.

The natural and abundant resources available to all of the HUmans were beginning to be *claimed,* and ownership of unequal amounts and proportions was being declared. The large crystals that supplied the power to the populace and intercontinental communication towers for many aspects of worldwide activities were *now* seen as a commodity. With greed, HUman advantage, and an indifference for others' growth, first as individuals and then, eventually, in larger groups, they made decisions and developed value systems based on *personal* gain. They chose to empower and identify their HUman needs, desires, and realities through the use of their minds and egos only. They omitted a key spiritual component needed for all HUmans to evolve and prosper harmoniously: the filtering of all creative endeavors through the intelligence of the mind as well as the *heart.*

When the Universe originally planned to assist 3D HUmans in the process of evolving their collective consciousness to a 5D capacity, they knew by having the choice of *free will* that a massive miscreation could occur. The project's oversight committee anticipated this possibility and believed that they had reduced the risk factor mainly by going slowly during the transfiguration of consciousness phase. With great awareness and precision sequencing, they introduced the higher teachings from a Love-based Universe over an elongated period.

The process of change and evolution on a planet should not be rushed, controlled, or misdirected. But in this case, it was extended over a 500–1,000-year period, doled out to HUmans over a span of roughly seven generations.

The aim of a peaceful transition of consciousness is why *free will* was such an important and immutable law of the land. It was put in place so that living HUmans would be in total control of their own choices, actions, and beliefs, at their own pace. They could choose or *not* choose these teachings and evolutionary options. Their freedom of choice assured complete integrity and transparency so that the will of the Lemurians, LightWorkers, and even Universal powers did not bleed through and control the direction or outcome of the project. The power of *free will* placed that decision in each individual's hands, *where it belonged.*

This cosmic feature, available to millions of HUmans on the planet, *increased* the probability of disarray, singlemind-edness, and the thwarting of many *bigger picture* plans. Although this was understood, it was considered more important, as an act of grace and rectitude, that space be made for the possibility of chaos, albeit a spiritual byproduct. *And occur it did.*

The changes that led to the subsequent demise of Atlantis didn't happen all at once. Some were subtle and slow, others, sLightly more obvious, but initially deemed benign. Although a few people were choosing different options and intentions for their creations, their views and behaviors didn't seem to pose any real threat or cause concern to those working in the Light. *Until they did.*

After a few hundred years had elapsed, many of the situations that eventually grew into great concerns were being cleverly hidden in plain sight. Many of the HUmans from both continents and regions beyond them dismissed the escalating fervor and potential for destruction. Ignoring the chaos was a miscalculation of cosmic proportion.

The First Call for Action Came *Early*

It was years *before* Atlantis and Lemuria sank into the oceans when the first group of LightWorkers were instructed to leave the islands, taking with them their assigned objects and responsibilities. In a calm, organized, and inconspicuous manner, a few key treasures, texts, and crystals were moved to various new locations around the world. Although there were many tiers of people serving on the transport committee, Group A/Tier 1, the *Aveidon LightWorkers,* were asked to quietly evacuate first.

There was no immediate crisis at the time, so most of these Group A LightWorkers left on small private boats and large cargo ships and traveled to their respective destinations without being in the throes of major duress from our continents being under siege. As some of the first *Light-Seed Settlers,* the members of this group were responsible for calibrating the frequencies of the land for others who would be coming and to begin creating "MU LightWorker comMUnities" before their arrivals. These home away from home "neighborhoods," constructed in many locations around the globe, eventually turned into cities. Some included areas corresponding with parts of modern-day Asia and Australia, as well as Egypt and the Hawaiian Islands. Mount Shasta in California is also known to host many Lemuria comMUities, both on the land and below the mountains.

Although, as time grew closer to the end, the departures became more frenetic, the early years of disembarking from the continent of Lemuria went rather seamlessly. While the oversight committees and high-level Light Commanders were actively implementing this initial level of the evacuation plan, most of the other LightWorkers on the project were not even aware of the transportation plan that was being put in motion. It was not considered withheld information, just part of a plan that would be revealed in different stages.

Many of the LightWorkers, including me, held an enormous amount of hope that this seemingly obvious trajectory would somehow cease and turn around. Even over time, as it became more and more apparent that Shadow-based influences were guiding many of the creations and rapidly catching fire, LightWorkers stayed the course. In fact, many chose to remain until the end and *"go down with the ship."*

I know I did.

The Last Call for Action Came *Late*

By the time the last call to evacuate came, there was a tremendous amount of fear and chaos on the planet. Several of Atlantis's main crystal power stations had already blown up with a dramatic force equivalent to an atomic bomb exploding with noise, debris, and billows of smoke. The explosions lit the skies, spread fires, and generated tsunamis throughout the oceans. They physically shook many lands near and far, and the smaller islands closest to the explosion sites began to sink first. Although Atlantis was a rather large land mass, with each subsequent explosion, it broke apart more and sank further underwater.

Lemuria, like other bodies of land on the planet at the time, was in close proximity to Atlantis and felt the initial impact. But the catastrophic effects of the crystal explosions, specifically those that were used as power stations were not experienced until several days, perhaps weeks later. By then, some of the Atlanteans had already read the "hieroglyphics on the wall" and evacuated the continent. Many were resistant and chose to stay. Some who were in denial, or just abject fear, remained behind and eventually perished.

In Lemuria, a majority of the HUmans were more receptive to the guidance of the Light-elders and trusted their instruction and sense of timing about when to leave their beLoved homeland. It was a *soul*-breaking time for our heart-based society to abandon their once-treasured, halcyon world.

Many HUmans were lost in the destruction, but contrary to popular belief today, many also *survived*. The LightWorkers who remained on Lemuria as part of the "last call" group, mainly left via *dematerialization*. Rare, few and far between, these HUmans were extremely advanced in their ability to dematerialize, then rematerialize. Because of this ability, they were able to safely transport themselves from HUman to energy, and then from energy back to HUman, in the process moving themselves from one location to another, both on the planet and elsewhere throughout the Multiverse.

These individuals were the special, upgraded *6D HUmans* who had created the programs that were taught in sacred schools across Lemuria, Atlantis, and the surrounding lands. They instructed people in the secrets of Light language, astral travel, remote viewing, biofortification, and multidimensionality. This group of 6D HUmans safely (*and effortlessly*) made it off the continent and islands.

Everyone was given the option to evacuate—even those who had accepted "stay-on-land" or "last-call" service contracts. *Free will* remained a choice up until the very end.

There were approximately 500 HUmans who remained in Lemuria when it sank. They consisted mostly of those who for one reason or another resisted leaving or genuinely couldn't find their way off the island. All efforts were made repeatedly to warn, assist, cajole, and plead with those who wouldn't leave before the energy field carrying the radiation arrived. The impact of the radiation fallout was anticipated to be the most *searing* of all the destruction caused by the explosions. We knew that it would arrive on MU first, before any of the destructive flooding from the main waves of the tsunamis hit the shoreline. The direct exposure to the high levels of radiation would be the most tortuous symptom for the remaining HUmans to endure physically, emotionally, psychologically, and, in the long-term, *Karmically*.

Although there were many others in Lemuria and its surrounding areas who were in leadership positions, I can only speak from my own personal experience. I remember, with a very heavy heart, feeling a deep sense of despair and hollowness. I was frozen, hesitating, and dreading having to make that "final call." What felt like hours after the obvious conditions dictated that it was time, I finally called it. I know my last instruction to the remaining Light team to evacuate came later than it should have.

I Am Jonathan III of Aveidon

Many years ago, before I taught my first class on Lemuria in New York City, I had a past-life regression session regarding the last lifetime I had in Lemuria. This was one of the most intense and informative such sessions that I've ever personally experienced. I was shown a lot of the details that I have described in this chapter, along with some extremely difficult to perceive traumatic memories of the months, weeks, and days leading up to the fall of both adored civilizations. It took me many years, *personally and professionally,* to fully process the information.

I *now* can clearly recall my last moments before the radiation arrived. I was standing with a walking staff in hand on the highest land elevation in Lemuria—my favorite place to be on the island. This was where I would go to connect with the gods and nature and to speak with all the animals on the land. It had the lushest green grass, trees the size of skyscrapers, and a vista overlooking the bluest blue-green waters in all of the Pacific Ocean. I was an older man with long, white hair and a beard, and, while still in the regression, I heard my name spoken: ***"Jonathan III of Aveidon."***

Looking out over the waters, although I never turned around while in this memory, I knew that standing behind me were approximately five to eight of my *key* Light commanders, all who had chosen to stay behind with me and remain on the island. Some of them carried the title *Soul Apostle.* They had been assigned in many different lifetimes to the mission of an Earth-based 5D Ascension.

Now, an estimated 27,000 years later, I have had the great privilege of reconnecting with several of them again, some as students and clients, others as my colleagues and dear friends.

Eons Passed Before Our Next Attempt at a 5D Ascension

The continents of Lemuria and Atlantis sank in our prehistory. THE EXACT DATE IS UNKNOWN. If ever there was going to be another time on the planet when the Universe, Earth, and HUmanity would be cosmically, spiritually, planetarily, and physically aligned enough to be ready to attempt another 5D HUman Ascension, we knew it wouldn't come for a very, very long time.

We painfully understood that we would have to begin again almost from scratch with HUmanity, as well as having to wait for all the energy coordinates of the Multiverse to be solidly lined up and in place again. The teachings and scriptures that were brought to the different lands, *initially kept hidden,* would have to resurface over a long period of time, in drips and drabs. The collective consciousness needed could only be recreated again by 3D HUmans following their own *free will, evolution, and devolution* process and by arriving both vibrationally and Karmically past where they were at the end of our time in Lemuria and Atlantis.

A significant number of the seed crystals hidden in the mines around the world would have to be recovered, their frequencies put back into the Earth's atmosphere, and their *coded information* released into the hands of the right HUmans, deciphered at the perfect times. This would allow for the widespread disbursement of the crystals' frequencies, teachings, and esoteric information needed to stabilize the *new 5D Ascension plans* and timetable.

A significant number of HUmans worldwide would have had to personally process lifetimes of Karma, Shadow experiences, *soul* lessons, and the like, to allow them all to be *(metaphorically)* "at the same airport, at the same time, boarding the same fLight." This same group would also have to be in vibrational resonance with the land and have developed advanced HUman bodies capable of carrying more Source Light with more activated strands of DNA than their forebearers. On a consciousness level, they should be so advanced that they would more often than not choose to create most things through the filter of both the 5D mind and heart.

All around the globe, old friends, family members, LightWorkers, ShadowWorkers, and *frenemies* of both Lemurian and Atlantean descent would have to reunite and pick up in the vicinity of where they left off. HUmanity and all its 3D/4D HUmans would then be ready and given another opportunity to attempt a successful Ascension through their own volition while on Earth.

Many millions of moving pieces would have to be in a precise alignment, not only on Earth, but across the galaxies. This possibility was a tall order even for most seasoned LightWorkers because, at the least, it would require a commitment to being involved in lifetimes of processing and perpetual LightWork through the shadow side of the 3D realities. But for those of us who didn't make it off the continents before they sank, the journey to the next 5D Ascension would also come with wading through an additional set of very difficult hurdles, *time spent trying to elevate one's being out of the darker realms in the lower dimensions and purgatories.* The last few months on Lemuria leading up to its final days came with major trauma and accumulated social Karma. Those who stayed behind chose to carry a lot of the collective's Karma as a scribe and witness for the moment.

Although this was truly experienced as a torturous and hell-like experience for those who *souls* traveled that route, it was not *"intended"* to be a Karmic punishment. In *bigger picture* terms, they became *ShadowWorkers—agreeing to a Karmic commitment* where they would immerse themselves in the unprocessed Shadow realms, giving them access and opportunity to help transmute denser, darker energies into Light when the next opportunity for a 5D Ascension came. Given all the needed parts, if we were to have another 5D Ascension on planet Earth, it would have to be an undertaking equivalent to a modern-day *miracle.*

Cut Once, Measure Twice

We had almost 27,000 years to figure out what may have gone wrong. Yes, *wrong.* Back in the days of Lemuria and Atlantis, we were still deeply steeped in 3D/4D consciousness and duality. Cause and effect (or spiritually speaking, the laws of Karma) were still alive and well. Our 3D system of opposites was the metric used to identify outcomes—good vs. bad, right vs. wrong. So, for a *very* long time, our consciousness (sub and un) was still programmed with the belief that the "end" went very "wrong."

In 3D/4D, and as far as project management goes, the earlier 5D Ascension project was a failure of epic proportions. But as far as an "attempt" goes, we went further than ever before in advancing collective HUman consciousness. HUmanity was also given a blessed, although *very traumatic,* HUman *experience* to label, use and learn from as our respective levels of consciousness and work contracts saw fit. Many of you, although bloodied and bruised by some of your past lives and harrowing *soul* assignments, *not only* saw the end of these continents as a 3D failure, but over time came to understand that we could also use the experience as a springboard for our next attempt at another 5D Ascension.

You and I alike believed if we were willing to "do the work" to face the lessons of both the Light and the Shadow aspects involved in our earlier attempt, the experience would be chock-full of grist for understanding our miscalculations.

Over what felt like *eons,* those in charge both in Lemuria and throughout the Universe meticulously belabored the details of the before, during, and after of the 3D to 5D Earth Ascension plan and its subsequent fallout. There were a few key findings, along with modifications that would be needed to launch a successful 5D Ascension in the future.

A *few* of the main discoveries and recommendations that were offered and considered were:

Light Force Requirements. Grossly underestimated was the amount of *collective Light force* that was needed to launch a successful 5D Ascension on a HUman-based *(embodied)* planet. It was believed that the collective Light produced from the comMUnity of LightWorkers higher level of consciousness would have carried enough torque for HUmanity at the time to shift from 3D to 5D. It wasn't. We came up *energetically short* for what we hoped would have been a seamless launch.

Double Duty. LightWorkers would have to *double or triple* down on the amount of personal work usually required and contracted for during a single incarnation to bring better Light balance onto the planet. Many of us Lightworkers would have to pick up the "slack" for those who couldn't do or complete the personal energy work they had committed to doing prior to incarnating, and this would add a lot of Shadow issues to their work agenda. In addition, their personal work would include both addressing and processing other family, ancestral, societal, and Earth-based matters.

Untransmuted Shadow Energy. There was a miscalculation of the potential impact of leaving untransmuted ambient Shadow energy in the fabric throughout the planetary grid, specifically at the ground zero energy fields of Atlantis, Lemuria, and the surrounding islands. Leftover Shadow energy that was created or still existed in the dimension *(3D)* that HUmanity was attempting to Ascend from had to be *energetically released* first before it could be brought to the surface in a tangible way for HUmans to collectively address. All frequencies comprised of any prior Shadow thought and beliefs that were not of 100 percent pure Light or higher, had to be significantly reduced or transmuted on a collective level prior to opening access to the 5D portals of the Ascended dimension.

Free Will Remains. A majority of the Shadow consciousness that was born out of 3D duality will be *purposely* drawn to the surface for transmutation. As difficult, distasteful, challenging, or dark as those truths are to hold, address, and face, we will still uphold and align with the cosmic principles that cloak an Earth-based society, specifically *free will*—even if that means another unsuccessful 5D Ascension outcome.

Karma Transmuted. Karmic law was based on *cause and effect* and a byproduct of 3D HUmans and their Light and Shadow creations. All major Karmic programs derived from that elongated dimensional cycle of cause and effect will need to be reexperienced and all their Karmic imbalances transmuted back to balance, Light and eventually *oneness*. Significant miscreations manifested and placed onto the planetary grid and still *in play* at the time of the next Ascension attempt, will need to be uncreated and deleted from its cache. *5D has no cause and effect, no Karmic law.* HUmans on *3D/4D* will not be able to vibrationally enter a higher level of consciousness with major *detrimental* frequencies of 3D/4D Karmic miscreations.

Animal Kingdom Healing. HUman/Animal-based projects, plans, and relationships from HUmans to HUmans, HUmans to the Earth, and HUmans to the Animal and Mineral kingdoms have to be reexperienced through repetitive gradations or variations on a similar theme, until all miscreations are transmuted and all creations are in alignment with the new *5D Laws of One.*

All these types of events occurring before, during, and after the fall of Atlantis and Lemuria went directly into the Akashic Library. The Mayans, our closest spiritual friends (*"heart-wise"*) and neighbors, were the main Earth-based scribes for what unfolded at the time. Their elders and seers carried a lot of mastery in the area of astrology, able not only to foretell imminent events but also to predict distant future events with uncanny accuracy and discern their potential astrological timelines.

During the 500 years prior to the end of Atlantis and Lemuria, the Mayans predicted the *possibility,* as opposed to the *probability,* of our continent's demise. The cataclysmic ending that we all encountered wasn't *predetermined* or etched in stone in the Akashic records. As a planet of *free will,* it was (*and still is*) always going to be the HUmans who decide the ultimate direction and outcome of all their experiments and evolutionary growth.

As we got closer to what became an inevitable ending, our Mayan friends offered up a 27,000-year period before HUmanity would reach a more evolved state with sufficient collective Light to attempt a 3D-5D Ascension again. one with, hopefully, a higher probability of a successful outcome. The future date HUmanity was given was December 12, 2012. The number sequence 12-12-12 was the vibratory source code that was programmed into our crystals, sacred teachings, and, most importantly, our individual strands of DNA.

Bigger Picture or Not, It Was *Devastating*

Many famous writers, historians, and world-renowned seers, such as Plato, Sir Thomas Moore, Edgar Cayce, and Helena Blavatsky, spoke about the former existence of these ancient civilizations. As one of my readers, you are likely to have been there, too.

Those who were on the continents during those final years of Atlantis and Lemuria and those who directly witnessed the apocalyptic ending were left with *many* painful, heart-wrenching memories. Buried deep within their *unconscious minds* were experiences of loss, disappointment, betrayal, confusion, and *traumatic devastation*. Besides experiencing our prized evolutionary project ending, we also lost our beLoved homelands, friends and Loved ones. The emotional imprint from those events was seared into our *cellular memory* and carried forward into our future incarnations hopefully to be addressed and eventually transmuted back into the Light.

When many of us were first informed that our Ascension project would eventually begin again, some of us couldn't wait to get back on the horse and get started; but the majority of us were apprehensive about returning. Many LightWorkers, both from the *past and the future,* were reluctant to come back to Earth again. Although we knew it was an honor to serve, knowing what we would have to endure during the many incarnations leading up to another 3D-5D Ascension, the possibility was daunting. There were no guarantees listed in the "fine print" of our *soul* contracts assuring that a successful launch would occur the next time around, especially with the laws of *free will* still in place. Some LightWorkers chose not to return at all and were assigned to other planets and LightWork during the same period of time.

Ultimately, once the Ascension project was officially reinstated, many Lemurians and Atlanteans did choose to reincarnate and work on the revised project once again. One of the main stipulations in the new Universal bylaws of the project was that we agreed the details of the *bigger picture* plan would be veiled from our awareness and that our memories of the original past life events would be recreated in incremental, *manageable* bits and pieces. We had a personal history with the trauma and events that we were recreating. If we had to begin again, we needed a more dialed-down filter, a lens that wasn't as clear, so we would not inadvertently self-implode. Because of this invisible, built-in protective element, many HUmans like myself, and perhaps *you* along with the many other LightWorkers around the world, often questioned their life's purpose, difficulties, relentless ups and downs, pain, and so forth. With much apprehension, it was the common stance for those working in the Light to feel ambivalent and confused at times about not even wanting to *stay*. Shielded from remembering, and without most things making any rational sense, the struggles were often personalized and hijacked by guilt and shame. Many of us suffered emotionally, spiritually, physically, and financially to a significant degree as we committed to facing our own Karmic wounding, not just for ourselves, but also for the higher cause.

To join the new, modified Ascension project, we not only had to be better prepared as a collective, but we had to be at an *emotional* place in our physical body that would allow us to cope with what would be the inevitable triggering of old source codes, reactions, and deeply buried memories. We would also have to be able to simultaneously address the 3D circumstances of our current lives and world that were recreated from the past, and to act on them in a more constructive way to transmute the original outcome. We would have to be stable enough as individuals and a society to endure all the personal emotional triggers and world-shaking events that often foretell the coming of epic change.

And finally, we would need to remember, *even though not being able to remember, that all our bigger picture LightWork will be seamlessly dovetailed into our personal work at the same time. Being a LightWorker wouldn't place us above doing our necessary "soul work" as individuals.* Our emotional traumas, personal reactions, beliefs, and life perspectives will also impact people, places, and the *bigger picture* outside world and situations. For better or for worse, we will have an impact on everything and, in turn, we will be impacted by everything. Both kinds of affects will always be Karmic in nature—that is, until you arrive in 5D where there is no more Karma. As LightWorkers we will not be given any special privileges, short cuts or *hall passes.*

All the events that will be occurring around us and that we will witness, experience, and possibly have very strong reactions to will only be mirroring *personal* unresolved or unaddressed issues that are up for transmutation, healing, and *deletion.*

Ascension: *Take Two!*

After 27,000 years in the making, Karmically, we had finally arrived at a place in our timeline where we were able to address our role and experiences of what happened leading up to the downfall in Atlantis. HUmanity, although it might not seem so on the surface, is currently reexamining much of our LightWork projects, understandings, and individual lifetimes from our elongated stay on both those continents. In essence, memories from our incarnations in Lemuria and Atlantis—reminders—are coming through from our cellular memory right *now* and manifesting in our day-to-day lives. We can also see them in the myriad of surrounding events around the world.

In 2012, we finally experienced a successful 5D Ascension on Planet Earth. It would have not been vibrationally possible to create a multilevel miracle of that magnitude without all the remaining 3D/4D Karmic "ghosts" of lifetimes past coming up for a complete and full transformation back to the Light.

In 3D/4D consciousness, Karma is still an active and present "spiritual law of the land." These mindblowing memories and their matching experiences essentially had to be spoon fed to us HUmans in nano-droplets over an extremely extended period of time. These events were buried deep in our unconscious minds, purposely hidden there to be eked out during the myriad of all prior 3D/4D lifetimes that we have lived between then and *now*.

The 3D/4D HUman, *at best,* was only able to consciously address small pieces of these traumatized experiences from our Karmic past. We did not have in place the bandwidth of consciousness, worldwide collective circumstances, or the *bigger picture* understanding to revisit these pieces as *awake* as we spiritually are today.

But *now,* after successfully assisting enough of 3D HUmanity to Ascend out of its repetitive chokehold, 5D for the first time, gives us a new perspective and the ability to more easily look back and allow the *bigger picture* of the *why* of it all to come into view. To previously address this, as it was being recreated on our planet throughout each of our lifetimes, would have been untimely without all the needed parts and players in place. We spent lifetimes (including the earlier parts of our current lives) in 3D/4D working through bits and pieces of the world's Karma. Because there is NO more Karma in 5D, it is *now* not up to us to chip away at it a little more but to lean back and finally put the puzzle pieces together that we have been gathering for what feels like forever. It's time to tell the story, make conscious what has remained in our unconscious and give that piece of our HUman history a long awaited 5D send-off. It is not up currently for the old 3D/4D rehashing and review, but for a total mind, body, and *soul* transmutation as we are finally able to *delete* it on a *permanent* source-code and cellular level.

In this lifetime, we had to go all in and use every morsel of our lives, past 3D Karma, and unprocessed issues, at least in regard to Lemuria and Atlantis, to raise the odds in our collective favor for a positive 5D Ascension outcome this time around.

Both vibrationally and situationally, we had to recreate the possibility of a 5D Ascension starting from where it last left off and reenter the plan again with a similar, current version. We had to be ready to experience some of the feelings, trauma, and other deeply held things in our unconscious memory. This recreation would include calling forth many of the original players, both from the Light and from the Shadow aspects of the downfall. In essence, we would have to create enough of a duplication that would allow the HUmans and the collective consciousness another opportunity to address it and its underpinnings, as well as transmute all that was needed into a higher form.

Much of the social and political chaos that we have been deeply traumatized and impacted by, especially in the USA since 2016, is directly attached to our Karmic past in Lemuria and Atlantis. Those remaining past memories and 3D/4D frequencies held in the collective unconscious from our lives back then contributed, not only personally but globally, to bringing to the surface many recreations of chaos, fear, and our current and constant impending sense of doom.

As you will come to see, your participation in this plan shows how deeply committed you and my other readers were to your *bigger picture* assignments.

CHAPTER THREE

FROM ATLANTIS TO ATLANTA

Be on the Lookout for an
"Orange Trip Switch"

November 8, 2016, was the first blatant indicator that we were approaching something bigger than just the outcome of the forty-fifth Presidential election in the United States. When Donald Trump was announced as the next U.S. President, the worldwide response of shock, disbelief, and abject confusion spoke to the depths of what was also unfolding in the macrocosm of the *bigger picture* plan towards a global 5D Ascension.

At the time Trump got elected, most people, including me, were veiled from fully grasping the landslide that was rapidly snowballing and getting ready to descend on our sleepy, unsuspecting planet. A television personality, real estate developer, and deceptively corrupt businessman was about to become the new leader of the free world. His day-to-day presence in our lives tripped a long-awaited, *Karmic switch* that inadvertently triggered the next stage in the final lap of our 3D reality.

Back in late 2015, during the Presidential campaign, something was beginning to feel very off. Even given America's often predictable political puffery, theatrics, and party allegiance drama, there was an unspoken sense that something *darker* was beginning to bubble to the surface. Meanspirited mocking, racist rants, and a surprisingly open disdain for the marginalized and disadvantaged were becoming commonplace.

Even the most radicalized individuals from either political party initially pushed back at the extreme rhetoric and uncouth behavior. For the first time in modern-day politics, everything we had formerly known to be true that was cleverly hidden under the radar was *now* being presented *unapologetically* in broad *dayLight*. It appeared to most who were awake that all hell was about to break loose.

From the onset of his campaign, Trump was a very influential force to be reckoned with. No matter what he did, said, or implied, he effortlessly engaged, excited, and riled up millions of individuals from all parties and walks of life. His caustic persona defied logic and his growing appeal defied common sense. Whether you were in favor of or opposed to his inciting views, his politics and perspectives were rapidly catching fire. There was no denying that an unforeseen momentum across the country was sweeping him and his divisive brand of nationalism into office.

As Trump's rhetoric seeped into the conscious awareness of the American people, his constant presence in our lives acted as a *trigger*, causing a massive subconscious awakening of many of our long ago programmed, Karmic source codes. He was a key *past-life player* in the overall storyline that was being recreated by the world's collective consciousness, all with the *bigger picture* intention as an opportunity to transmute it to something higher. Directly for the USA and indirectly for the rest of the world, if we ever were to arrive at a post-5D Ascension period on Earth, we would have to, at some point, return to a *version* of the 3D Karmic actions, events, or miscreations that originally led to the demise of our last 5D Ascension attempt.

The *"orange trip switch"* was the *Bat-Signal* in the evening sky that globally alerted all the HUmans on the planet whose life work was deeply ensconced in the *Karmic return* of Lemuria and Atlantis that our collective Light was ready to begin the next stage of our post-5D Ascension. We were *now* entering the transmutation journey of releasing the vibrational remains and cellular memories of our 3D/4D lives and the traumatic apocalyptic ending of those incarnations from long ago. His strong presence and enormously supportive platform of American people, let us know that everyone involved, *for better or worse,* subconsciously was ready to *"return to the scene of the crime,"* revisit this very early wound of HUman division and attempt to do it again, only this time with *hopefully* a better outcome. Most of the HUmans who were there then, reincarnated to be here *now,* specifically to be part of his political return.

As all this unfolded in our 3D/4D reality—as the world was getting angrier and spinning more and more out of control— quietly playing out in the background was our 5D reality. We finally made an evolutionary "crack in the egg" and began to allow all *the good, the bad, and the ugly* to surface and show itself without any filters, doctoring, or coverups. As a collective, we had finally risen high *enough* above the unconscious ashes of our apocalyptic trauma, and were vibrationally strong enough to take personal responsibility for our Karmic actions back then and *now.*

In a post-5D Ascension world, we were *now* in position, although unknowingly, to work towards the common goal of reconstructing a world scenario comparable to the scene we created in the months and years leading up to the previous, unsuccessful 5D launch.

As Trump came on the scene back in 2015, we neither had the full *bigger picture* nor the bandwidth to fully grasp how the 2016 upcoming election would be directly tied to the next stage of our 5D Ascension process. It was only in retrospect that we can see how his win, followed by his loss of a second term, and all the accompanying insanity before, during and afterwards, was laying groundwork for HUmanity once again to *choose* a new direction to go in.

It was at this crossroads where 4D became the prominent dimension throughout America and many other parts of the world. Many of the political events since 2016 have acted as catalysts, perfect backdrops for the whittling away of our old, disingenuous 3D facades. The often-upsetting political discourse, sparring, and value system divides were exacerbated under the *polarizing* frequencies of the emerging 4D consciousness.

Once again, as 2016 rolled around, we were in a place on the planet where we were attempting to move HUmanity forward from an accustomed, but outgrown, 3D level of consciousness to a more evolved and expanded 5D level of HUmanity. The chaos and subsequent meltdown of what was once familiar and commonplace was just a byproduct of the intensely polarized standoff between the part of HUmanity that was still vibrating in 3D consciousness and the part that had recently awakened from 3D thought. Although out of 3D consciousness, this rapidly evolving group of HUmans were not yet completely awakened to their 5D selves. These eclectic levels of mixed consciousness—some half-awake and others half-asleep, vacillating between dimensions—formed the 4D bridge of Earth-based consciousness.

Some woke up *"raging"* while others woke up *"peacing,"* but as more individuals awoke, more chaos ensued. Family, friends, and many of our venerable political institutions became undone. Our 3D duality became exalted in 4D as it became electrically charged in the form of *polarity*. The intense 4D polarity field did not cause *all* of the chaos that we were and still are facing today. Instead, it was *projecting* a *new* reality that mirrored the energetic eclipsing of these two major, yet vibrationally different, levels of HUman consciousness.

Karmically, this allowed for the 4D HUman collective to set a *wakeup fire* under previously dormant conflicts and *Shadow aspects* of 3D consciousness that still remained *grossly* out of balance. *Now* awake, gathered, and aligned, this unusually large group of 4D HUmans were perfectly positioned in their *vibrational role* to create a modern-day post-5D Ascension world, albeit 27,000 years later.

Comeuppance or Karma?

One of the main Universal laws of energy is *"Like attracts like."* As 4D *polarity* escalated, it drew to the surface one of the most *polarizing* figures on American soil, or perhaps in the world, Donald Trump. Nobody was more able to trigger, enflame, and set in motion this final piece of our 5D Ascension process. No one (to my knowledge) had come into this lifetime with as vast an amount of personal Karma that he carried regarding the demise of Lemuria and Atlantis. No one had the same *personal soul* agenda or *bigger picture* need for penance (*not Mike)* to be in his position. On a *soul* level, *unbeknown to him,* he was being given an opportunity to right a longstanding Karmic wrong that he not only was part of but *directly* created. In my opinion, no one had more culpability or need to take more responsibility in assisting to reroute this recreation of events back to higher ground.

Under Trump's watch, before and after his four-year Presidency, he served as a catalyst, magnet, and mirror for many of the key HUman foibles that not only plague us today, but also plagued us back then. Similar to *now,* not all the HUmans displayed these lesser qualities. But, if we choose to ignore, minimize, or downplay many of these Shadow aspects both in ourselves and HUmanity, there is a very good chance that once again we will be creating our final demise.

An Ascension Revisited

After four tumultuous years of the Trump Administration and Presidency, the USA, with bated breath, awaited the outcome of our next Presidential election of 2020. In retrospect, LightWorkers around the globe were confused, disoriented, and distraught with the political discourse and unraveling state of the planet. It was a very dark, scary, and critical time for many of us HUmans who were trying to make sense of life in a 3D world from a once-valued 5D perspective. Equilibrium of heart and mind was very hard to come by, as the depth of what appeared to be a *major setback* had quite spun us around. Just a few years prior, an enormous infusion of both Light and Love descended upon the planet, and *now* many of us were questioning if any of it was real or just wishful thinking or spiritual nonsense.

By the time the USA's next election rolled around, many of us were deliriously waiting for the other shoe to drop. Feeling off balance for many years, most of us couldn't with much confidence rely on our intuition anymore, especially regarding the outcome of the next election.

Months before November 2020 rolled around, 5D Astrologer Stephanie Azaria, always a step ahead, shared some poignant pieces of information about Donald Trump's astrological chart on the day of the USA election. She shared that the planet Mars was prominently positioned in the sign of Leo (for him) and, along with other significant aspects, indicated that there would be a lot of unveiling or exposing regarding either him or his political practices. On that day, he also had a *Karmic return* of a nineteen-year cycle *and* the position of his Sun sat *directly* on the Mars positioning in the chart of the entire United States.[2]

During that same period of time, the planet was going through a Mars Retrograde. *Retrogrades* gives us a chance to *re*think, *re*visit, and even possibly *re*do something related to that particular planet and where its retrograde is positioned in the chart being observed.

With all this activity happening around the planet Mars for both Trump and the USA, it appeared that Trump was about to get *yet* another opportunity to revisit something very Karmic in nature to him personally. This particular aspect of his *Mars* specifically sitting on the USA's *Sun* indicated that *if* he won the Presidency, or not, his impact, either way, would be very significant.

Either directly through his election win or indirectly through his loss, he was once again slated to become an important piece in the Karmic puzzle of the return of Lemuria and Atlantis.

It's interesting to note how his last name clearly speaks to his soul's need to *reverse* some of the damage he once did. The middle letters in the name Trump, "um," are MU—the nickname of our beloved Lemuria—spelled backward.

In America and globally, 3D was in the last of its full-blown stages. This was particularly evident in all the political platforms throughout the world. As leader of the free world, the USA needed a very strong wind to come along to potentially disrupt, if not completely take down, our outworn two-party political system that was born out of 3D *duality and opposition.*

On a *soul* level, President Trump at the time was given *yet* another opportunity along with the *"free will" choice* of "how" he was going to address things regarding the election this time around. Like all of us, most of the time our options boil down to either *Light or Shadow*, Love or Fear. In turn, Americans, as a people *and* on an individual *soul* level, were also given their Lemurian/Atlantean Karmic *opportunity* to *choose* either to remain apathetic, complacent, and powerless, as many of them had once done, back then, *or not.*

Our collective consciousness had to decide what path we were going to take in a post-5D Ascension world. From a spiritual perspective, one could argue that the first four years of the Trump Presidency was Karmic in nature and possibly was even needed to set the stage for an opportunity for HUmanity's unprecedented quantum leap. But after four years of all that transpired which the world witnessed a second term would not have served any additional *bigger picture* purpose. It would have only reflected a devolution of the HUman collective consciousness. The remains of the 3D world, including all its energy fields and leftover Karma, belief systems, and accoutrements, had a decreasing small window of time to possibly rise to the Karmic moment and this time around be awakened through LOVE.

The *bigger picture* blueprints for our new 5D Ascension plan had to include all the modifications, upgrades, and reevaluations from the prior unsuccessful attempt. In addition, as a *collective on a higher soul mission,* we had to be in a learning place, not *dozing off* again, or resting on our laurels. For the first time ever, we were experiencing a post-5D Ascension period on a planet that exercises individual *free will.*

As Promised, We All Showed Up

You needed to be here. I needed to be here. And Donald Trump and his entourage all needed to be here for this Karmic moment in time. He was an integral part of the leadership back in Atlantis and he had some very serious personal Karma to revisit—*for better or for worse.* The way the Sun in his astrological chart hits the North Node of the United States also indicated that Trump was meant to be a significant player in *changing* how we see ourselves and how the world as a whole reflects that image back to us.

After our very successful 5D launch in 2012, the post Ascension period *could* have reflected a society of aligned and undivided Americans. Our Earth's health *could* have been in much better shape. Our government and its leadership could have looked *entirely* different. America was and still is the most abundant country in the world. As a collective, Americans could have created and had waiting in the wings, a utopian existence for *all* to flourish in, but that's not what they chose during the years leading up to this period. It was certainly not from a lack of trying, on the part of LightWorkers. We have been working diligently behind the scenes for lifetimes and, truthfully, peddling our "bikes" as fast as we could. For eons we were navigating through a very dense world that was being shaped, and still is, every second by individual *free will*. At times, our Light work had the equivalent complexity as a futile exercise equivalent to trying to *herd cats*—billions of them.

Even in the role as the nontraditional, caustic, outsider President, if Donald Trump would have been reelected again in 2020, he *could* still have done the same thing *Karmically on a soul level* that he was personally slated to do—break down the remains of 3D duality—but differently than he did his first time around. Those of us living in a post-5D Ascension world had energetically arrived at a place on the *cosmic timeline* where his "Karmic services" were needed. And just like every other 3D, 4D, and 5D HUman who is serving and residing on our planet of *free will,* he could have *chosen* to follow through with the same exact *soul* contract through actions that were filtered through the energies of the higher vibrations of Light and Love.

But He Didn't—*or Did He?*

Doing his part, even *unconsciously,* in helping to blow up the remains of the quickly fading 3D world was apparently an item on the to-do-list of his Earth contract. From a *bigger picture,* his *soul* contract could not have received clearance before he incarnated, if not green-lit by the Universe, as well as Trump's higher self. All contracts, no matter how egregious they may seem, are initially structured to unfold with only the highest good in mind. We also agree to subcontracts, thousands of them that never actually come to fruition.

What aren't approved, cleared, or locked in are the unpredictable factors or *individual choices* on how those contracts get executed, specifically on a planet governed by *free will*. That is, and always will be, both the blessing and consequence of living free. HUmankind, first individually and then collectively, gets to choose a lot of its own fate and timing, as we swirl through the *bigger picture* plans on our journey through time and space, back to the unified field of Oneness and God-Light.

Yes, it was clearly part of Trump's Karmic contract to be on call, *if needed*. But his HUman was not at a very consciously evolved place when he was finally called. He could have been a great President, done great things, and led the free world by representing a higher example of kindness, strength, and Love for all HUmans. He didn't. Was that good or bad? The story, even years later is still ongoing, active, and creating more Karma versus clearing old Karma.

Only time will tell how his actions will be assessed and if the choices he made, and continues to make, are placing him in line for a comeuppance. His life, input, and actions continue to be full of drama, deceit, and disruption. From his lost election bid in 2020 up to the publication of this book, a series of cascading events, political reveals, and legal entanglements has Shadowed him at every turn. As aspects of this story continue to remain front and center throughout all media, as depressing and exhausting as it has been, it also has served to awaken HUmanity and hopefully keep them awake.

We still have a very long way to go before this storyline changes. Going forward, the resurfacing of hidden political details, deeply disturbing truths, and many other past Atlantean moments, *if* used constructively, can help jar more memories, feelings, and, hopefully, opportunities for others to also wake up out of their 3D slumber and roll over into *our full potential* 5D world.

Donald Trump himself is neither the exclusive reason nor the absolute power behind the resurfacing of the Shadow energies of 3D thought. But he was and will continue to be a main player through the 2024 Presidential election cycle in the United States. He will serve our cause as the *barometer* by which we measure the remaining state of 3D HUman consciousness. He himself does not have much power; he is only able to carry and reflect back what the collective of HUmans ascribe to him. And in doing so, we can blame him and others or we can move through the collective Shadow by being brave enough to face and transmute our own.

Trump has deep Karma not only with America, but with the whole world. Most likely, if you were around back in the Lemurian/Atlantean age, he had a personal Karmic debt, directly or indirectly, to repay to you too.

As I came to remember, walking alongside everyone else during the last seven tumultuous years, I had some very personal Karma with Mr. Trump as well as one of his key people back then.

I Was Struggling Too

Like many Americans, I was disturbed and very disheartened by the state of politics and the actions of our leaders, especially those of President Trump. He had already been in office for approximately three years, and from my perspective, that's when everything that once made *some* 5D sense to me didn't anymore. I knew we were going through a difficult post-Ascension period as a collective, but I was beginning to feel personally beaten down, spun around, and disconnected from my usual objectivity and *bigger picture* slant on life.

Back in July/August of 2015, it started to become painfully obvious to me that Donald Trump might be a dark horse candidate in the upcoming race for the Presidency. By nature, I'm not one who comfortably rests on anything being absolute and I always try to leave a lot of space for the Universe's long-shot possibilities, but even the fact that I had to consider his possible candidacy was distressing to me. Not because I was rooting for another candidate and didn't want to see my choice or party lose, but because I spent countless years in this current lifetime and many others working for the greater good and the evolution of HUmankind. I was proud of being an integral part of contributing to the planet's successful 5D Ascension just three, very recent years prior.

Spiritually, I was often confused and getting progressively more concerned that something was seriously amiss. I often wondered, *"Have I misread or misinterpreted the signals? Am I wrong about us having reached 5D Ascension?"* I went through periods of feeling empty, cluelessness, and lost. My inner compass spun around a lot, and it was hard at times for me to get my bearings. I chose not to teach classes during those years because, for the previous thirty years or so, I only taught when I felt inspired and directed to do so by my higher guidance. I often felt the connection to my guides was lost—as if my "Bat-Signal" stopped working.

As a Feng Shui Expert and 5D Ascension Guide, I was always "downloading" some important information, direction, or transcendental "intel" to pass on to my students and clients. But, during this period, I found myself living in an unfamiliar place of "radio silence," confused and at times scared. Often when guidance did come through, it was choppy without my usual familiar frequency. It felt like the cadence of a message embedded in an old telegram: *"Teach STOP. On STOP. Blank STOP. Blank STOP."* It seemed only when working with my private clients that I felt aligned and experienced *my* familiar version of peaceful, grounded channeling and still connected with Spirit.

At this same time, the political world was spinning out of control, and I often found myself so saddened and disappointed with our devolving, 3D world. There were periods when I was flabbergasted by the meanness of the rhetoric, the disrespect, and the flagrant bigotry that I was watching come directly from President himself. As a therapist, I was alarmed by what I believed to be obvious mental health issues, behaviors that demonstrated clinical narcissism, dangerous impulsivity, a sociopathic lack of empathy, and emotional immaturity. I was baffled, not so much by the amount of people who, for whatever reason, chose to support him, but because there were so many people—some very smart and otherwise kind—not seeing how *unstable* he was. I think this was the most difficult piece of the never-ending puzzle for me to make sense of in my new 5D world.

For the first few years of his Presidency, I experienced low-grade depression, frequent headaches, floaters in my eyes, and insomnia. To reiterate, this was *not* because the candidate of my choice didn't win, but because, as I eventually came to understand, something was stirring deep in my unconscious, bubbling up to the surface that turned out to be bigger than you, me, President Trump, and the apparent unraveling of the American democracy.

I Remember *Now*

Akin to the impulse of not being able to look away from a bad accident, I frequently watched the nightly news shows during the first few years of Trump's Presidency. Like many other people, I often found myself staring at my TV quietly in a chronic state of disbelief. With each passing headline of a new Trump-related firing, scandal, or *inHUmane* practice, I felt more concerned about the massive division that was unfolding within HUmanity. It was getting difficult for even the most perceptive among us to discern what was real, what was truth, and . . . *what the hell was happening!*

Around the middle of January 2019, I was watching the Senate confirmation hearings for President Trump's latest appointee for attorney general, William Barr. For me, it was the first moment in time since 2015 that everything made *bigger picture* sense and began to fall somewhat into place. I had my first "aha" moment, followed immediately by an exclamation, "Oh no!" I remember feeling frozen, sitting on my couch and although my mind was racing, I physically wasn't able to move. I had a flashback, as if it was yesterday, and I remembered a meeting I had with a man who turned out to be a key player in what was unfolding politically in real time. Here is an excerpt from my journal about that recollection.

The first past-life memory that I recalled about the current political situation was when I was living back in Lemuria. I was standing outside a large, almost castle-like structure, not ornate or very tall, but made of large slabs of pristine white stones. Although it looked more like a fortress, it didn't feel intimidating or off-putting. The surrounding area was quiet and the structure itself felt like it wasn't used often. It appeared to be located in a beautiful, remote area, away from the main surrounding and more populated cities.

Although I couldn't see the ocean, I felt the coolness and breeze coming off its waters and knew it was close by. I stood outside the front outer wall for what felt like an hour, waiting for someone to come out to greet me. I didn't recall how that individual was supposed to know I was there, but I knew they were aware of my arrival. The building was designed with clean and simple lines. It felt peaceful, but I had the impression that at one time it had been much more bustling and was originally built for something other than government activities.

I was living in Lemuria at the time, although over the years I often traveled to Atlantis for both business and pleasure. I was older then than I am now—perhaps in my early seventies? I sensed that I hadn't been back in Atlantis for quite a while and didn't feel the same comfort or familiarity that I felt during my previous visits to this beautiful sister land.

Although I appeared apprehensive, I also seemed relieved. I was finally going to meet with several high-ranking members of the Atlantean government (for lack of a better term). At least this appeared to be the equivalent of what we would call a "government" today. I knew they were individuals who had the "authority" to meet with me and address my concerns. After many attempts over a long period, they finally acknowledged my request, and an appointment was arranged.

I remember being escorted into an open courtyard off to the side of the property. The furniture was marble or stone-like. Some long, rectangular tables were installed around the periphery of the exterior wall that also shared the entranceway leading into the interior space. The furniture was sparce, heavy, and appeared unmovable. It was the equivalent in function to the chairs, chaise lounges, and buffet stands that we might currently use in our backyards and on our patios today. There was an overall ancient Greek or Roman feel to the architecture, but it was not as colorful or engaging as the architecture from modern Greece and Italy. The atmosphere was quiet, at least in my memory, as I waited for several individuals to come out and our long-awaited meeting to begin.

A man walked out into the courtyard. He stood at medium height, approximately five-foot-seven or eight. He was rotund with short, dark hair along the sides of his head. The top of his head seemed mostly bald. He was personable, friendly, and we immediately sat down next to a small, round, white marble table with a heavy, white stone pedestal base. I sat down on a structure that seemed like a simple marble or carved stone chair, and he sat down on a white stone chaise lounge with his legs extended across the footrest. Although neither of us ate, food was displayed on the long, rectangular table against the wall. I recognized some of the food: a roasted fowl and a variety of exotic fruits.

I do not remember the name he went by back then or what his official title was, but the man I was meeting was former U.S. Attorney General William Barr. I do know he was able to speak from a place of authority on behalf of the other leaders who had great influence in Atlantis. I did not consciously recall the specific hierarchy, governmental structure, or assigned political positions of any of the Atlantean people. I did remember, as part of this specific past-life memory, that he apologized to me before we began our talk for the absence of the "other leader" of that political period, who was unable to attend because he had been called away unexpectedly on business.

I was crystal clear that the leader he was referring to is the Donald Trump of today. Although I vacillated back and forth with this particular detail, I could not definitively land on whether they were equal in the line of power or if Mr. Barr worked for him or if Donald Trump was his right-hand person.

Lemuria had a different system of representation, which was structured around egalitarian principles. This was the closest to what we considered to be a form of government. The Atlanteans, specifically those in power during the last few decades before the great fall, never chose to recognize Lemuria's authority as either a formidable opponent or a neighborly ally. During the final years, due to their increasingly self-serving and insular approach to decision making and government-based agendas, they never responded or followed up when the Lemurians (and others) made a multitude of earnest requests for the development of a "good faith" collective HUman alliance.

I was not a part of Lemuria's political structure. I was Jonathan III of Aveidon, a Light Commander of the Intergalactic 5D Earth Ascension Project based on Lemuria. Although I did not come to that meeting representing all the people of Lemuria, I felt compelled and authorized to speak on their behalf.

Although I was not privy to all the ways that the Atlantean quartz generators were being exploited for financial gain and personal power, I did know this much to be true: The inherent capabilities of the crystals piezoelectric circuitry was being extended beyond the range of their natural abilities. The power was being supplied (sold) to other surrounding areas, forcing the crystals to produce a larger output at a greater speed than was originally intended. The generators were being dangerously overtaxed.

I explained my deep concern about the escalating misuse and the mishandling of their powerful, crystal-based energy supply to our current-day Mr. Barr. I wasn't there to morally argue how many of the Atlantean and *some Lemurian HUmans had misused our sacred teachings, abandoned our coveted alliance, or acted in ways that reflected a society whose heart and mind had separated. I was there because I inherently knew that we were rapidly approaching the end of life if something did not immediately cease, and I hoped that I would be heard.*

He leaned in and gave me his undivided attention. Appearing concerned and truly empathetic, he expressed a desire to help in any way that he could. He was empathetic about planning to speak to the "other" leader in his group to apply an immediate intervention of some sort. He was cordial and appreciative and thanked me for bringing the matter to his attention.

As I was walking out of the courtyard, I looked back and remembered noticing that his energy field was now vacant. Although he was "technically" still in his body, it seemed like only a ghost of him remained. He was gorging on a plate of food, consumed in the meal, acting as if I was never there and as if he was not present for our talk just seconds earlier.

I walked out past the white stone walls that surrounded the compound and never looked back. I kept walking. I knew then that most likely my life and everything we LightWorkers had worked for and believed in was over.

I traveled back to Lemuria, and we continued to get as many HUmans as we could off the island along with the artifacts, seed crystals, and sacred scrolls.

It could have been days or weeks that passed, I truly am not sure, but an explosion equivalent to the impact of an atomic bomb in today's world was heard and felt for hundreds of miles throughout the Pacific and Atlantic Oceans. It appeared to me that underwater volcanic eruptions, disrupting the ocean floors, occurred first. Nothing profound happened immediately. Time seemed suspended amidst an eerie sense of calm. There was nothing to do, nothing to say. All I could remember was sitting down and waiting.

Five or six days may have passed. My conscious mind clearly knew it was daytime, somewhere around noon. The sun was out, and the temperature was very pleasant. Possibly we were in the last week of August. I saw myself (Jonathan) suddenly running down from the top of a very lush mountain, zigzagging towards the shoreline below that ran along the backside of the mountain. I was down on one knee, leaning the weight of my body against a low rock formation. I was bending over the structure and looking down into the water, as it was forcefully hitting against the rocks below. I was stretching my right arm out, trying to reach for something that seemed approximately ten to twelve feet past its extended reach. I saw lots of debris floating in the water. There were objects in it that I couldn't immediately identify being washed up by the increasing rough waves.

It was the beginning of the end.

Lowering the Barr

When I met the man before the fall whom I've come to understand is *now* William Barr, I recall he was similar in appearance—portly, balding, though without facial hair or his signature round glasses. Ironically, I only began to recognize him as the same man today when Barr decided to publicly don a "beard." His *beard or coverup* was Donald Trump.

Although, I am still not clear on who was the top guy back in Atlantis, or who worked for whom, I've come to understand that my confusion itself is more telltale than I first realized. In this lifetime, power in the Trump Administration was wielded in the same blurry manner. At any given point, it was never clear to the American people or our friends in foreign countries, who was in charge and making key decisions.

Three years into his Presidency and several Attorneys General later, Donald Trump was again shopping for an AG. The traits on his wish list included being willing to show unwavering loyalty and serve as his personal attorney, and mostly sharing his view of the executive branch as having broad authority, few checks, and unlimited power.

William Barr had already served once as U.S. Attorney General (1991–93) under another one-term Republican President, George H.W. Bush. His tenure back then overlapped with two significant social issues of our era. Back on March 3, 1991, he was the head of the highest office in the U.S. Justice Department when a video of the Rodney King beating by several white police officers in Los Angeles, California, was released to the media. This excessive use of violence, followed by a jury's acquittal of the police officers involved, led to massive social unrest that erupted in coast-to-coast protest demonstrations. During the same period, our country's horrific AIDS crisis was raging and the HIV virus responsible for the epidemic was rapidly spreading around the world.

Barr left that administration with some of his past-life memories possibly stirred (but *definitely not shaken*). He unconsciously tested the waters, but the correct timing, President in office, and level of the collective 5D consciousness was nowhere in place at that juncture in our evolutionary process. Pieces were missing that still hadn't been created or come into play yet by the LightWorkers and HUmanity. Specifically, our successful 12/12/12 5D Ascension was still way down the road. He, like most of us, was unconsciously waiting in the wings for all the aspects of the *potential* 5D Ascension to fall into place, both personally and politically.

With a strong Judeo-Christian faith, staunch conservative views, and decades of moralizing opinions, Barr finally got his long-awaited call back from his stage rehearsal in 1991 when Trump appointed him as the country's new AG.

Our post-5D Ascension indirectly helped Barr and Trump rekindle their old Karmic *"bromance."* Like all of us who came from Atlantis and Lemuria, specifically during its last decade leading to the end, they also subconsciously began to unmoor a part of their past together, one that they were getting ready to reclaim in this lifetime. Barr and Trump both had an enormous amount of unmitigated Karma from their Atlantean lifetimes. The vibrational pull for him to reenter the political fray with his old comrade in arms was unavoidable.

Like some of the "social Karma" that unfolded during his first AG reign during the President Bush era, he would also be reentering the Justice Department while the Black Lives Matter movement was coming on the scene after the heinous murder of George Floyd at the hands of a White police officer in Minneapolis, Minnesota. His reappearance also directly coincided with the arrival of another rampant killer virus that threw the world into a pandemic of inconceivable proportions.

From a Karmic Perspective, the Replay Was Perfect

Trump needed to hire a sympathetic Attorney General who would be friendly to his self-serving agenda. Barr needed to disguise his actions and agenda by serving behind someone who pathologically needed the spotlight and whose narcissism, if things were to go awry, would be almost unaffected by any of the blame, consequences, or repercussions. Trump was a perfect decoy. The perfect partner for Barr, just as Trump had been for him in Atlantis. Like moths to a flame, these two men were drawn to each other once again, and they both had a lot of unfinished past-life business to address for themselves, with each other, and with many of the HUmans on the planet today.

Although he remained biased and protective of President Trump throughout his tenure as Attorney General, once William Barr realized the political tides were changing and Trump was not going to be reelected, he decided to step down before he was let go by the incoming administration. He resigned a few days before Christmas in December 2021. Some might argue he stepped down because he didn't want to participate in the upcoming attack on America's Capitol Building during the insurrection on January 6, 2021, or have it happen on his watch. *Did he choose to grow a conscience in lieu of a beard?* Maybe. But complacency, inaction, and silence are as powerful forms of culpability as violence.

Most accomplices to a crime never come forward or speak up until it somehow serves them. Barr was true to form, as were many other associates and former Trump administrators. The former Attorney General later wrote in his book *One Damn Thing After Another* that President Trump went "off the rails" in the aftermath of the 2020 Presidential election bringing on *"whack jobs"* who fed him a supply of "unsupported conspiracy theories" about the election, according to excerpts published by the New York Times.

For better or worse, when Karma calls—especially on a *free will*-based planet—it will always bring with it an opportunity, even if sometimes it's just a sliver of one, to elevate yourself, others, or the situation at hand. What Barr, Trump or the many others who were involved in the fall of Atlantis did or do during their stay this time on Earth and the opportunities that they will be given are ultimately between them, the Universe, and the *bigger picture plan;* just as all 3D/4D Karmic experiences are for all of us.

I sent the email on the following page to everyone on my 5D mailing list on Wednesday, January 6, 2021, 3:16 PM, as events of the day were still unfolding.

From: Andie SantoPietro

Subject: Current Political Situation

Hey Everybody:

I am very much aware of what is going on—as I know you are all also. It's scary, but we have been preparing for this place of total undoing of what once was for a very, very long time. In and of itself this is an emotionally alarming and disarming time. But for many of us it will also trigger a lot of deep cellular memories of the end days of Lemuria and Atlantis. Lots of different emotions, fears, and abject disbelief.

Let this flush out. Let it run its course. Be with it, allow it, and release it. Don't hold on to it. Let it move through. We are going through a mind-blowing timeline shift, Multiverse transformation, and Ascension like no other. As disruptive and frightening as all this is, remember we are going to get through it and eventually be better for it. Not right now, but soon. Don't get stuck in the reality of the moment. It's transient. If we can steady ourselves, we steady the country, and then the world.

Please hold the space, hold love, and create the intention that this will soon be under control, pass, and peace will prevail.

The universe, as well as all the guides that were with us during calmer times, during our classes are here now with you, me and holding the spiritual energetics behind all that is unfolding.

Don't lose sight of this truth. Hold your own. This is our work... this is our destiny.

I'm sending you all my love and light.

Espavo, Espavo, Espavo.

Andie

Back to the Future

Donald Trump's win of the 2016 Presidential election was a surprise to many of the HUmans who did not see it coming. He was a dark horse in a race that appeared to be going to his opponent, former Secretary of State Hillary Clinton. That is, until the head of the Federal Bureau of Investigation (FBI), James Comey, *intentionally or unintentionally* sabotaged her campaign at the last minute.

I believe that Donald Trump and William Barr, his comrade in arms, as well as a long list of his revolving door staff and friends, came back during this time in history to be given the *dual* opportunity to serve as both villain and/or hero, *based on their choices,* to play out the hands that they were Karmically dealt.

Because the story of Trump's political future and personal life are still unfolding as of this writing, I will withhold my opinion on the final role his history and Karma will play in the *bigger picture* plans on the world stage. What I do know for sure is that Donald Trump is a controversial figure whose mere presence on the campaign trail back in 2015 *"poked the sleeping Atlantean bear"* of our 3D past. And during the years that followed, he also shook a lot of people from their *"gentle Lemurian slumber"* once *again.*

And yes, all of us HUmans reconvened, and it was indeed our Karma to be experienced. But at the same time, please don't lose sight of the fact that Trump, Barr, and everyone one else on the planet today, for that matter, personally carry some piece of our current-day social Karma. No matter what your political preferences are, or which lens you choose to see life through, no one gets a Karmic pass right *now*. And not because of the old 3D "fire and brimstone" belief in punishing wrongdoing, but because we wouldn't be on the planet, *now*, then, or in any lifetime between without a certified 3D-5D Earth passport.

All our Earth HUman passports come standard with a *bigger picture*, two-fold incarnation plan. Every one of us is here for the following two reasons:

1. Our *soul's* personal evolution, and
2. Service and contributions to the greater whole.

Doing our *passport* work here, via the Light or the Shadow, evolved or not, doesn't give anyone a *hall pass* for avoiding the Karmic work and experiences that we all came in to do.

On Planet Earth, if you miscreate or somehow contribute to any prior 3D Karma, you are expected, at some point before you Ascend to a higher level of consciousness, to assist in transmuting all of it back into balance. That's why so many of us during this lifetime feel energetically exhausted, like sponges that were wrung dry. We had a lot to get to and clear up and out—not from a point of punishment but from accountability. It's similar to the way you would be expected to make the bed you slept in or clean the dirty dishes you left in the sink.

Good People Do Horrible Things, Horrible People Do Good Things

Some HUmans commit crimes on this earthly plane, get caught, and then go to prison. Other HUmans commit the same crime, or a worse one, and evade what we would believe to have been justice. Understanding the rhyme or reason of how one person is held accountable for their miscreations whereas another isn't is way above my *bigger picture* level of understanding. What I do confidently know is that there is a very broad difference between *HUman law and Spiritual Law*. How those two realities interplay remains an enigma to most of us. For HUmans, the reasoning of Spirit is most often veiled.

A lot of people in Lemuria and Atlantis, as well as the people in charge of HUmanity's public health at the onset of our current COVID pandemic were asleep on their watch. This is not a statement made to ascribe blame, for no person alone causes any one outcome. No single person has that much power. Nonetheless, *positions of great power come also with great responsibility*. When we are called to those higher office positions, Karmically, the appointment always comes with bigger stakes. This is so, not only on a mundane level but also on a *soul* level. This truth applies whether the individual is conscious of it or not.

Approximately 63 million eligible Americans voted for President Trump in 2016. And although he had two million-plus fewer votes than Secretary Hillary Clinton, the Democratic candidate, he won based on the logic of the electoral college. Every state has a specific number of electoral votes and the popular vote in the state customarily dictates which candidate those votes are cast for. Only occasionally will an electoral college member deviate from their responsibility to do as the people have indicated.

Many people from both political parties, for a variety of reasons ranging from heartfelt and sincere to hostile and angry, saw Mr. Trump as someone representing their desires/wishes/agendas. Many people just wanted a change. Seen as an outsider, others voted for his celebrity persona from his hit TV show *The Apprentice*. Some were angry and frustrated at the direction the county was going fiscally and morally. As in most elections, some were voting against the other candidate. Some liked his bigoted rhetoric at election rallies. These are just a few reasons he received votes. The win itself had its fair share of drama, a myriad of twists and turns, and was peppered with foreign interference that shaped, if not swayed, the election process in unpredictable ways.

In retrospect, I am *now* able to say Trump's election win back in 2016 was clearly a result of our collective past Karma and was inadvertently called forth by all the people and the surrounding elements which aligned and came back into play. We all had a part, for better or worse, in recreating the outcome that put him in power in Atlantis millennia ago. We all had Karma, both personal and social, to process, purge, and transmute. He gave us an opportunity to do this very important "*soul* work."

The four confusing, frightening, and at times mindblowing years of Trump's term in office brought to the surface the disturbing remains of 3D HUman competition, separatism, elitism, greed, ego, apathy, complacency, mental illness, White supremacy, and blatant disregard for the well-being of the planet and its resources. Most importantly for our HUmanity, each of these remains was a Karmic aspect of our existence which we specifically needed to address for our collective 5D Ascension.

Other times and other attempts to raise HUman conscious-ness to a 5D level did not have all the pieces in place as we have *now*. We have been fighting and transmuting these causes for over 27,000 years. The evidence is in our ability to have been able to create the first successful 5D Ascension launch on our planet back in 2012! If we weren't chipping away at this intent lifetime after lifetime, for eons, we wouldn't have been able to excavate the quantity of Karma that we have pulled up from the deepest part of our past HUman experiences. But because we *now* have drawn these remaining pieces into the Light with the 5D level of HUman consciousness available to us, we can also step firmly into this monumental moment in cosmic time. With all of this HUman Shadow truth laid out before a *now* awakened populace, our direction, going forward, is more consequential than ever. Once again, we get to choose on a *soul level,* to either recreate what once occurred or evolve into a better potential version of what can be.

Donald Trump and many of his cohorts obviously owed a huge Karmic debt to many people, not only in the United States, but across the planet. He served a very large purpose during the years of his tumultuous and often destructive Presidency. He shook our democracy, turned a blind eye to the rule of law, and inflamed, as well as helped further polarize, HUmanity. How all those actions eventually will contribute to our evolution versus another devolution has not yet been determined.

In the *bigger picture* storyline, it is looking like Trump came back again as a leader in part to lead the *darker side* of our HUman condition to these exact crossroads. And yes, his part in the outcome, for better or worse, is his personal Karma for him to either transmute or continue to accrue. But what we do and where we go from where he delivered us to as a collective is ours to act on, create with, and ultimately determine.

Those who voted for Trump in 2016 and those who didn't were granted the same four years' tenure of his Presidency equally through which to witness, experience, create, and recreate our perceptions and reality.

Without implying blame or judgment, we all witnessed record-setting administrative turnovers, daily chaos and drama, emotional instability, clinical narcissism, social unrest spurred by elitism, White supremacy, racial divisions, and allegiance with foreign autocrats and governments. Even so, in 2020, another 74 million eligible Americans attempted to vote him back into office for a second term. He lost to his opponent, President Joe Biden, for whom 81 million voted. It was not a close election.

Many people, for many different reasons, once again cast their votes in favor of Trump. Clearly, not everyone was of the same mindset. Nor should all people who voted for Trump be clumped together or seen in a negative light. But no matter what the variations in thinking were among them that had brought them to their personal decision to vote to reelect him, these voters were part of a collective that Karmically shared an intended outcome, creation, and *potential* reality.

As we saw during the insurrection at the Capitol Building in Washington, D.C., on January 6, 2021, and the subsequent attempts of Trump constituents to overthrow the 2020 election, this Karmic movie is far from over. There is an upcoming presidential election in 2024 that he may decide to run for as the Republican candidate. Even though Mr. Trump may have been voted out for a consecutive second term, millions and millions of people are still actively reflecting and vibrating to a significant piece of their unfinished 3D/4D Karmic pasts.

Maybe the spiritual purpose of this is to spur the growth of their Light. Maybe it's for the transmutation of leftover 3D/4D consciousness Shadows. But like all of us, we are here *now* together experiencing all this life stuff that remains before us to choose how we want to both dimensionally perceive it and then, more importantly, transmute it so we can elevate all of HUmanity.

Many people back in the days of Lemuria who were once living on automatic pilot have *now* finally awakened. A lot of the people of Atlantis have also been given another opportunity to reevaluate their own past beliefs and priorities. We are *all* getting another opportunity to revisit our values and what we view as important.

From Atlantis to *Atlanta*

The 2020 election was fraught with so many twists and turns, political propaganda, lies, distortions and manipulations to alter and change its outcome in favor of a President Trump win. The degree of violence, HUman polarization, recounting of votes, attempts to seize voting machines and change the electoral votes was a frightening display of a democracy being put under duress and a 3D society whose scaffolding was the *rule of law* showed signs of cracking.

There were many states where the former President lost both the popular and electoral college vote. In many of those states, he, his administration, and many appointed local, state, and federal Republican party members collectively fought to overturn the results. But of all states that proved the most pivotal and significant, especially at the end, the one that mattered most was Georgia. A specific community in Georgia that was pivotal was *Atlanta.*

Trump not only lost in Georgia, but he was recorded on tape attempting to intimidate and coerce its Secretary of State into "finding another 11,780 votes," an amount that would have given him one more popular vote than needed to win that state's electoral college votes. Georgia's district attorney went on to sue Trump for his corrupt actions, and as of the time of this writing, the lawsuit was still pending.

Georgia also added to its significance as a prime player in this Atlantis to Atlanta *bigger picture story.*[3] After a very close runoff election, they managed to eke out winning back two seats from the Republicans, giving the Democratic party the majority in 2020 of the U.S. Senate.

In addition, two years after being a key player in taking control of the U.S. Senate, news headlines about Georgia abounded once again! In January 29, 2022, a headline of an article referencing the November 2022 midterm elections read: "Control of Senate Once Again Hinges on Georgia!" With even more Karmic skin in the game *now,* the historically Republican suburbs in metropolitan Atlanta—the most populous part of the state—are leaning heavily Democratic.

I do not know what all this will mean going forward. Nor am I implying there will be a particular outcome. But I am truly clear that the people throughout the great State of Georgia, some of their stellar leadership, and our very own, 5D candidate Stacey Abrams are playing particularly important roles in our full-circle return from our days past in Lemuria and Atlantis.

No matter what dimension you choose to pontificate from, words, in any language, have both a meaning and a vibratory field that surround them. A word can signal a warning, a statement of Love, or a *subconscious memory*. Words are powerful and deliver us to a position or stance that we often don't even know we arrived at, way past its intended meaning.

Atlanta is, was, and will continue to be a deep reminder, a symbol, and a subconscious trigger for many of us who have been impacted by our lives and years during and leading up to the fall of *Atlantis*. Trump, Barr, Stephen Miller, and a whole cast of HUmans who were around during that failed 5D Ascension attempt and the demise that followed also were and are subconsciously impacted by *words,* Karmic timing, triggers, and contracts.

Much of this coalesced off the Atlantic Coast but the tornado landed on the good soil of Atlanta, Georgia. I suspect that the name Atlanta was also a main town back then, possibly *Atlanta, Atlantis.* It was our version of what we today refer to as the capitol of a state. Atlanta today is also the real-time capitol of the State of Georgia.

Many of the power crystals from the monolithic energy towers back in Atlantis and Lemuria were detonated due to misuse and the personal greed of the people who were influential at that time. Large pieces of those crystals sank deeply and spread into our many *oceans and waters* around the globe. Starting in 2020, through earthquakes, tsunamis, and global warming, the crystals began to make their way to the surface, through deep rock and from buried sands to more accessible levels where their gravitational pull, vibrational fields, and hidden programs could be felt and possibly accessed once again.

Quartz crystals are live entities within the mineral kingdom. Life force has consciousness, and consciousness can never be destroyed, only transmuted. Some of these crystals have traversed both the Pacific and Atlantic Oceans and are starting to get closer to specific areas and lands that have people living on them from back in Lemuria and Atlantis. Many LightWorkers around the globe are waiting to receive the messaging, consciousness, and most importantly, *the programming they carry*. This information will only be accessible to us when at last we achieve full 5D Ascension on Planet Earth.

Some of those crystals and their embedded teachings are currently within range of Atlanta, Georgia, and are helping the people, including political leaders, not only to awaken, but activate their *soul service contracts*. These powerful crystals are also showing up throughout the globe, coded, alive, and carrying higher vibrational Light to support HUmanity towards a higher, more advanced world creation.

Hello, Old Friend

Vladimir Putin, Russia's current President, had what appeared to be a very interesting relationship formed with Donald Trump during Trump's first campaign in 2015 that extended beyond his lost Presidential bid in 2020. Putin and many of Russia's oligarchs, had a vested interest in supporting and helping Trump to get elected, then reelected. Putin waged an unprecedented "disinformation" campaign in an effort to accelerate the further division of the people of the United States, while at the same time supporting the candidate of his personal choice, Donald Trump. Through political camaraderie and allegiance, the two superpower *leaders* created a mutually supportive relationship that had little to no benefits for the people of their respective countries.

Although on the surface they appeared very different, these two leaders shared a similar vibration and understanding of the *world, money, and personal power.* Their relationship baffled many. They both may have had overlapping autocratic desires, but what was at the crux of the world trying to figure out their true connection was their shared past lives in Atlantis. Putin and Trump were *colleagues* back then, expressing similar politics, beliefs, egos, and self-destructive tendencies of eventually *"flying too close to the sun."*

In this lifetime, both men have shared a similar ideology that was born out of the remains of our old, out of balance, *3D duality paradigm.* Their mutual pathology and personal Karma—*narcissistic entitlement*—was further nurtured by privilege, supremacy, and a penchant for unchecked power and greed. They, along with many others throughout the world, over eons of time, have helped carry, but more importantly *reflect,* the Shadow energies that exist throughout all aspects of HUmanity.

Putin's past-life persona began to reveal itself worldwide on even a deeper level with the annexation of Crimea in 2014, and the invasion and attempted takeover of Ukraine, currently happening in real time as I write this today, on February 2, 2022 (2-22-2022). Each of these egregious acts of maniacal greed and blatant disregard for HUman life were cast from Putin's original playbook from his time spent in Atlantis. But coincidentally, the first big reveal of his Karmic return was back on August 8, 2008 (8-8-8), with his invasion of *Georgia.* And like his Karmic colleague, Trump, all the way on the other side of the globe, *Georgia* was a player once again.

The genocidal war waged by Russia in the Ukraine under Putin's command in our real time 3D world was and continues to be a horrific HUmanitarian tragedy but, from a 5D perspective, it has surprisingly incited many other HUmans around the world to *wake up and get involved*. After so many times, throughout our 3D/4D history that HUmans, as a people got caught sleeping at the proverbial "Lemurian wheel," we are once again being given the opportunity to collectively rise against the darker side of HUmans and HUmanity and use our *Light and Love* actively to transmute what is unfolding into something greater and unified. This bloody conflict is an opportunity not only for us to support the Ukrainian people but to help the people of *Russia* wake from their "Lemurian sleep" and rise out from under the terrible regime which passivity and helplessness created.

No matter what unfolds on the planet during this heart-wrenching period of HUman loss and displacement, our world has been forever changed. Since World War II, we have never witnessed a war of this nature or been as *awake* collectively as we are *now*. Although we often focus on the downside and confusion about many of the world events occurring during our post-5D Ascension period, the outpouring of vocal, financial, and active support is tangible evidence of a planet unified in their *hearts*. The people of Ukraine, and their leader, Volodymyr Zelenskyy, are reflecting back to our new 5D world the power we hold by *how and where* we choose to focus our attention, through *Love and with Light*. This is clearly our first 5D war. In the short run, this war is a painful reminder of the difficult path that *bigger picture change* sometimes takes. We are in this 5D Ascension for the long game and, for better or worse, *the only way out of it is through it.* We can choose to parlay all this chaos and suffering for something greater, just like our heart-based 5D brothers and sisters in Ukraine are modeling for us.

Atlantis sunk into the sea first, before the continent of Lemuria was severely and horrifically consumed by the fallout of radiation from explosions in the electrical crystalline grids in Atlantis. As described previously, the impact of the radiation on the plants, landscape, and remaining HUmans is beyond description. I have had very difficult past-life memories of being there and the impact that the radiation had on me personally.

Just days after Putin invaded Ukraine, he made an unmitigated, bone-chilling threat to NATO countries, *reminding* them that he had access to nuclear weapons. The inference was clear, he was willing to engage in nuclear bombing if he deemed it necessary. A maniacal dictator of today's 3D world openly expressed total disregard for people's lives and their potential suffering for many of the same reasons of *greed, power, and narcissism* that many individuals exhibited in Atlantis. Putin unapologetically showed the world that he would be willing to engage in nuclear mass destruction, the type of war that is always followed by the larger, longer-lasting damage of *radiation poisoning.*

Only a *spiritually* deranged HUman who is terrified of what might lie before him would be willing to go out in infamy, recklessly dying on his own sword, for all the world to witness. Only someone with a very dark, unresolved Karmic past could possibly need to recreate some of the exact circumstances of the moment in time when Atlantis fell. For he too, as Shadowy a HUman as he may be, is here to transmute unresolved soul issues and bring them back to the Light. Like Trump and the rest of us who have come here *now,* he is here to reroute and release the past through newer, higher choices.

The 5D Light in all of this 3D darkness is how, in this lifetime, his Karmic involvement in our modern-day version of some serious devolution actually gave those committed to living in the Light a golden opportunity to rise, empower themselves, and take more "action" this go-around.

What happened and continues to unfold in the nation of Russia and to its people will be an important element in the narrative of our 5D post-Ascension world. They, the Ukrainians and all the HUmans around the world *now* hold the Karmic opportunity in their hands and collectively can contribute to a mutual release of yet another major piece from our karmic past in Lemuria and Atlantis.

And in keeping perfect step with the crossover of current and past events, the Universe has a very interesting way of placing pieces together of equal value. In Kostroma Oblast, a federally controlled region of Russia, lies the town of Shunga. This is the only place in the world that mines the highest quality of the stone named Shungite, which is a *rare,* black, naturally occurring, carbon-based stone that conducts electricity and has very powerful healing properties. High quality Shungite absorbs and diffuses electromagnetic frequencies (EMFs) and other forms of, you guessed it, *radiation.*

Help Came by Way of Three Major, Multilevel Service Interventions

LightWorkers and non-LightWorkers alike will often experience 3D realities and Karmic miscreations that, no matter how *advanced* of a spiritual being they are, never *feel* fair or make any sense to the subject. Living as a 5D being sometimes brings situations related to personal and *bigger picture* issues that are inexplicable to the heart and too much for the sane mind ever to process.

The "whys" for many of the events in our current timeline are veiled from us, often leaving us feeling defeated, frustrated, and angry. Life and all our efforts appear so pointless at times that we rightfully wonder if even one of our prayers has been heard or . . . *if there is even a God.*

The political chaos and social uprisings around the world, particularly in the last decade, have not fallen outside of this fold. It's often hard to fully believe that we are actually part of a benevolent *Universal game plan* with unlimited support and a back-up cavalry.

Although there are thousands of service contracts in play every second of our lives, most of the time we don't identify them as such. Such *soul* agreements are invisibly woven into the fabric of even our most simple decisions, such as to make a left or right turn while driving, or in fleeting thoughts. We don't usually experience them as *higher guidance* or *divine interventions because* they are so subtle and unseen, *except* on an etheric level. Many of these events are cleverly layered into our regular, everyday routines, as well as into the great and terrible moments in life. As difficult as it is to fathom, these types of service contracts are also in play when we are experiencing the world's darker moments and unspeakable 3D/4D HUman tragedies.

Our 5D Ascension in 2012 brought with it a more advanced HUman with newer capabilities for cocreating on higher levels within the framework of Universal law. We created an evolved collective of advanced beings of Light that are *now* able to call in and activate certain *bigger picture, intergalactic intervention* contracts.

The more advanced our levels of individual and collective consciousness became, the more able we were to receive and utilize some of the greatest levels of Universal help available to us *now* on our *free will-based* planet Earth.

Although there are millions of contracts at play at any one time, the three that magnetically came into my *bigger picture fold* were as follows.

Earth's *Merger* with Planet Eargo: The Divine Feminine Cavalry Arrives

A pivotal year, 2020 brought with it a long series of destabilizing events that could have turned out to be cataclysmic in nature for our 3D-5D world. It's important to know that for all our understandable internal questioning about topics like *"Where was God through all this?"* the Universe was diligently working behind the scenes on behalf of our 5D Ascension mission. For the past 27,000 years, many Light beings, both those in and out of physical bodies, have been on a mission to help HUmanity evolve from its longstanding lower vibration of 3D into a higher 5D level of consciousness on Planet Earth.

Thankfully, the benevolent Universe did not assign us to Planet Earth to navigate this monumental, multilevel Ascension miracle without a lot of help from beings of the unseen world. One of our planetary allies, making good on a prearranged Earth contract, helped us align a much-needed intervention on our planet at the time we required the assistance the most.

During the second half of 2019, Earth's vibrational orbit, both spiritually and energetically, stepped into a *time merger contract* with the vibrational orbit of another planet in our Multiverse, *Eargo*. Although we have *crossed* timelines with other planets many times before, we had never previously *merged* timelines with another planet to this degree.

In general, timeline crossings are common throughout the Universe. Many of them occur by agreement. And these agreements are found "written in the fine print" of intergalactic contracts as "if needed" back-up plans. A *timeline crossover* is when two planets vibrationally eclipse each other's vibrational field, and for a cosmic moment brush elbows, sharing or exchanging something that the other planet (or its HUmans) needs a homeopathic "infusion" of at a precise moment in time. When they occur, the crossover is usually short, quick, and experienced as just a cosmic blip in time, often with both planets not even recognizing that the overlap had happened. On a more personal level, sometimes we experience these crossover moments as a flash of *"déjà vu"* or the feeling of familiarity when we have met someone for the first time. Sometimes this uncanny sense of ease also happens when we walk into a particular environment or step off a plane in a totally new place that we have never traveled to before.

Technically, what's happening at that precise moment is that the vibrational fields from two different planets or energy constructs are identical in their frequency notes. This in turn, adjusts, fine-tunes, or injects an outside vibration to activate or trigger pre-programmed contracts, source codes, reminders, or adjustments.

Our *souls* and overseers of a planet could schedule a plan B crossover for a variety of reasons, including the purpose of advancing timelines, sharing events, staging an intervention, or simply connecting the vibrational field of their inhabitants.

HUmans, animals, and environments may interact in unusual ways during a timeline crossover *or not*. Once the crossing of two frequencies has served its energetic purpose (perhaps it is a Karmic *soul* meeting to release or repeat an old experience, a past-life memory, or make a vibrational adjustment, and so forth), then the two vibrational fields quickly morph back into their individual timelines and orbits. Then the veil is placed back on and the seemingly off moment in time returns to normal if you will. The weird perception or experience passes, as if it never happened.

By contrast, when two timelines *merge,* the eclipsing aspect of the two individual fields or planets isn't just a momentary blip, but an actual joining together for a longer period. This is a very rare occurrence.

Even a brief exposure to another energy field will transmit both the *compatible* and *incompatible* frequencies of that field, object, or person. Through osmosis, we could pick up both the wanted and unwanted energy patterns in the process of exposure to their vibration. More often, however, the frequencies that remain with us tend to be those we already are vibrating to or are under contract to receive.

A planetary merger is much riskier than a planetary crossing, as we run the chance of being overexposed to frequencies that can be disruptive or unhelpful.

Although energy transfers are not guaranteed during timeline *crossovers and mergers,* especially on planets that are based on *free will,* if an individual or planet has the *vibrational receptors* to magnetically attach, then hold onto a frequency that they were exposed to, then the transfer usually occurs. The recipient would need to have the emotional, spiritual, and energetic conductors to integrate, maintain and *host* the new frequency and all that it brings on a long-term basis.

In or around October/November 2019, many LightWorkers around the world were called to join our 5D mentor, *Steve Rother, and the Group* for a class and channeling session regarding Planet Eargo and its upcoming merger contract with Planet Earth. He shared the information that during the week of November 16–23, peaking on the 23rd, we were going to have the first of three energy infusions through a timeline *merge.*[1]

Eargo is similar to Earth in many ways. Its civilization had qualities that we were in desperate need of, and we had some advanced attributes that they needed. The Universe and many of our allies working in the unseen world gave both Earth and Eargo clearance for a planned *bigger picture* contract to go forward. When a plan B level of support is intergalactically greenlit in this manner, it usually means that some aspect of plan A has failed or is about to head off the rails. Planetary mergers are implemented when a *significant* intervention is needed.

Eargo's society is super advanced in *governing*. Its history reflected eons spent working on and reducing the negative impact of an unbalanced political system. Through a lot of hard work, trial and error, over time they arrived at a profound and constructive system of governance that worked with *feminine energy* as its primary focal point. Planet Earth was in the period following its 5D Ascension and trying to break free from its old duality based political structure, which was anchored in patriarchal *masculine* 3D energy. On a mundane level and from a *bigger picture* perspective, we needed this energy infusion to restore our balance, as we were spiraling down what seemed like a bottomless political rabbit hole.

Let me put this in context. At the time, in the United States we were knee-deep in the Trump Presidency, democracy and the rule of law were dissolving, and many countries around the globe were on shaky ground. The planet was destabilized and all HUmans, aware or not, were in desperate need of a higher reasoning, more fleshed-out model of government to grow towards vibrationally. Eargo offered those things to us. As advanced as Eargo was in this area, it was lagging somewhat behind in the areas of technological advancements and 5D spiritual acumen. Planet Earth, for all our shortcomings, has led a lot of the Planets throughout the Multiverse in the areas of spiritual evolution, technology, and science.

Higher law placed our planets together and both benefited from the other's infusion of chi. Our Light team did not know then how this was going to work, or even if Eargo's higher-frequency governing would be enough to assist Earth in overcoming the massive political and social divides that were rapidly escalating worldwide. This energetic standoff was one of the byproducts of a fading 3D and increasingly 4D level of consciousness. We were reaching an extremely *dangerous* impasse.

Without knowing at the time what was to come both politically throughout the USA and especially with Russia's recent, despicable, genocidal invasion of Ukraine, it is self-evident, *now* more than ever, how much our planet needed the high-level intervention of the Planet Eargo merger. Our governments and politicians are still operating within the old, *soul*-destroying 3D Shadow model. I believe our merger with Eargo was an important "behind the scene" component to why we are still able to move forward as a viable planet today. The rise of HUman consciousness that has emerged from our planetary infusion of Eargo's feminine energy, specifically *governing* energy is quickly becoming a significant piece in our *bigger picture* untold 3D–5D story.

As bad as things were in 2019 and as bad as things still are, without the unseen forces carrying balance, good, sensibility, and calm through the vibrational fields of the LightWorkers around the world to everyone else, everything we know would have escalated into an even harsher alternate reality that we wouldn't have been able to make our way back from. The role of LightWorkers regarding our current state of affairs, especially in the Ukraine, is to continue to download and disseminate the feminine energy and make this atrocious war the last 3D war *EVER* on our new 5D planet.

Eargo was the behind-scenes puzzle piece that supplied the additional fuel and laid the feminine groundwork for HUmans to continue to evolve and for the *bigger picture* plan to move forward, despite the world's current appearance. We are seeing this energetic shift in leadership and how "feminine" power is displayed in the real-time actions, steadfast commitment, and heartfelt words and strength of President Zelenskyy. We are getting to witness what governing looks like with the Divine Feminine at the helm.

Over the few years since then, additional important *infusions* of feminine energy have proved invaluable to Earth, as HUmanity was about to enter a very dark time on the planet. Ever so slightly, this energy has helped us to keep our hearts open as we began moving through an intense post-5D Ascension period replete with life or death choices and decisions to *evolve or devolve.*

187 LightWorkers Sacrificed Their Lives for the Greater Good

Approximately seven weeks after the first infusion of Eargo energy occurred, the world experienced a shocking, heart-wrenching HUman tragedy. Once again, Ukraine was involved. On January 8, 2020, FLight 752, a Ukraine International Airlines civilian aircraft, was shot down by an Iranian air defense crew who mistook it for an incoming American cruise missile. A hundred and eighty-seven people, on a *soul level,* had made a crucial decision to be passengers on that plane as a form of service to the planet. From a HUman heart-based perspective, the loss of life, families destroyed, and the impact that a tragedy of that magnitude leaves behind was inconceivable. And although it doesn't change the outrage and the senseless loss of HUmans lives, I choose to see those *souls* as heroes. What apparently seemed purposeless from our limited 3D perspective, that horrific crash inadvertently also served in the *bigger picture* plan as an intervention to prevent what would have been a much larger loss of life, a *third world war.*

The two opposing leaders in office at that time, Iran's supreme leader Ali Khamenei and the U.S. President Donald Trump were known to be as emotionally unstable as two vials of nitroglycerin during an earthquake. Leading up to that day, the tension between them was mushrooming. Neither person possessed the leadership qualities or mental health balance needed to deflect, negotiate, or deescalate what was looking like an international crisis on a grand scale. When the plane was shot down in error, the hearts of all HUmans around the world were thrown into shock. In turn, these two leaders were also jolted out of their obtuse disregard for what the repercussions would have been if they had pursued their escalating hostile actions.

On any level of consciousness, 3D, 4D or 5D, *make no mistake about it,* this loss of life was a devastating tragedy for the people who were on that plane, their Loved ones, and the rest of HUmanity. The event left a big hole in the hearts of many. Did those passengers and crew know what fate awaited them? Consciously, *probably not.* But unconsciously, I believe they did. This is not in any way to excuse the behavior of the political players and Shadow aspects involved. It's not meant, in any way, to diminish the HUman tragedy that occurred. Any of those reactions would be narrow, emotionally cut off, and cruel. And my perspective is surely not meant to excuse responsibility or diminish blame. But from the *bigger picture* of "why" we are here, our *calling* to incarnate into a life as an earthly HUman is a coveted blessing.

We make the choice consciously to volunteer to incarnate before we are born. It is not only a great honor to come down, but to be *chosen* to become an Earth-based HUman. With that choice, however, comes one of the most difficult challenges in creation, one everyone here will experience from the perspective of the HUman body. The beauty of HUman incarnation also means that the HUman heart will at times endure the pain of loss and grief. For it is only in the HUman body that *souls* experience emotions, both the happy ones and the not so happy ones. Grief is grief. Loss is loss. These emotions can be painful and devastatingly life altering.

Without remembering that there are *always* many moving parts to every tragedy, loss, and aspect of life that is not going as planned, you will be relegated to seeing life through the single, narrow lens of your 3D experiences and thinking. 3D experiences are not wrong; they are as real as any other perception. But 3D only delivers one tile in a situation's multidimensional mosaic. Life in 3D is like having access to numerous cable networks yet choosing only to watch the same program night after night. After a while, you might start believing that what's playing on that one station is the only show in town. It's *not.*

The duality-based principles of 3D thinking have conditioned us into a belief system of this or that *opposites.* Conditioning puts our HUman backs (*and emotions*) against the wall and tells us that we must choose only *one* reality and dismiss all others for us to arrive at the *real* truth. As we and the rest of the people in the world grow into our 5D HUman selves, it becomes more obvious to us with each passing day that *truth is transient and relative.* It's not as fixed as we once believed.

I know that those 187 passengers were ordinary citizens. Mothers, fathers, sisters, brothers, neighbors, and children of somebody. I know that they were innocently going about their days, traveling, working, or just grabbing a fLight home to their Loved ones. But I also know that there were 187 LightWorkers that day, leading with their hearts, who were working for a higher cause.

If we don't look beyond the tragedy and dismiss the part of that event that was inexplicitly connected to their *soul* purposes, then we fail to honor, Love, and bow our heads to all aspects of who those people were. If we see them only as victims and not some of the most honorable and generous *souls* in the Universe, then we will be failing to understand their *bigger picture* work and gifts to HUmanity. More importantly, we would not be "holding space" for the unfathomable sacrifice that they and their families contributed by way of their return trip back home. They hold a venerable place in the LightWorker chain of command. With deep gratitude and honor, I acknowledge them, thank them and bow.

The following writings and information occurred during the editing state of this manuscript. It was a very interesting synchronicity to both acknowledge and add to the section above, which was written almost a year before it.

During the month of July 2022, there were several televised hearings put on by the House of Representatives Special Committee on the January 6, 2021, insurrection at the U.S. Capitol Building in D.C. As the bipartisan committee interviewed hundreds of *witnesses and reviewed documents, they came across a section of time during the day of the insurrection where records of President Trump's actions, inactions, and usual documentation of a President's whereabouts were inaccessible. Newspapers and various TV outlets often began to refer to that period of time when he first left the "Stop the Steal" rally at the Ellipse in Washington, D.C., to the time he first appeared to make a public statement or take any action to intervene regarding the attack of a mob of his followers on the Capitol Building as the "**missing 187** minutes."*

I believe each brave soul on that fated Ukraine International Airlines fLight gave their life that day in exchange for one of those missing 187 minutes. Hundreds of HUman lives, all the top levels of our United States government—from then-Vice President, Mike Pence, House Speaker Nancy Pelosi, members of the Senate and House of Representatives, along with several other leaders in the line of succession to the Presidency and backbone of our democracy—could have been assassinated in a period of several hours.

Instead, a Karmic miracle took place that day at the Capitol. Despite the horrific unfolding of real-time trauma and violence, while witnessing unspeakable acts of destruction with no leadership or backup forces to assist, given what "could" have unfolded during those very dark hours paled in comparison to what actually did. Without knowing it, the entire world witnessed a 5D timeline cross of events that inadvertently stopped the

potentially cataclysmic end of the democratic system of
the USA via a coup to overthrow the government.

That evening, in the midst of a modern-day war zone,
the U.S. Congress reassembled and the votes were cast,
just as planned, declaring Joseph R. Biden the forty-
sixth President of the USA.

Two More Divine Infusions Complete the Eargo Merger

With each passing day in early 2020, the world seemed to need more and more assistance to stay out of the rising wave of tension, anger, injustice, and fear. The *second infusion* of energy from the timeline merger with Eargo occurred in April 2020, and the *third and final infusion* came in August 2020. The same type of energy, attributes, and strengths were shared between Earth and Eargo as the first time. Each "hit" reinforced the original contract exchange, just to a lesser degree, as the planets were slowly moving away from their original vibrational connection. On these occasions, we nonetheless were exposed to, and downloaded more of Eargo's source codes related to feminine governing principles and the feminine energy in general. Also on those heightened occasions, we shared our 5D Ascension and technology source codes with Eargo.

In retrospect, those downloads turned out to be crucial, as the world was about to begin meandering, for a few surreal years, in ways that we had not foreseen. These years would require us to remain painfully awake, keep our 5D hearts open, be accessible, and stay the 5D post-Ascension course.

Despite the trauma that was about to be unleashed around the world, these infusions helped stabilize our hearts and seeded many, many gifts and creations within us and throughout our ever-changing civilization. The extra infusions or *energy hits* that we absorbed and in turn, released into the world will continue to grow for decades to come. They paved the way for many more HUmans to *wake up* and enter a new stage of personal empowerment and change. The feminine merger energies contributed to the newly awakened consciousness reflected in the majority of Americans who voted in the 2020 Presidential election and indicated not needing another four years of President Trump in the White House for their evolutionary growth and Lemurian/Atlantean lifetime healing. Although the 3D/4D world around us continued (and continues) to breakdown, the collective consciousness broke through the surface and helped reveal many layers of imbalance that were long hidden. This massive awakening and shift of 3D Shadow consciousness to 5D Light consciousness laid the groundwork and contributed to the election of President Joseph Biden in 2020, a very strong, heart-based, *feminine-energy male.*

The feminine energy infusions also activated dormant social contracts and provided the torque needed for powerful movements, such as "Me Too," "Times Up," "Black Lives Matter," and the kind of challenges to our outdated 3D paradigms such as the one led by athlete Megan Rapinoe for equal pay for female soccer players to emerge. It paved the way for the exposure of many masculine-dominated institutions such as the Catholic Church, and more currently the release of the Southern Baptist Church's "secret" list of sex abusers among its ranks and congregations. Bills in New York City, for example, were passed where victims of childhood sexual abuse could *now* come forward to sue their abusers, as the old 3D patriarchal statutes of limitation had been lifted.

This energy also supported us through two of the most consequential events that have occurred in our 5D post Ascension journey: the historical election of U.S. Vice-President Kamala Harris and Senate confirmation of U.S. Supreme Court Justice Ketanji Brown Jackson.

President Biden and Vice President Harris were inaugurated on January 20, 2021. This date (1-20-2021) is a *palindrome*—the numbers read the same way back and forth—a phenomenon that is numerologically significant. Palindromes, spiritually speaking, represent glitches associated with overlapping past, present, and future timelines. Such dates are seen as auspicious, having almost magical powers to reset the energy of events in history both in the seen and the unseen worlds.

Remember, *no* one single factor creates anything. On the other hand, we can never fully know what that one single factor might bring to the total equation of a life, situation, event, death, or anything for that matter. The playbook of Ascension, our multidimensional reality, and the *bigger picture* plan often presents itself in incremental pieces, and on the surface feels like one big, confusing dichotomy.

Many of us have suffered greatly during the last five to ten years as we tried to wrap our heads around what was unfolding before our eyes, and often feeling helpless, unable to do anything about it. Perhaps we had an idea once, a sense of what we believed was right, good, fair? We struggled with questions like *"What is the rule of law?" "What is justice?"* and *"What is acceptable in a democracy?"* We have also often asked, *"Is anybody in charge?"* And more painfully, *"Did God forget about us?"*

As we move forward, one of the things that will help buffer those living here is to remember there is a very big difference between *HUman law and Spiritual law.* HUman law is flawed. It's limited. It's based on opinion, feelings, randomness, imbalance, and the misuse of power, etc. God's law is Divine and it's just and fair. Throughout the majority of our stay here, we are blocked from seeing the *bigger picture* that is often being played out multidimensionally.

The Universe is constantly cocreating many different, alternative roads, timelines, and events with us. Often, during some of our darkest moments, these are veiled from us, not by God, but by our limited HUman bandwidth to take it all in. Although we believe that we'd be better off knowing, in actuality we're just placating our old 3D/4D masculine brain that wants to be one step ahead of the curve, needing to control our actions, and reactions. In 5D, the only time is in the *now.* There is no advantage or need to be anywhere other than where you are in the moment and facing the task that is right before you. Its challenging at first, but in 5D, it's the law of the land.

What can you do when you feel confused and upset by events? Start by reminding yourself at every turn to at least consider that many of the realities you are witnessing in your own life, on the news, in politics, and elsewhere, are playing out on different levels simultaneously. The same events are always serving as pieces to different puzzles.

Even without understanding any or all of the details of the unseen *bigger picture,* try to make the space for the possibility that other realities do exist. Each is part of a greater plan to direct us to create a life and ultimately a reality that contains more value, greater Light and an expanded state of unified Love. We are multidimensional beings living in a multidimensional world, constantly in service for the greatest good of all *souls,* sentient and insentient, bodied and of spirit.

Sometimes the Universe sends a good opportunity to us by means of what initially appears as a problem like a health challenge or a setback. Other times, the Universe takes something that HUmans themselves have miscreated and tries to use it instead for our highest good, in spite of our missteps. Worldwide, the most profound Shadow opportunity of our post-5D Ascension period may have presented itself in the form of a *virus.*

CHAPTER FOUR

A PANDEMIC
ENTERS THE FRAY

2020: Numerology Sets the Stage

In January 2020, we moved from the 20(1)9 year (a decade of numbers beginning with ones) to year 20(2)0, which was going to lead an entire decade that would be vibrationally guided and directed by the number two. Upping its numerological intensity, year 2020 held *two "2s"* and *two "0s."*

In numerology, the energy of the number *one* is primarily about new beginnings, ideas, and leadership, as well as providing the *context* of the individual: I, me, self, and so forth. "1" is a singular number, so it reflects singularity in its energy and manifestations. It is also considered to be a *masculine* number, energetically speaking.

The number "2" has quite a different energy field. It holds softer frequencies and represents relationships with others (as well as with yourself). The significance is more related to couples, pairs, and partnerships, and the feminine energy in general. It also can reflect different choices, paths, opposites, and *duality.*

The year 2020 also showcased double "0s." Vibrationally, 0 speaks to moving towards and into the energy of *potential*, an unknown territory. Zero holds the space for creating *opportunities to take you where you have never gone before.*

Vibrationally speaking, we were headed away from the "me" decade of the *1s* and into the "we" decade of the *2s*. Leading the decade off with double zeroes indicated some new energies were on their way in carrying the promise of something *unforeseen.*

A Powerful *New Moon* Crossed Paths with a Chinese New Year *Rat*

New moons graciously offer themselves to us in every month of the year with one appearing in all the twelve signs of the zodiac. They carry with them the magic of potential, cosmic energy that can support us in creating brand-new beginnings. New moons tend to offer us a reprieve from what was just completed by the preceding full moon. The specific zodiac sign that it appears in will influence and shape the gifts, opportunities, and challenges that it brings.

All new moons are important. But when the first new moon of the *year* is also the first of the incoming *decade* it becomes particularly significant as its impact is exalted. In 2020, our first new moon set the energetic tone not only for the rest of the year but for the entire upcoming decade of 2s and 0s! This first new moon of 2020 was in Aquarius and occurred on January 24. Aquarius is a sign known for rebellion, innovative thinking, and community. Its energy set in motion everything that the epic year was about to hold space for and encompass.

The *Aquarian new moon* was almost sitting on the exact day of the *Chinese New Year of the Metal Rat,* January 25th. Ironically, the Rat in the eastern zodiac was the first of twelve Chinese zodiac animals to show up when Buddha first put out a clarion call for all the animals to come forward to serve. With the energies of both the Aquarian new moon and the Chinese New Year combined, the planetary stage was set for the remains of our 3D lives, as we had known them, to go *ka-boom*.

Unbeknown to the world at the time, China was already in the throes of becoming ground zero for COVID and the initial catalyst for the massive paradigm shift in 2020 that was about to unfold. As if on cue, the Republic—still celebrating the onset of the New Year—was positioning itself to become the epicenter for the initial outbreak of the novel coronavirus and the subsequent worldwide pandemic.

To shake the playing field further, later in 2020, the so-called *inner planets* of Mercury, Venus, and Mars all went retrograde. Because their three orbits are the closest to Earth's in our solar system, by proximity, their energy fields tend to impact us more directly. The three retrogrades helped to create a continual reprieve, slowing down some of the hardwired aspects of the longstanding grip that 3D consciousness had on our lives and the planet. This *contributed* to assisting some of our remaining 3D constructs, beliefs, fears, and so on to break the surface, be released and restructured, and more easily transmuted into the new Ascended 5D matrix. Even though an unfathomable chaos was about to erupt on one level of our lives, in the *bigger picture* of the overall "Divine Plan" all was unfolding *exactly* as it was supposed to.

Failure to Launch

After 2012, many more HUmans on the planet began to move deeper into their Ascended 5D consciousness while simultaneously moving further away from elements in their 3D lives, beliefs, and perspectives. Awareness and understanding of the process was *not* a prerequisite for this unprecedented shift from one paradigm to another. Despite only some people being consciously or actively involved in it, energetically everyone was impacted, directly or indirectly, by its huge frequency shift.

Although it was happening in drips and drabs over a 27,000-year period, once we were able to reach critical mass and Ascend, 5D became the new vibrational law of the land on planet Earth.

Higher frequencies *reflect,* as well as *create* massive changes in HUman mental, emotional, physical, and spiritual bodies. You might feel angst, depression, fear, and the inability to make sense of what is not only happening around you, but inside you. Even the most evolved among us, people like you and me are still having a very challenging time adjusting to a 5D frequency because we live in physical bodies with a lower density. Can you imagine those on the planet who are energetically or *bigger picture* clueless? How mindblowing it must be for them to cope with these incoming forces! Many of those being thrown about and challenged by these increased energies on the planet are our partners, family members, friends and neighbors, and the many HUmans who are making horrific headlines on the six o'clock news every day.

Remember, energy is another form of consciousness, and consciousness is an alive entity. When something senses its life force is changing or being threatened, it will resist and *fight* for its survival. Thoughts, beliefs, ideologies, and opinions are living entities that can go haywire during periods of massive change. Sensing that there was a new *vibrational sheriff in town,* 3D consciousness did what any living entity would do, it rolled up its sleeves, leaned in, and prepared to fight.

With 3D and 5D consciousness holding opposite ends of the same "rope," the tug of war created an even wider separation in our 3D–5D world. 4D polarity escalated, fears abounded, violence ensued, and, sooner or later, something had to give. We drifted back into "me, me, me" and lost complete sight of "we, we, we." This was most apparent in our dueling politics, social unrest, and HUmanity's intense divide.

The world has been in a do-or-die state for the last several decades. Back in 2000, we had a golden window of opportunity not only to save HUmanity, but also to reduce some of the environmental stresses on Planet Earth. Year 2000 moved us out of the "1s" (me energy) of the 1900s and into the "2s" (we energy) of the 2000s. With three "0s" in tow, we ushered in the long-awaited turn of the century. Its numerology carried with it the energy of hope, new potential, and the opportunity to redirect our priorities back to the people and to the Earth itself. Although all the energies were lined up, *the stars weren't.*

Our collective consciousness was not vibrationally ready to launch. This was reflected, as often the pulse of HUman consciousness is, in our political stage and choice of President. George Bush was *barely* elected in what was the century's first questionable recount and Vice President Al Gore, who would have led the planet in a much-needed direction away from the broken state of global warming we have today, was sent packing. Instead, the years to follow presented a horrific attack on USA soil, 9/11, the ground zero of the war on 3D western values. All was followed by the longest battle in USA history, the two-decade old Afghanistan War. With trillions of US dollars spent, and an unjustifiable amount of HUman lives lost, it finally ended almost twenty-two years later during the

Presidency of Biden and Harris, as we approached the triple 2s of 2022.

Not until we plowed through twenty years of purged HUman Shadow could we have peeled back to this *next layer* of our post-5D Ascension period that we are currently in. The Shadow dredging during those years of the remains of 3D consciousness set in motion a lot of the upheaval that the world, most especially in the United States, was challenged by after 2012. From political power grabs and government deception to a novel coronavirus causing a worldwide pandemic, our old 3D consciousness found creative ways of spreading *fear* and *anger*. Intense feelings, yes, but they were only able to be present in the face of a void. When activated, they reflected back to HUmanity all the places in *us* where Love was absent. Both of those emotions are valuable parts of our HUman experience here on Planet Earth. They are not wrong or bad. But when misdirected, they can become powerful tools of manipulation. When we are experiencing them, they place our HUman selves in a weakened emotional and spiritual state where we fall more easily into a posturing of singularity, entitlement, and HUman separation.

We were very *ill* as a people and a planet long before the coronavirus was ever hatched and spread from China. The virus itself and the pandemic that followed were physical manifestations of the widespread psychosocial diseases of hate, fear, judgment, and isolation. The vibrational vitriol and lack of compassion and Love for the planet and our brothers and sisters were the energetic building blocks for the global spread of the virus. Something of an equal or greater magnitude to the first out-of-control disease had to have a counterpart of equilibrium proportions. Nothing short of a widespread, international killer virus would have come close. HUmanity was already far into a disease of the *heart*.

The virus is very real. It has been dreadful. It had taken almost six and a half million lives worldwide as of September 1, 2022, infected 500 million HUmans, paralyzed economies, and bankrupted people and businesses, putting a halt to modern life as we once knew it. The pandemic played out in technicolor for all of us on our 3D channel, to watch as well as experience. We all suffered from the 3D conditioning that has shaped HUmanity for eons. We were all duality-based thinkers at one point prior to the arrival of the pandemic. Feeling a need to divide HUmanity into separate races, nationalities, socioeconomic tiers, genders, religions, and the like is a byproduct of 3D consciousness, a fractal of 3D ideology.

Economic repercussions, political perceptions, and other lesser priorities directed the initial onset of COVID, both in China and in the USA. Many did not care the *same* way about old people dying or HUmans from other countries losing their lives by the millions. HUmanity began to become more alarmed by the impact COVID was taking when the media began to report that children were being affected. Kids getting sick became the game changer. And the bigger question is, why might we believe that one HUman life is more important or valuable than another? *Right?* As we evolve and grow, it's important for us to look at why we are often more disturbed when children are involved. All HUman life is valuable. That often-callous division of our compassion, and who is and who is not deserving of our priority or Love comes from our 3D belief in scarcity, a deeply reinforced non-truth. For scarcity is a belief derived out of 3D duality, created by HUmans, not the planet or God, to justify our actions and false perceptions that there is not enough money, Love, food, and resources to go around.

If you, like most of us who are trying earnestly to scratch and claw our way out of our 3D comas, buy into even a little piece of that false narrative, then perhaps we too have contributed to how we live in a society that allows us to forget about elderly people in nursing homes, and focus only on the importance of our children.

Many people reading this book are over sixty, or at least getting up there. If we live long enough, each of us will be at some point moving into one of those categories of people that society has often marginalized. This is yours and my heart chakra work to look at why age matters so much, or why we value one life, race, or gender identity over another. Every *soul* comes into this life with different responsibilities, but of *equal* importance.

It might be very hard to hear this. But the truth is that everybody who has left the planet, especially during the COVID pandemic was somehow part of the *bigger picture* plan to leave the planet regardless of their age. This doesn't take away from the enormous loss of life, Loved ones or in any way justify their deaths. There are so many multidimensional pieces to every moment of our lives and our deaths that it is important to at least make the space for this broader truth, even if the HUman level facts make no rational or *heart sense*.

Similarities to the HIV/AIDS Crisis

In the 1980s, I was in my twenties, living in New York City, working on a master's degree in social work. This period of my life is indelibly etched into my memory for it corresponded with the early throes of the AIDS virus crisis. During that very dark time on the planet, I lost family members and friends, and like others, I walked around as one of the *worried well*. None of us had much idea of what was killing a group of Humans that appeared to be mostly gay men.

The rapid spread of the AIDS virus *at first* was partially because it was considered to be a *gay man's disease*. Some of the pervasive thinking at the time—*good, bad, or indifferent*—was that the virus was God's punishment for homosexuality, and, even more egregious, "Let *them* just kill themselves off." The bottom line was nobody dealt with it or took charge early on, so the virus spread. After a period, it spread to the next group, which was mainly prostitutes and IV drug users. All those groups were composed of marginalized HUmans whose well-being was unimportant to the powers that be.

The only time that the AIDS virus garnished any significant attention was when mothers infected with the virus gave birth to babies who were infected in turn. Then the unaffected world and the people in authority began to *grow a conscience* and decide to take more aggressive action. "Oh my god, this AIDS virus is terrible. It's *now* killing babies." Not that they became any more important to the powers that be, but suddenly, by reverse osmosis, all the various marginalized groups of AIDS patients finally were able to reap the benefits of medical research, treatment, and care.

A PANDEMIC ENTERS THE FRAY

HUmans have a way of prioritizing, then justifying, other HUmans' worth. Often it is the children who ultimately step in to wake us up. It really never should come to this, but time and time again it does. As a people, adults need to evolve past the point where we require kids to step up to remind us that *everybody* should be valued. God doesn't make a lot of "junk."

As the COVID pandemic erupted, HUmans were very upset at the possibility that the original source of the virus may have been from bats. Interesting to note, the AIDS virus also came from the animal kingdom. HUmans were selling bat blood as a form of medicine, in an open market setting when COVID was contracted. Even if spreading a highly contagious virus from the animal kingdom to the HUmans wasn't the original intention, HUmans did willingly cross the energetics of the animal kingdom with HUman life. And although cross contamination might sound horrible, let me remind you that as a species we do *eat* animals. We hunt them for pleasure and food, domesticate them, cage them, and we also abuse them. When COVID rolled around, we were very worried, and still are today, that we contracted a virus from the animal kingdom that might *kill us.*

In Lemuria and Atlantis, experiments involving crossover breeding between HUmans and animals took place. This produced a group of hybrid HUmans that were considered *freaks* and *throwaways.* As we step back into that Atlantis to current-day review, we must consider some of the leftover Karma from that time period and the choices we made back then. Leftover Karma is not necessarily for punishment, but the virus in this *bigger picture* context also played a role in allowing us to release and delete old 3D actions and miscreations. Part of healing and transitioning out of our 3D lives involves looking at how we have dealt selectively with the animal kingdom. This piece of the Ascension puzzle is very, very important for us to become conscious of and explore. The challenge or "wrong" doing is not in the fact that we are carnivores, but the *level of consciousness* in which we *approach* the killing of animals for game or food, our exploitation of them for medical experimentation and the conditions and circumstances that we claim them as pets, to name a few. All this is coming through and showing itself in various ways in our post-Ascension 5D world. There is a growing need for compassion, applied especially to how HUmans share the planet with other forms of life, and the Earth itself. This time period will bring a lot of these very difficult and painful truths forward. We have arrived at a collective level of consciousness on the planet, where, without defensiveness, finger pointing or blame, we can begin to consider other choices. It is the perfect time for these things to start balancing themselves out.

A *"Black Swan"* Event

Back in 2019, I was living in Lido Beach, Long Island, New York, on the water. Temperature wise, it was an unusually beautiful, warm day for the middle of October. I remember it very clearly because it was my birthday. A few of my friends and I went for a walk and, lo and behold, there was a structure sitting on the sand that had washed up on the beach which wasn't there just a few days before. This section of the beach was directly parallel to where my back door was, approximately 1,000 feet

away. If it was there prior to when I first noticed it, I would have seen it sooner.

As we walked and got closer, I realized that it was actually a portion of an uprooted tree that washed up on the sand. It was very, very old, worn down from a long time being in the water, had hundreds of barnacles attached to it, and was lying on its side. The angle that it was resting in showed its uprooted bottom and created, even when up close a perfect sculpture of a Swan. We were all pretty amazed by what we were seeing.

I visited that swan daily for the next two weeks and meditated with it, spoke to it, and tried to understand why it was there, and specifically, on my birthday. Although I am usually very good at reading the signs and deciphering *bigger picture* messages, I never really got a clear impression of what its significance was for me or why it appeared at that point in

my life. One day, I went out to pay my animal guide a visit and found most of it washed out to sea. What remained behind were a few branches and twigs.

None of this made any sense to me until many months later. When we entered the New Year, specifically the Chinese New Year in January 2020, COVID first *surfaced* in China. Shortly after that, like wildfire, the virus rapidly spread to a lot of unsuspecting countries around the globe including making its way to the shores of the USA. All this coincided with the beginning of my personal changes that I wrote about in the Introduction, which shifted my life path and redirected my work, leading eventually to the writing of this book.

It then became clear that the Swan was a personal indicator for me. Was it a "source code" trigger, giving me the heads up about the upcoming shifts and changes that were about to unfold on the planet, and my *bigger picture* part in all of it? In retrospect, I believe so. Several months later, the coronavirus turned into a full-blown worldwide pandemic so rare that it was a "Black Swan" event.

A *Black Swan event* is an unpredictable event that is characterized by its rarity, severe impact, and the widespread belief that it was obvious or predictable in hindsight. If you look closely into the large, ominous sky of the photograph on the previous page, in the *dark clouds* you will see a silhouette of a very large Rat figure from a side view profile, completely equipped with a tail, two front legs, and an eye! The Black Swan event of the pandemic came as I previously indicated in 2020 the *Chinese New Year of the Rat.*

The Universe *Didn't* Send the Pandemic

Although the virus was *part* of a major unleashing of forces from the galaxy into the planet, it was not caused or sent by the Universe as a stop gap measure or angry punishment because the HUmans were not playing well together. But when the unthinkable happened and the virus arrived, the benevolent Universe figured out a way to "use" its presence for a conduit of at least some good. All viruses, including COVID, start out as being relatively *neutral.* It's a biological entity and there are millions of viruses and bacteria throughout the planet. What helped turn this virus into an *international serial killer* is that it picked up a tremendous amount of torque, I believe, because of the condition that the world was in *before* it came into play. As a people, we were so destructively polarized. We were at odds with our neighbors, our politics, and our values. 4D was raging and at an all-time high. The virus, little by little, found its way in when the world was *already* at a weakened breaking point. And, more importantly in a post-5D Ascension period where HUmanity was moving into position to address, face, and rip off its next bloody Band-Aid covering up traumas from the final days of Lemuria and Atlantis.

COVID started out like every other virus that grows within us, and on the planet. What turned it into a worldwide pandemic was that it vibrated to the same low-frequency energy as all of the *thought forms, projections, fears, and ambient energies* that its new, vibrationally parallel host, HUmanity, was emitting. Both were a very good vibrational match and in the laws of energy, like attracts like. The same war we have been fighting among ourselves spilled over into the lack of unity around the treatment, protocols, and politics of how the virus was going to be navigated. The more options we had, the more we fought. The more we fought, the longer the pandemic hung around to disrupt our lives. At every turn back then and *now,* how we chose to use its presence and what we choose to project onto it is going to make the difference in how it is allowed to disrupt us.

I'm not necessarily saying that the virus is a *good thing.* But what will ultimately determine its value in retrospect will be how we choose to play the hand that we were dealt. Will it be used to break down differences and unify the world or will we allow it to keep creating more negative emotional states, like fear, greed, separation, and hysteria? If we don't start moving into a place of owning our healthy, balanced power and waking up from the stupor of 3D opposition, then we are not *choosing* to transmute at least a piece of it into something greater. In turn, we are not going to be effective in using our new 5D HUman selves with all the source code upgrades that were downloaded during this crisis and the *bigger picture* background in of our transition from 3D to 5D consciousness.

The *ESPs* of Illness

My last book, *Feng Shui and Health: The Anatomy of a Home,* breaks every illness or disease into three parts: the Emotional, the Spiritual, and the Physical—aka the ESPs of illness. HUman illness is never just a one-dimensional, physical manifestation. Anything from the common cold to a life-threatening disease has at *least* those three components. Every physically related imbalance, injury, or sickness of any kind also has an emotional and spiritual aspect as well because we HUmans contain these three main interrelated aspects of ourselves.

All those categories represent different components or the *anatomy* of what that particular illness, for that specific individual is about. If you want to dismantle an illness, anything ranging from a common cold to something life threatening, at some point you have to move through those three main aspects. Most of the HUmans on the planet tend to deal with illness primarily on the physical level. But in totality, before the health challenge became physical and manifested into a disease, such as cancer or a retrovirus, there was a spiritual and an emotional component first.

The physical realm of any illness is the *last place* that discord surfaces; but ironically it is the first place that usually gets our attention that something is wrong. So, when it's on a physical level, *without making a disease a negative,* it has already moved through two red Lights. It already came down through the spiritual realm, then passed through the corresponding unresolved issues held in your emotional body. Over time if either of those components do not get addressed, acknowledged or the energies surrounding them get resolved, then it may eventually surface on the physical plane via the physical body. Often, although hard to imagine, certain *souls* actually factor in an illness into the life experience as a learning event—part of their work while here on the planet or as a vehicle to return them back to the Universe at a predetermined time. It's usually a much more tragic experience for those who are witnessing the sickness or the great loss of a Loved one who is impacted the longest.

The coronavirus is similar. Getting ill from it follows this same sequence and anatomy. It hit us so hard and broadly during the time that we HUmans had just entered onto the brand new, super-fast timeline of 5D. Although the virus may have entered our 3D world on the physical level, impacting millions of unsuspecting people around the globe, as well as their families, friends, and communities, the truth is that it has been running rampant for an even longer time throughout the world on a *spiritual and emotional realm*. On the 3D level, the world had finally reached a tipping point where HUmanity had a collective meltdown and broke apart on a *physical level*.

The pandemic's devastating effects were and continue to be a very real and extremely frightening reflection of what was already playing out on the spiritual and emotional Earth planes. All aspects were significant and intense components of our old 3D/4D reality, consciousness, and paradigm.

The virus, pandemic in nature, does not change its path of destruction because enough time passes, herd immunity sets in, or a vaccine gets developed. It changes because the collective thought consciousness attached to it alters. That shift on an energetic, social, or emotional level will always run concurrent with a medical cure, breakthrough or arriving at herd immunity. A virus that is as contagious and as deadly as COVID initially was is hugely different than a virus the average person picks up for a ten-day run. The emotional or thought form attachments are *collective, worldwide in nature* and not just based on your personal history, family predisposition or recent exposure to a sick coworker.

Instead, the COVID virus erupted in our 3D world while the planet had already transitioned to an increased 5D timeline. And yes, COVID killed a lot of really good, innocent, and unsuspecting HUmans. And those millions of significant beautiful *souls* should be the main reason that we give it our best shot in making some purposeful sense out of *why*.

The impact from the virus happened on a much bigger scale. A few people from your office, town, or convention that you attended didn't just get sick, the *world got sick*. It happened in a relatively brief period of time; the world had gotten a massive timeout. COVID affected economies globally, not just the stock market in the United States, but finances for every country across the board. It didn't just hit you or me personally or our families. It touched *everyone*. An exceptionally large swath of the world was collectively impacted giving us our first internationally shared HUman crisis. On a 3D mundane level, it was clearly due to the spread of the coronavirus, but on a 5D *bigger picture* level—what kept the pandemic and the multiple variants of the virus prolific—was and continues to be lower vibrational ambient HUman thought forms that are attached to it and feeding its stay.

As a virus, COVID *may or may not* have killed many people anyway, but throughout its tenure it was the attached *thought forms* that turned the virus into a pandemic and sickened, bankrupted, and killed more people than the virus would have done on its own.

The virus in a way became a "victim" of all our ambient thoughts of judgment, fear, anger, and HUmanity's divisions.

All those *same* things had existed in a "highly contagious" way on the planet long before the virus was transmitted to HUmankind by a wild bat, an animal on sale in a wet market, or an intentional political sabotage plot carried out in a lab in China—whatever the physical truth of its emergence may be.

None of these causes or all these causes could be true, but even if they are not, truth is created on all dimensional levels by the collective consciousness rubberstamping its idea of what is true. All versions and dimensions of what truth is *determined to be*—the good, the bad, and the ugly—played a significant role in people's reactions to the virus. Each of us, including those working in political arenas throughout the world *combined* the energy power behind belief systems with the already existing HUman foibles such as greed, racism, elitism, judgments, competition, hate, and so on. All these variables together contributed to how this pandemic played out.

The Coronavirus:
A Spiritual *Hail Mary* Pass?

COVID also had at least one other important perspective to consider, its 5D *bigger picture* piece in our post-5D Ascension evolutionary purpose. For all the devastation, loss, and havoc that the virus caused, especially in 2020, ironically it held a remarkably interesting frequency for an earthbound virus. HUmanity was at the tail end of breaking away from its very long relationship with 3D consciousness. Prior to the outbreak of the pandemic, the collective consciousness was being massively stretched as HUmans around the globe were polarized in a 4D suspension.

A PANDEMIC ENTERS THE FRAY

Years ago, one of the more brilliant 5D astrologers and forward thinkers of our time, *Stephanie Azaria*, reviewed the astrological "birth" chart of the coronavirus. Her analysis revealed that it carried a high vibration of consciousness, as its chart showed that it had come in as an awakening to help unite and heal us; that is, if we were *conscious enough and chose to utilize it* for that *bigger picture* purpose. I believe this virus and the pandemic were presented to us as a *Hail Mary pass*, a last-ditch opportunity to wake up the masses and hopefully save ourselves and the planet, and complete the final stages of our 27,000-year 5D Ascension process.

The virus proliferated into a widespread pandemic, but it was grown in the emotional Petri dish of thought forms such as hate, judgment, and anger in an age of separation of HUmanity. All our individual emotions, feelings, actions, and *inactions* are enmeshed in powerful vibrational energy fields and are very much alive and exalted in a common level of dimensional consciousness.

A virus, if only biological in nature, can only multiply itself within the living cells of an able and willing host. As a planet and a people, we were running out of opportunities, as well as valuable time. Sadly, it seemed like HUmanity had lost its moral compass. Nobody was budging on their position, and the self-righteousness holdup was doing the planet tremendous harm. It felt like somebody accidently hit the **PAUSE** button on our life's remote and we got stuck in a dark period of some of the worst remains of 3D reality.

Intergalactic Support

It is important to *remember* that at no time are we ever taking our Ascension journeys alone. We are partnered with the Multiverse and there has been an enormous amount of help coming in from the unseen realms. The place we arrived at in 2020 was a watershed moment on our long journey into 5D. We were at a critical time, in the throes of an intense standoff, and HUmanity was not able to move forward or out of the energies of 3D polarization. An undertaking of this magnitude could have only been accomplished with all beings, both in the physical and in the spirit world, working in tandem on behalf of the greater good and the *bigger picture* plan. The planet, and all its earthbound LightWorkers, ShadowWorkers, and LoveWorkers had and will continue to have a tremendous amount of help from those energies that work in the Light.

Eargo came in. Our timeline merger enabled us to pull in the much-needed feminine energy to counter the old, antiquated patriarchal government system that needed to be dissolved. Then, suddenly, boom, the coronavirus erupted. A global pandemic then became part of the *bigger picture* plan. Though we had to face an enormous amount of dark times and energies, through a lot of dark repercussions, it helped accelerate us, in often mindblowing ways, to make that *connecting fLight* that was so close to leaving the runway without us. The pandemic was a shortcut, the fastest means available to begin to heal the *soul*-destroying cancer of HUmanity's 3D separation disease. If we did not seize these few opportunities, as horrible as the choice may have seemed, HUmanity would have self-imploded. We had a choice either to use the coronavirus to heal us, shock us awake, and unite HUmanity, or to use it to finish the job that HUmans had started and let it destroy us, thus arriving at another heartbreaking, *soul-wrenching* end. The kind that many people reading this experienced during the last days of Lemuria and Atlantis.

One of the benefits of the pandemic was that it forced HUmanity to become more compassionate. The stark reality is that it allowed yet another group of HUmans to raise their frequencies and join the 5D grid with the already awakened. As our collective 5D frequency increased, we improved the odds of an energetic restructuring from 3D to 5D happening once we came out the other end. The rewards would be a new planetary paradigm. Everything we wanted for the world and HUmans *over time* would finally have the possibility to actualize. No part of this 5D Ascension journey has ever been guaranteed, but if we did not take our chances *now,* there would not be an opportunity again, perhaps for eons.

I know it is often *horrible* out there, especially of late. Planet Earth has not been the easiest of schoolrooms in the galaxy, especially for injured, traumatized sensitives who often have been working overtime on triple shifts. Whether or not you identify as a 5D person, we all still live fulltime in a 3D world. People are still scared, sick, dying, losing Loved ones and jobs, and having no feeling of inner peace or safety. None of those realities escape me. But at the same time, we have all been made privy to a miracle unfolding. That is, if you are willing to open your mind and heart and be flexible in how you choose to see all this.

What I will tell you with a certain amount of confidence is that because of all these, horrific, malevolent tragedies, we are extending the amount of time HUmans would have had on this planet by another seventy-five to one hundred years. Without learning to reprioritize and live our lives through the lens of a genuinely loving heart and HUmanity-based conscience, we will never get back to the basics that make us good, and ultimately none of *life versus extinction* would matter anyway.

Omicron, Vaccines, and Masks

The omicron variant that came after the delta variant was significantly more contagious but less life-threatening than prior mutations. *(Ironically, in real time as I edit this section, I am in the throes of recovering from the Omicron variant.)* This reduction in loss of life reflected how much *fear and thought forms* the planet had transmuted since the first two years when the Delta variant was predominant. Being less severe, it allowed people who were burned out physically and suffering from pandemic fatigue to start saying "OK, fine, I have COVID," not reacting with the same fear and/or arrogance initially expressed during the onset of the virus itself. Our newfound bravery and more hopeful tone overall reflected the movement of our beliefs, thought forms, and fears of life and death that are deeply embedded in our cellular memory lifetime after lifetime and in particular from the tragedy and losses during our final incarnations in Lemuria or Atlantis.

The division of HUmanity during those past incarnations was revisited in part throughout the various stages of the COVID pandemic. Issues regarding the use of masks and vaccines divided more HUmans at a time when unity and alignment could have ushered us through the Omicron variant more quickly. The pandemic *was not prolonged* because of the different choices HUmans were making regarding whether or not to wear a mask or get vaccinated and boosted. Instead, it was the energies, belief systems, emotions, and thought forms *behind* the decision that each person arrived at which contributed to the continuation of COVID and its *bigger picture* counterpart—HUman separation.

As previously discussed, the planet moved from the decade of the "1s" (me, my rights, and so on) to the "2s," which held the vibration of the shared collective "us." Meaning, we moved from the vibration of the *ME (men's empowerment = masculine)* to the *WE (women's empowerment = feminine)*. Although it has overall gotten a little bit better, not having our *hearts aligned* as a society was the bigger issue clogging the wheel, and it was those particular arguments that both reflected and highlighted the core of our planet's struggle at the time. Two people can make the same decision but for varied reasons. The impact that each of our choices had either contributed to the healing or to expanding the great post-5D Ascension divide of HUman separation. As we were all thrown sideways into survival while simultaneously moving out of the remains of 3D consciousness, the *bigger picture* repercussions were not often considered or factored into our decision-making processes. Not for many of us, including those who consider themselves evolved.

Managing Coexisting Realities

As they present themselves, and they will, please try not to see some of these situations from only one dimension or perspective. They are not unidimensional. The lens through which we view an event is only one of the many realities that are playing out in the totality of the situation or experience. As our consciousness evolves, our advanced 5D selves become more amenable to seeing several simultaneous realities and no longer feel the need to dismiss a version to validate a perspective or invalidate another's sense of truth.

Expanding our TV cable contract from the basic to the deluxe package empowers us with more choices by giving us more "channels" to watch. Sometimes having choices feels overwhelming because making a choice means taking responsibility for what you are choosing to watch on the screen. Sometimes, we forget that we can just simply change the channel if we don't like the perspective that's playing.

Having various dimensions of reality coexisting in our day-to-day lives can be mindblowing on occasion. Understanding multidimensionality stretches our vibration, as well as our overall collective frequency. One day a situation presents itself to you, such as a breakup, getting fired, an illness, or a virus and you are in your higher mind, responding with, *"I will definitely be able to get through this or there is a higher reason for this situation."* A minute later, you find yourself in fear and panic, thinking, *"Oh my god, how am I going survive? Make ends meet? Live without him (or her)?"* Living in two dimensions at the same time often keeps us vacillating and feeling conflicted about choosing one or the other as the "real" feelings or the truth.

COVID's presence in our lives is also here as an opportunity to learn to move in and out of our down pat, conditioned beliefs on how we still draw on the 3D thought of duality to perceive all things as good or bad. In fact, in 5D they are not anymore. Our lenses have broadened and we are not very capable of living in our *now*-true state of multidimensionality. We can *now* apply some of COVID's bigger lessons to retrain our everyday reactions to change, fear, disappointment, and life.

That's a good example of why LightWorkers are so challenged and spread thin emotionally. By bringing into view other dimensional options beyond the limitations constructed by the old paradigm—the one truth, one-choice, *either/or* thinking of 3D—you inadvertently create an alternate belief system for others to rise, Ascend, and download if they choose to. That's what many of us came in to do: to lead with a visceral knowing that reality is larger than what we could ever imagine it to be. Living a veiled incarnation often prevents us from recalling and accepting this as a given.

COVID has allowed a whole world to finally be scared together, worry about money together, be frozen by the unknown, drop into vulnerability, and "consider" a life where we are all, at the end of the day, truly one race, the HUman race.

Feel free to have your fears and grieve deeply when needed, but always remember that 3D life as we once knew it is no more. If you liked parts of your 3D life, or if you hated them, the bottom line is that we are still going to experience the absence of our old lifestyle as a major loss. Shifting from one paradigm of consciousness to another, especially after living in one paradigm for so many lifetimes, creates a loss of a familiar identity that has been part of us for such a long time. Our 3D egos were cemented in duality consciousness for eons. It's painful and often unsettling to move away from it without completely understanding why it's all happening.

Every new experience we have that no longer falls into the 3D brain's computing system, including COVID, the rare Black Swan occurrence, feels like a threat to our reality—*as we once knew it*. Initially, the new 5D perspective feels frightening as hell to our HUman egos because its presence means that we are letting go of our 3D premise and its corresponding duality. Choices create freedom, but also an overwhelming sense of premature emancipation.

As HUmans transition through the last phase of polarity or the severing of 3D duality, there is always an explosion of many feelings, especially anger, frustration, irritation, and fear of the unknown. This unprecedented shift in frequency, consciousness, and reality can often feel like a life-or-death experience. Dimensionally speaking, *it is*. Our new 5D HUman is going to need a lot of Love, kindness, patience, and humor to navigate our new physicality and reality, along with helpful ways of living our new life while still alive in a 3D/4D world.

Higher Help Came Immediately

Once the coronavirus exploded throughout every nation on Earth, the Multiverse, along with all their incredible guide teams stepped in to assist us by acting on our collective prayers for some *higher-powered intervention*.

Later in this chapter, you will be introduced to a few of the key ethereal support figures who worked en masse with us on an energetic level not only to contain the pandemic, but to support science in developing vaccinations, that were created at record speed. Although, vaccines are and continue to be not for everyone, the speed at which they were developed was most confusing to many because the science of vaccines unfolded on our new superfast 5D timeline. Additionally, many of these beings of Light and Love guided us in understanding how we could best use the virus/pandemic (which we ourselves created out of the energy field in our polarized 3D reality) as a tool to help heal HUman separation, hatred, fear, and any other feelings we have when we think about COVID and its various impact.

When HUmans can individually and collectively own all the pieces of their HUman Shadow *without* judgment or shame, then we will be able to Love those aspects of us into higher-level thought forms. These, in turn, will deliver us and the world to a brand-new place in 5D time.

Our 5D hearts and *souls* all want a monumental level of deep peace and freedom for all sentient beings. Let this knowing seep into your conscious and subconscious minds. Please remember that this is what many of us came here to do. In many ways, the pandemic is our *opening night*. The curtain went up. We've been rehearsing this opportunity to lead with our hearts for eons. The pandemic—*after all is said and done*—is going to be another huge, higher awakening that will finally give us the collective breakthrough we needed to not only follow our hearts, but to let it lead us back towards the unification and healing of all HUmankind. That is if we are awake enough, and brave enough to run with it past the waves of our constricting fear (*F*alse *E*vidence *A*ppearing *R*eal).

The pandemic has given us a plethora of opportunities to expand on our constricting beliefs based in the lower energies of 3D fear, limitation, and lack. When we lead with our hearts, we often feel vulnerable and protective of ourselves at first.

When you are going through those times when you feel stuck in a particular situation, it is usually due to the unconscious compression from our old friend *fear*. When that comes up, think of ways to create *opposite* experiences in other areas of your everyday life. Energetically, when the fear releases its chokehold, and eventually it *will*, be ready when that door reopens for you. Walk out of it as fast as you can, keep walking, and don't look back.

If you are feeling some stagnation in moving through these or other areas of your life, most likely it's an opportunity cleverly disguising itself as an old remnant of fear giving you yet another chance to *open your heart and choose Love*. When this arises, don't think twice. Thank it and let go to it. Allow it to serve *"your" bigger picture,* assisting you in stretching beyond your heart's current comfort zone.

Tragedy? Opportunity? *Both?*

Our post-5D Ascension is also serving as a *cosmic dispensation* period from some of our leftover 3D/4D personal Karmic lessons. With a 5D level of consciousness *now* accessible on planet Earth, *Karma (a byproduct of 3D/4D)* is being both resolved and dissolved very rapidly. Most remaining Karmic experiences that we are struggling to release from family issues and financial woes to relationship patterns or even our past lives in Lemuria and Atlantis, are undergoing a major dissolution.

Did the virus come in *specifically* so we can participate in the undoing of Karma? Absolutely not. This is an important point to clarify at the get-go because our first impulse is always to process life through the lens of our conditioned 3D dualistic thinking. *"Was it this or was it that? Was it a blessing or a horrible curse? Was the pandemic brought upon us by the Light to break down our 3D free will, which has run amok, or did it emerge through the Shadowy, nefarious efforts of bad actors?"* Our 3D ego wants us to arrive at one specific truth because it is functioning outside of our recently arrived at level of 5D HUman *multidimensionality.*

As horrible as the pandemic was, it gave the world an opportunity, to begin recognizing and then healing some significant social problems that were comorbid and just as contagious as the virus and all its infections. And although we haven't completely maximized the *silver lining* that it carried, the disease of HUman separation did begin to heal. Ultimately, the pandemic helped to highlight our commonalities as Earth HUmans and our species dire need to unite in order to continue on and hopefully Ascend to something greater. The fact that we even began the process is a *miracle,* given the broken state the world and most HUmans were in leading up to the pandemic.

The virus did not sicken us in ways that we, as a world collective, weren't already ill and dying from already.

The speed at which we were evolving between 2012 and 2021 was mindblowingly fast. Although it didn't seem that way at the time, 2020 blew apart the *world's* foundation of 3D consciousness, not just yours, mine or the woken. After living lifetime after lifetime as 3D HUmans within the constraints of the limited principles of duality the world had a *massive collective upheaval followed by a massive collective meltdown.*

The speed at which the virus spread was only mirroring the pace of how quickly our consciousness was evolving.

You might ask, *"Consciousness is evolving?"* This idea might seem counterintuitive given the struggles, oppression, and ugliness that we continue to see coming from our fellow HUmans. However, these wounds are symptoms of a society in turmoil whose scars are in plain sight—bloodied and oozing on the surface—paraded for *everyone* to see. That is, everyone brave enough to look.

Shifting out of a 3D life is easier to do in theory, than in actuality. Our 3D egos, which are based in duality, still believe that the source of all our personal and world-related "problems" lie outside us. Tenets of 3D are inherent to a system of opposites and the constant opponents of what's good or bad thinking that leads to beliefs like *"If I'm right, then you must be wrong."* Everything from personal arguments to international wars has been a byproduct of our 3D polarizing system based in duality. In order to transcend to a higher vibration as a 5D HUmanity, *honesty is a requirement and emotional risk a given.* At one time or another, with all the lifetimes that we have lived, most likely, either intentionally or unintentionally, we have contributed at some point to creating these post-Ascension, leftover 3D Karmic patterns. Without the heartfelt willingness to remain both *awake and reflect on our part in all of this*, no matter how difficult looking at the truth is, it becomes a steeper climb to get to a higher, peaceful, and authentic world.

COVID Protocols Mirror Society's Core Wounds

Before governments around the world had access to COVID vaccines, their main attempts at trying to control, or at least slow down, the transmission of the virus was through a series of three main protocols: *social distancing, wearing a mask, and the washing of hands.* At first, the lack of HUman contact felt awkward, weird, and lonely. It was an unfamiliar way of interacting for social beings living in a hug and handshake society. Many of the early COVID protocols served as metaphors for deeper truths underlying the ways that we have conducted ourselves for centuries. Before the pandemic, we hid our true thoughts and feelings behind invisible *"masks."* If things didn't align with our beliefs, perspectives, or skin color, we would often *"wash our hands"* of a situation. This was how we ignored or denied HUmanity's needs and the planet's repetitive "calls" for help.

Each of us, at one time or another, has engaged in *some* form of social distancing. Sexism, racism, homophobia, transphobia, xenophobia, and the like are examples of 3D's flagrant versions of *social distancing*. The strong, self-righteous beliefs and judgments that separate and divide us also reflect the core wounds that our 3D/4D HUmanity is suffering from. If you are willing to look closely at the events of the last few years, you'll see that there is nothing new that the virus has presented to us, even the various protocols took a page out of the 3D HUman separation playbook.

Over the last ten years, it has appeared to the naked eye that as a collective we are actually *devolving*. Insane political theatrics, social upheaval, and the worldwide pandemic turned 2020 into the poster child for a world growing backwards. From a 3D perspective, that assessment is very true. From a 5D perspective, however, we are rapidly evolving in bigger leaps and bounds than ever experienced on the planet before *now*. We are in a state of massive expansion *as well as* social contraction. This paradox might be quite confusing at first because most of our mental conditioning comes from our 3D brains dictating to our deducing minds that only one of those things can be true.

Devolve, Revolve, Evolve, or Dissolve: It All Comes Down to *Love*

As challenging as life was at the height of the pandemic, it was important that we stayed the course through the Shadow pieces of our post-5D Ascension process. And it is *still* very important to keep a *bigger picture* perspective no matter what you are currently facing in your own life or what's being presented to you on the larger stage of what often seems like a very perplexing world.

In any given situation, we have full authority over every *decision, reaction, or perception we choose*. This responsibility can feel completely empowering or like a horrible burden. But ultimately, each individual circumstance contributes to the *bigger picture* and our evolutionary choices that we face on a personal and collective level.

We Can Devolve

Vibrationally, as a people, we can go backward, slipping into prior tiers of 3D consciousness. Levels that we have already Ascended through will be repeated and reexperienced. When we devolve to earlier states of consciousness, we reduce the collective supply of **Love** energy in our lives and throughout the world. Look at the word *devolve*. If you reverse the letters, starting at the L, you will see it spells *Love*. The past tense *devolved*, incorporates the past tense of the verb Love, *LOVED*.

We Can Revolve

We can continue to live in a 4D level of consciousness as long as we need or choose to. But over time, after it served its initial purpose, it will feel very stressful. This dimension was meant to act as a *bridge* for HUmans to pace the raising of their vibration while transitioning across the huge frequency gap between 3D and 5D. Many LightWorkers and ShadowWorkers periodically get stuck in 4D. A main indicator often is when you find yourself running in circles in different areas of your life. More aptly, you are actually traversing back and forth over the same proverbial bridge, making it quite difficult to move to the next stage of your personal 5D Ascension. This can feel like we are turning, spinning, or just plain running in place with certain aspects of our lives. We're not necessarily devolving fully back to 3D when this happens, but we don't have a more complete, forward-moving 5D experience either.

Many choose to hang in 4D long past its purpose. This state of consciousness can lull you into complacency because it *feels* comfortable. It can give you a skewed version of the journey because although you *are now* much more awake and aware from how you once saw life, you might experience the increased consciousness and growth, as your final destination. It is not. By keeping one foot in 3D reality and the other occasionally stepping into the realm of 5D consciousness, you can easily be duped into believing that you learned to ride the surfboard managing multidimensionality. Your 4D stay is just meant to be a buttress for your 5D Ascension journey. This is what this dimension is supposed to be used for, but the length of stay is only meant until you get your pole-vaulting skills down pat. Remaining here past that point only delays facing the risks, fears and changes that come with a 5D transition.

We all have to eventually take a leap into the abyss of the unknown world of 5D consciousness. Straddling 4D doesn't allow for your *soul's* innate need to expand into more God self and Love. It can often be a chaotic place to be, although at times it may feel safe and other times stressful.

If you're stuck here, you are revolving. *Now,* look at the word *revolve.* Reversed from the letter L, it spells *Lover.* You're still energetically carrying the frequency of Love but 4D is like having an affair with a *former* Lover. It could be fun for a short period of time, but then you realize at some point, it's time to move on.

We Can Evolve

We can actively seek growth and welcome change, as we expand into more of our God-selves while still hanging around the planet in a physical body. We can integrate our new superpowers that come with being 5D HUmans. We can embrace our advanced ability as creators of the Light and use this higher energy for the good of ourselves and HUmankind.

In essence, we can do all this and actively evolve HUman consciousness. 5D relates to the word *evolve*. When you read the letters backward from the L they spell *Love*. Not Love in its past-tense version or in its romanticized, hiding-place version but Love, straight up. Pure and simple.

No matter when we choose to evolve, under any circumstances and conditions, that's where we will find Love at its strongest. Love's power and the gifts it brings are multiplied exponentially in the moment we choose to grow into more of it. *Love is our soul's highest state of being.*

The long and short of it is this: The more we evolve, the more of our God-Light radiance we carry and emit, the higher our consciousnesses and vibrations are raised everywhere we go, and with everything we come in contact with. Under this illumination, Shadow issues are revealed. Under this illumination Shadow frequencies are given the opportunity to transmute back to Light. The vibration of Love brings up everything that is *unlike* itself!

Because it carries so much more Love and Light, the 5D frequency magnetically acts like a poultice on our collective wounds, siphoning out all that is hidden, not of the Light, and not for our personal good or the greater good. In 5D, we are transmuting our lower frequency *creations and miscreations* into something higher, although at first we tend to see them exclusively in their disruptive Shadow form.

We Can Also Dissolve

Collectively, there is one other *choice* we have besides evolving, which is extinction. If we lose our HUman capacity to uphold and expand our core vibrational element of Love, we will *dissolve* as a species. If you look at the spelling of the word *dissolve* in reverse from the letter L, it spells *loss*. The last four letters from·the E backwards are *evlo,* a complete scrambling of the word *Love*. HUmanity—meaning all the billions of individuals that comprise our species-have a choice at every turn and in every situation to choose Love over fear.

The coronavirus pandemic held our feet to the fire when it came to our *evol*utionary process. It placed all HUmans on a worldwide timeout. This allowed for many of the planet's issues such as political divisiveness, warfare, healthcare, entitlement, poverty, racism, greed, elitism, white supremacy, and other social issues to visibly move to front and center, without all the busy that they are usually surrounded with and hiding behind. Truth is, we haven't been playing very well together for a long, long time and the pandemic with all its bells and whistles illuminated these problems.

Those working in the Light on this planet and elsewhere have extrapolated yet another miraculous window of opportunity for HUmanity to rise up and out of what COVID left behind. Although we have successfully moved out of the dark hole that the pandemic created, it is important to realize that as a civilization we are not out of the woods yet—not by a long stretch. As long as we are alive on this beautiful planet, we are still needed to hold the space for the energy of Love and Light to take hold until everyone has the opportunity to Ascend if they choose. There is still a lot of work to be done. It's so important right *now* not to rest on your laurels, go backwards or even worse, lose your *bigger picture* perspective.

Send the Virus LOVE:
And Send *Yourself* Some Too!

Yes, the pandemic was a 3D HUman tragedy of epic proportions. But from a 5D perspective, it also forced to the surface so many opportunities to bring a lot of unspoken fears, dark secrets, inconvenient truths, and ugly aspects of HUman culture to the surface. *Now* more than ever, we must move forward and complete the work on the remaining Shadow energies that have miraculously, and finally, been squeezed to the surface for all to see.

Pause for a minute, and take a deep breath in. Allow that remembrance to move through your new 5d consciousness, effortlessly. Trust on some level that your very wise, all-knowing *soul* knew not only that these truths would be unveiled, but that you yourself were an intricate part of the *bigger picture* plan. This is a *sacred Universal truth*. But always, as with everything, feel into this reminder and ask your heart if it aligns with your *personal truth.*

No matter where we are right *now* on the continuum of the virus and its aftermath, as long as it is still active, it's important to remember to send it Love. Yes, I know this sounds backwards, especially with how disruptive it's been and how many beautiful lives it took. But *Love* is the energy the virus needs to be transmuted back to spirit. No matter where it resides and what degree of havoc it is creating, directing the vibration of Love to the virus will ultimately help counter the remaining thought forms of fear, hatred, and separation that it still carries in its energy field for *our* healing. The energy of Love with its high frequency vibration has the ability to calm the virus, and to help the people and the society it has impacted, and is currently impacting, to move through yet another piece of our 3D Shadow consciousness. The more Love it receives, the less it is hated, feared, and blamed. With a new infusion of higher Light, the virus can be more quickly flushed out of HUman bodies and family narratives with less immediate and long-term damage (as we have witnessed with the lesser strains such as Omicron).

The more we send the virus and our rapidly transitioning culture Love, the more we add the high-octane fuel of *God Love* to its tank. Higher-power "fuel" allows the journey to 5D that everyone on the planet, at one point or another, has made or will soon be making, to come to fruition. We are all part of the greater collective on Earth, and even more so, we are a very elite part of those who already have in some form begun to *Ascend.*

Advancement into the higher-vibrational realms comes with a contingency clause. As we expand into more of our new individual 5D Lightbodies, we have the responsibility to also *pay it forward*, to consciously use and direct our SuperHUman power of Love to assist those who are in line right behind us, working towards their long awaited 5D Ascension. Applied at the appropriate moment, pound for pound, the energy metrics of Love won't disappoint. Like a homeopathic remedy, a tiny dose of this vibrational medicine can counteract and transmute not only the virus, but more importantly the fear-based, 3D thought forms that are keeping it and everything else in our lives that we would like to move on from alive.

What is the one important factor that might prevent you from activating your SuperHUman power of 5D Love? It must be received by *you* and directed to healing *your* own wounds, fears, worries, and personal challenges *first*. You must direct Love inward every time you need to use it or choose to send it outside of yourself. You have to be willing to *receive* your own big, beautiful Love energy before you can give it away. This sequence is needed to energetically release the safety latch on your Love Taser. It has been coded into your *soul's* DNA as a stopgap measure so you won't override your new 5D HUman system with old 3D/4D victimization programming about codependent Love.

The more we commit to addressing the personal ways that fear shows up in our daily lives, the more quickly HUmanity will be able to Ascend. When we *choose* Love over fear in every area of our lives—from our finances and health to relationships, and even COVID, we create a *new energetic matrix* around the situation or perceived problem. This choice creates an opportunity for energy and its thought forms to rise and integrate into the higher frequency of Love. This helps us stop experiencing fear as the only possible reaction. The vibration of fear is the lowest vibration of any emotion known to man, including hate. Fear constricts, tricks, manipulates, and keeps you locked into spinning on an old 3D emotional hamster wheel. It's a no-win frequency that will never truly offer up a higher *soul*-ution to the issue at hand. The frequency of fear, as experienced in our 3D emotional bodies, was never intended to be used as a transformational tool or for creative problem solving. Nor was it meant to be an emotional state that we should stay in for long, debilitating periods of time.

Fear was originally meant to act as a warning to initiate a short-term rush of adrenaline and snap us quickly into having a crazy-fast reaction to a potential danger. It wasn't meant for us to have an intimate relationship with it or to allow its *soul-destroying* impact to dim our beautiful Light, steal our peace of mind, hijack our happiness, and make us sick with worry. Do you think the cavemen sat around the fire, passing out equal parts of Xanax and Rescue Remedy while talking about their anxiety about being successful as game hunters? As we evolved in the last few hundred years or so, supposedly into a more sophisticated level of 3D society, fear was more frequently used as a weapon to control, limit, redirect, and suppress the rising Light of consciousness that was growing in the 3D HUman wanting and trying to reach for more.

This vibrational upleveling became a greater threat to those who wanted to remain in power. HUmanity's new growth in Light and consciousness needed to be contained and controlled. 3D, with its very clear lines of division and categories, falsely led us to believe that abiding by "the rules" of the status quo would keep us safe. Those who reinforced them, whoever they may be, helped to keep these guardrails in place. Many people may have not liked a lot of those structures, but the paralysis that fear instilled, allowed for millions of millions of people, over centuries of time, to follow them anyway. It held us in a perpetual Shadow reality for almost 30,000 years, and it still does today.

Like Attracts Like:
A Fundamental Law of Energy

Each of our individual reactions, experiences, and emotions—especially those which are loving or fearful—energetically vibrate to a specific frequency. These frequencies, once released, will always find their way to a vibrational match. HUman emotions and feelings, among them happiness, anger, fear, even when only experienced within yourself or in a one-on-one exchange with another person, also become part of the same ambient thought forms throughout mass consciousness. Collective frequencies become thought forms and thought forms create our realities and most of the defining aspects of the dimensional levels that exist.

Thought forms are like *lumps of clay* that can be shaped into poverty, hopelessness, illness, and so forth, or abundance, creative opportunities, happiness, and perfect health. And as we witnessed, a lump of clay can morph into a deadly virus and a devastating worldwide pandemic.

When the collective's thinking shifted into a higher vibration, we saw scientific advancement in the form of vaccines developed at Lightning speed. Necessity is the mother of invention. When the collective's thought form shifted, milder versions of COVID appeared because the collective fear shifted *first*.

The frequencies that our thoughts carry are some of the many very powerful SuperHUman abilities we all possess. The more we step into our 5D HUman selves, the more dominion we have on how to use our thought abilities as a constructive tool for self-care and to serve the highest good of all. Our

187

3D/4D HUman selves had little awareness of the dormant capabilities and the miracles that were deeply hidden in the underutilized consciousness of our 5D selves.

Responsibility Is the *"Ability to Respond"*

No matter who or what triggers us, ultimately it is *our* responsibility to address where fear resides in us. It's nobody else's, ever. If you're afraid about not having enough money, being alone, or riding elevators, you've come to the right place. You, like me, were once a fulltime member in the exclusive organization for 3D HUmans, the *Cray-Cray Club.*

I *knew* I recognized you! So nice to see you again. . . .

From centuries of living according to 3D doctrines, our emotional bodies have come to contain a lot of potentially debilitating fears. Still, our fears, however acquired, belong to us. The most recent global pandemic helped us look at some of our fears together. These fears became less shameful because everyone was addressing one fear or another, all at the same time. In many unexpected ways, the pandemic *broke the news* on some of the deepest, personally shameful, hidden secrets that divided us but that we all secretly shared, probably since the beginning of recorded history.

As HUmans, we spend a copious amount of time and energy covering up the Universal truth that we are inherently *vulnerable.* We never learned to fully embrace, with pride and self-esteem, that we were given the blessings of being able to feel feelings. Unfortunately, not only our feelings, but our "feelings about having our feelings" have been repeatedly used against us in the form of shame and control. Exacerbated by numerous lifetimes immersed in 3D duality, we became conditioned to believe that there were "good" and "bad" feelings. *Internal polarization creates external polarization.* When we feel conflicted, the world feels conflicted. We are all part of everything we see around us. Heck, we created it.

While the horrible pandemic was running rampant in our 3D world, the invisible world of 5D consciousness was trying to salvage something positive from it. As we tried to make our way, from moment to moment, through the world's collective anguished thought forms, on a 5D level, the virus was giving us an opportunity to transform the world. As our shock and confusion were playing out in real time, the virus, like a well-aimed bowling ball, was delivering a strike. It knocked down many, many old 3D pins in one precise roll.

Many people in the industrialized world built what they have with the bricks of 3D privilege, power, and HUman separation. Without coming from blame or sounding chastising, many of us got a small taste of what our global neighbors in less developed or affluent nations were accustomed to facing on a daily basis, without a deadly virus in tow. Fear over not having enough money, food, shelter, health care, medicine, or fuel—suddenly appeared in our reality. Like a homeopathic remedy, it imbibed us with a relatively small amount of the larger situation to stimulate, recreate and ultimately help heal what ails us. Our familiar comforts, many of which seemed formerly cemented in place, rattled loose. The pandemic metaphorically banged the stuck jar lid on the side of our sink and helped to loosen the grip of its seal.

Experiencing scarcity scared the *"bejesus"* out of us—enough to crack the shell of our entitlement egg and let some higher, 5D Light shine through. When your hidden truths and fears come to the surface, grab them with open arms and an open heart. Create a safe place where they can rear their ugly little heads for a transition back to the higher realms of perfect God-Light and Love. Facing personal fears and breaking free of the 3D handcuffs they inadvertently place on all of us, will move you through those last final remnants of 3D consciousness that exist in your life and in the larger collectives' vibrational field. *Now* is the time to commit yourself to facing them, loving them, and dissolving them.

If you want to make a monumental difference in your life, entering more deeply into the new 5D world, and accelerate taking your incredibly challenging, often scary leap of faith, then I have just handed you your personal *marching orders*. Face and Love your fears. Do not rise above them. Embrace them and Love the 3D parts of yourself. In turn, you help others to Love away their 3D selves as well.

Your 3D/4D self is not going away completely anytime soon—not in our lifetime anyway. We are in a very early stage of recognizing and becoming multidimensional. We have much to learn, Grasshopper. Even so, multidimensionality is not a rare occurrence on the planet anymore. It is no longer an exception. It is *now* the rule of our new existence.

It is important to begin to continue to look at our old beliefs and levels of consciousness and then take notice of who we have grown into today. We must find the courage to look our identities, *all of them*, straight in the eye, so we can begin to distinguish the different aspects of our multidimensional Earth selves. Even as a 5D HUman, you will go back and forth on a regular basis into and out of your still hardwired, 3D/4D consciousness. Once you deepen your acceptance of these new bits of information and the truth of what it means to be *you* these days on the planet, you will automatically increase the kindness and Love you direct to yourself and others.

The new 5D spirituality is not for the thin skinned. 3D utilized religion for the purpose of holding power. It was and is, for many, still needed. But that was your momma's spirituality, not ours. Know that you are one of the greatest *souls* that *ever* existed, and you are alive to complete what you had started 27,000 years ago: 5D Ascension for Earth-based HUmans. Nobody else could have done the job that you have done, especially the piece that was specifically designed for you.

At our core, we all know what we came here to do. The math is simple. Whatever you have or have not done, whatever your actions or inactions were, both of those measures were what you came in to do. Stop the searching for the perfect job and exhausting yourself by going on interview after interview about your life's purpose. Those things are red herrings.

SPOILER ALERT:

You were *already "hired"* before you arrived because you had the perfect *spiritual resume* for the job which was called your life!

The Story of *Everybody, Somebody, Anybody, and Nobody*

"There was an important job to be done. Everybody was sure that Somebody would do it. Anybody could have done it, but Nobody did it. Somebody got angry about that because it was Everybody's job. Everybody thought Anybody could do it. But Nobody realized that Everybody wouldn't do it. It ended up that Everybody blamed Somebody when Nobody did what Anybody could have."[1]

This story by the late radio and television personality Charles Osgood, which circulates the internet on business blogs, is so on point that I wanted to share it with you. The story may sound a little Abbott and Costello-ish, but its message is very clear. No one took responsibility, so nothing got accomplished or addressed. It's a familiar story that has unfortunately played out way too often throughout our lives, but especially during our childhood years. Like any other conditioned, 3D patterns, if we learn them in childhood, we tend to repeat them throughout our lives in our own interpersonal relationships, especially with our families, work, and romantic partners. When "looking the other way" or "passing the buck" becomes the norm, this often morphs into ambivalence, passivity, and a sense of powerlessness that curtails the ability to positively affect our reality and lives. 3D HUmans are often conditioned not to take dominion over their own lives, and so, rarely get to experience the power that they can unleash when they take an action.

This is often hard to see in ourselves, until it is reflected to us through our collective, worldly manifestations, such as in our political leaders, organized religions, societal conventions, and oppressive laws. Anywhere there is an individual, group, culture, or society that lacks *accountability,* you find this kind of *"passing the buck."*

As you understand and move into 5D HUmanhood, your life will be ripe with opportunities to step into your truth and *personal* accountability. Sometimes it will feel . . . *almost too ripe. Inner* authority comes from within. 3D has taught most of us to rely on and follow *outer* authority. You already have all the puzzle pieces you need to play your key role in the *bigger picture* mosaic of the Multiverse. This is what you were hired for: being *you.*

If we do not address things like hardwired 3D ideas, beliefs, and falsehoods, process them, and do whatever we need to do to delete them, then the world we live in won't change. Each of us is the hope and the change we seek in this world. This means, *you* are the cavalry coming over the hill just in the nick of time. You are the savior that you've been waiting for. You've come here to live out your life with all its good, bad, beautiful, and ugly experiences as part of a collective effort in helping to create a *miracle.* That is Earth's 5D Ascension story in a nutshell. *Crack.*

This Is Your *Passion,* Your *Moment,* Your *Clarion Call*

The pandemic disarmed us, constricted our lives, and broke down the majority of our familiar comfort routines. And because of all that habit-changing noise, we were forced to wake up from a deep, long, lazy slumber. To adjust, we found ways to be creative, resourceful, and face our worst fears. As a result, we *now* have a lot of new tools at our disposal, as we were stretched beyond our limits. A couple of years living in the unknown, cracked apart the old, stagnant 3D constructs that our new 5D paradigm outgrew.

With its accompanying reduction in emotional intensity and overall lessening of drama, 5D consciousness brings with it advanced levels of spiritual growth and evolutionary Ascension. On the physical plane, it will also bring more advanced scientific discoveries and breakthrough cures for the diseases that all of us have been impacted by including cancer, heart disease, and AIDS. At first, this good news will feel almost hard to trust, because it may feel like the treatments came into being too quickly for our much slower 3D brains to wrap themselves around the idea or faster timeline. Similarly, many HUmans had initial hesitancy to the mRNA vaccines that sprung up in record time to bolster our immunity and prevent a lot of additional deaths from COVID. It was the 3D vibrational division spillover between various groups of HUmanity before and after the novel coronavirus began circulating that had contributed to some of the vaccine fears.

As we begin to move more consciously into 5D thinking and further away from 3D thinking, which *polarizes* good vs. bad, right vs. wrong, allopathic, or traditional, medicines vs. various forms of natural remedies, such as herbs, homeopathy, and acupuncture, and so on, we will see more options and *combined treatments for improving our health*. Once we expand into 5D triality, both views will move off the ropes and find collaboration. That's the unpolarized 5D way. These new treatment options won't encounter the same polarized mental opposition. At that point, everybody on Earth will feel comfortable expressing their freedom to *choose* between modalities and not come from an energy that opposes or shoots down the others. This will remain a constant for how we treat viruses, our wants, desires, and lives going 5D forward.

Even a Broken Clock Is *Right* Twice a Day

As conscious and caring HUman beings, when our choices harm others or adversely affect their lifestyles, then we have a responsibility to rethink our behavior. A variety of healing modalities might one day be available to mitigate the impact of the virus or other HUman health challenges, but we are unlikely to discover or develop them as rapidly as we are *now* capable of doing. Our remaining 3D/4D polarity filters are still coloring our thinking and fueling our HUman character flaws. We won't be able to help everybody who needs these medicines and new approaches to HUman life here on the planet unless we address, and at least try to transmute, our underlying social divisions.

As previously mentioned, the responses of different HUmans to mask mandates and other COVID protocols were a sign of 3D polarity running amok—another repercussion of HUman separation. If we are willing to look at our responses openly, not from a place of 3D duality but of 5D triality, we will find thought forms of judgment, anger, and self-righteousness, which create disharmony, and a world of people who are deeply out of sync. Whether or not you take vaccines or chose to wear masks is not the point I am trying to make. Instead, I'm trying to shine a spotlight on an underlying problem with negative thought forms, fear, anger, and HUman division.

So many more healing modalities will be coming into our new 5D world in which we will be able to do mega transformative healing. Many of these at first may provoke suspicion, resistance, and doubt. In 3D, our minds reign, and our old conditioning dictates what usually feels right or wrong. We learned only to use our five senses to evaluate what is real or correct. Although taking a course of medication or a specific treatment should always require critical assessment, as we move into 5D we will learn how to validate what's real and true with the intelligence of our *intuitive heart's knowing.* The Ascended heart/mind processor in our newly acquired 5D HUman body will use *both* approaches side by side together. Going forward, this is how Earth's 5D advanced HUmans will be making sound decisions.

Even many of the super-evolved among us will have to revisit their decision-making processes when 5D kicks in fully. Just like us, they too will also benefit from reconsidering everything from their spiritual belief to how they impact and interface with people wherever they go. What none of us has fully grasped yet is that in the higher realms of consciousness our 5D HUman system has access to so much more power than we had in 3D/4D. If we were cars we would all be (electric) versions of Lamborghinis and Maseratis! Our 5D "engines" use fewer filters and emotions inappropriately. But when we do direct our emotions towards another person or put our weight behind an opinion, 5D emotions will carry a lot more G-force.

5D HUmans will use their emotions less, but when they do they will be more *impactful.* As 5D LightWorkers, we are already carrying more higher frequency God-Light around than most other people, and because this is anomalous, we often do not realize what we are capable of, and how sensitive we have become. We pick up more ambient energy than other people and are impacted even more intensely by what we expose ourselves to and take in. The suspicion and fear that enters into 3D decision-making by *contrast vs. choice* hijacks our brains, distorts our thinking, and blurs the lens of ultimately what is best for us.

Higher Dimensional Beings Are Actively Working on Our Behalf

Back in 1998, approximately two years after my first book**, *Feng Shui: Harmony By Design*** was published, I created an international nonprofit program called *Feng Shui Around the World*. I, as well as many, many other Feng Shui Consultants provided free Feng Shui services for individuals affected by AIDS.

On September 27, 1998, my spiritual mentor, His Holiness the late Grandmaster Professor Thomas Lin Yun Rinpoche, Spiritual Leader of the Fourth Stage Black Hat Sect Tibetan Tantric Buddhist School of Feng Shui, exalted my efforts by joining me and leading the international Feng Shui community through a *worldwide blessing ceremony* for the eradication of the AIDS virus. 108 people were invited to join us in person at the Lin Yun Temple, Long Island, New York, as he led several hundred HUmans around the world in a groundbreaking prayer and BTB transcendental rituals. The numerology of that day was nothing short of profound and divine: 9-9-9 with 108 people adding up to another powerful 9! The number 9 in BTB Feng Shui is the strongest of all the yang numbers, and in numerology represents massive spiritual change, transformation, and completion.

In retrospect, both the onset of the AIDS virus during my mid-twenties and my subsequent FSATW program a decade later set the vibrational stage for my current *bigger picture* work, tying together all these various pieces from Lemuria, our HUman 5D Ascension and all that has surrounded it. I was already on board, *spiritually speaking,* with the impact of the AIDS virus long before COVID came about. But it hasn't escaped me how back then His Holiness Grandmaster Lin Yun helped plant the "dreamer" seeds in the etheric grid of mass consciousness around thought forms, viruses, and the vision of a world healing. As I will explain in the next few paragraphs, even *now,* over a decade after he left his HUman body, he is still working with me on behalf of the Multiverse and this current transition through COVID moving us into a 5D world.

Back in 2020, I was directed to do some personal work with Patrice Fields, Psy.D., a renowned teacher, healer, and current-day metaphysical maverick.[2] As part of her initial review, I started talking about my Feng Shui work and mentioned my teacher and spiritual guide, His Holiness Grandmaster Lin Yun. I shared that as one of his disciples, it was my honor to study BTB Feng Shui teachings and spirituality for over twenty-three years. I still get emotional at times just mentioning his name. He continues to be one of my greatest gifts and blessings in my lifetime.

While I was talking to Patrice about him, she said, *"I know Grandmaster Lin Yun!"* Surprised, I asked, "How?" She said, "Twenty years ago, he came to my house to do a Feng Shui consultation." My jaw dropped open.

If you're in the Feng Shui world, especially in the BTB circle you would know that His Holiness did not show up at just *anybody's* house to do a consultation! I didn't know what was unfolding at the time, but I was both shocked and riveted by the serendipity of the moment.

Patrice shared with me that just prior to the time that we connected, His Holiness appeared during one of her meditations, and she started talking to his spirit about the coronavirus. It was in the very early stages of the pandemic, and frankly, no one clearly knew what was happening or where it was all going. His Holiness told Patrice it was not his area of expertise, but said, *"You know what, I know someone that I want to connect you with, someone that you have to meet who deals with these sort of things.* He is a very high-dimensional being who specializes in *viruses* and also works on the *writing of Spiritual Laws."* In her meditation, His Holiness Grandmaster Lin Yun then walked her over to a place where this *spirit being* named **San J Pan Wan G** was and introduced them.

Like His Holiness Grandmaster Lin Yun, he is a very informal, but incredibly high-dimensional being who likes being called *San J.* San J's energy field specifically works from and resides somewhere between the 8th and 9th dimensions. He shared with Patrice that some of his most important work is to *transmute* the energy of the coronavirus and help us realign our planet through the higher principles of Spiritual Law. Patrice generously shared San J's teachings throughout her work and classes during some of the most intense periods throughout the height of the COVID pandemic.

He shared with her that he was calling on all the *dreamers* on Earth, those among us who can use our *daytime dream states* to shift the current reality by *dreaming through* to the other side of this pandemic. He encouraged us to believe and *dream* something bigger and higher to evolve from all of Earth's current Shadow. He reminded us about the power of the *awakened dream* and how by using our new abilities not just to visualize things into manifestation, but to *dream* them into manifestation. He emphasized that the energy force behind our current *dreaming ability* is more powerful *now* in creating a new reality. Manifestation through dreaming, employs the *divine feminine energy* field and magnetically pulls the creation or desire to you. Visualization utilizes the old masculine energy, still very impactful, but slower and vibrationally outdated. As we become more fluent in this approach to *creating,* collectively, we will then be able to use this effectively for *bigger picture* change and a greater world alignment.

San J Pan Wan G is here to help HUmanity mitigate the powerful force of the thought forms that exist *behind* the virus. He is working on creating new Spiritual Laws, especially laws that help diffuse the forces that are currently out of control at this time on the planet. He works with thought fields specializing in those related to viruses. This is a very powerful, verbatim quote that Patrice Fields channeled from him and shared with her students.

He said: ***"I am the peace that moves you to dream."***

San J is one of the most significant *dreamers* in any time or dimension throughout the *Multiverse*. He holds the space and also *dreams* into reality the relationship between the individual and the land, the individual and the elements, and the individual and mass thought forms. He vibrates to a very high frequency of integrity. Ask him to work with you and to help you be a better *dreamer*. He is an incredible resource.

Dreaming is not a spiritual cliché; it is a force of nature from the unseen realm that can help you manifest what you need to move more smoothly through your life and your 5D transition.

This is the honored lineage that we are *now* a deep, venerable part of. I am so grateful that His Holiness Grandmaster Lin has come back into my life from the great beyond to guide and join me once again in finishing the work that we began together many decades ago for the next stage of HUmanity's 5D evolution.

CHAPTER FIVE

THE NEW 5D CODEX

Fear Divides Us, Love Evolves Us

As already established, fear is constrictive in nature. A simple way to begin to release its invisible chokehold on your beliefs related to truth and safety, is to challenge it with the litmus test of *contrary action*.

During 2020-2021, for all our issues reflected in our struggles with HUman separation, the one thing that connected us all was the emotion of *fear*. If you had looked under the "hood" of the pandemic, you would have seen that fear was the main emotion behind our political beliefs and subsequent actions long before the virus erupted onto the world stage. Fear surfaces for all of us when we are feeling threatened, unsafe, or constricted. When we are catapulted into a place of fear, we can never be at the same time in a place of *Love*. Love is expansive. It creates an energy field where we feel safe, and it's within that peaceful equilibrium that we are clearer and able to make decisions in our best interest. 5D consciousness teaches us how to make decisions that empower and grow us through the lens of choice, *not fear*. In 5D, you still get to decide not to spend a certain amount of money on a car or a vacation, or to stay in a job that you might not like or to choose to take or not take a vaccine—but these decisions are not made through the old, 3D control filter of fear.

If we are being honest and allowing ourselves to "check under the hood," some form of fear is usually present when we are going about our daily lives. No matter how evolved and spiritual we might believe we are, the vast majority of us were born into 3D/4D, not into 5D, and fear is a constant companion to all that we believed to be true. This applies to us personally and collectively. In 3D, we were conditioned to believe that fear is the friend that warns us about imminent harm or danger. In actuality, it's the bully part of our original psyches that manipulates us and runs serious interference to Love.

In 5D, fear is understood to be an illusion. Love is God. God is Love. God is you. God is me. God is everyone. At the core of our existence, everything is synthesized down to Love. When we entertain fear for any long period of time, we allow it to move us away from ourselves, God, and Love.

We learned fear in 3D but its false narrative created a wedge between *us and Love, and us and Trust*. It duped us out of remembering that we were and are *always* safe. Earth suffers from a chronic, deadly case of HUman separation. Our misguided sense of individuality was never meant to divide us, cause wars, or rob us of our dignity—*or others of theirs*. But when fear sets in, it often becomes a justification for greed, self-righteousness, abuse of power, and a sense of supremacy related to race, gender, and sexuality.

Shake Things Up. Be Contrary!

Several of the common fears that our 3D aspect has often struggled with are money, relationships, and health. Pause a minute and jot down or at least think of two or three specific issues that are germane to your existence right *now*. For example, *"I feel lost and without direction," "My son is doing* drugs," or "I don't know how I will ever be able to get out of debt."

Once you've thought of a couple of fear-based issues, I'd like for you to come up with one or two actions for each that seem totally *contrary* to everything your fears are directly and indirectly saying to you about them. For example, if you have worries about money, do something contrary to that belief or fear, an action that would force your image of your financial constriction to shift and unconstrict itself. The next time you spend some money, even if it's for a practical reason, such as buying groceries or medicine, claim prosperity and joy for having the money to spend, even if it's on a credit card. Let yourself feel relieved that you *had it* to spend, even if that's not the case or your usual *go-to* reaction.

Worrying about going broke? Donate to a charity or give $10 to a homeless HUman. How much you give should be relative to what you can afford . . . but push yourself slightly out of your comfort zone. Get "consciously" in the way of your old reaction or thought form, even if that thought reflected a current truth.

In a 3D/4D paradigm, the situation or concern is probably representing a specific reality or fact. The objective here is not to deny it or make believe it's not true. Your goal is to create an alternative reality through changing your usual response to the situation at hand. If you don't like the "movie" playing, as a multidimensional being you get to change the channel! In doing so, with full awareness, you engage your 5D mind in another scenario. You begin the process of rewriting the "storyline" by separating out the situation—which might be very real—from your emotional, knee-jerk reaction of fear to it. This allows you over time to deescalate the situation and diffuse the high-end vibrational charge that is the real catalyst which is keeping the situation on a hamster wheel.

As you move into 5D, you will realize that those are two very different components of any one situation. Fusing old 3D/4D emotions to the situation keeps you in a perpetual loop fueled by *fear*.

The final caveat in this exercise is to make sure the action that you are taking is also new. If you are donating, the donation needs to go to an organization, cause, or someone whom you have never donated to before. The best would be giving to someone or a cause that you previously dismissed or judged as unworthy or believe might already have *enough* money. Try to move past your immediate family or friends for whom giving can be easily justified in your consciousness, or that your mind might read as a familiar way you usually do gifting—such as to your children, nephews, or cousins. Unless it's a relative who always complains that they don't have any money, doesn't work, and borrows often. Yikes. That one's hard! In this case, it's even better if your gift is anonymous and has a surprise element to it like placing money in their wallet without them knowing it came from you.

Get as creative as you can! How about a direct deposit of cash into someone's account, picking up the dinner check for a stranger, or leaving a $20 bill in your friend's pajama drawer? Paying an electric bill for someone in need or the toll for a stranger in the car behind you would shift your energy and theirs!

Maybe leave a note at your neighbor's door reading, "Just wanted you to know you are Loved," along with flowers picked at a local park. These are all ways that we can really, really become *very* generous with Love and it doesn't have to cost a dime.

Apply these principles to everything that scares you. The point is to do something that is totally opposite the behavior of your biggest fears. When we fall into lack and fear, it's harder to see our way out of it to higher ground. Come up with creative ways to address the fear with an act of Love or generosity. Keep your Love flowing in ways that you haven't actively done before. Apply contrary ways that challenge the truth of what fear wants you to believe is real. Stand up to the bully in your head.

And yes, on one timeline, whatever is worrying you is real. That is, it's real to the degree that your experience of it is reflected back to you. But as a 5D person, you also have the choice *now* to utilize some powerful new tools that are perks of your expanded consciousness. As you remember that there are other stations of *reality TV* also available to you, all you have to do *now* is learn how to work the timeline "remote control device" in your hands and "change the reality channel." Do you want to watch the scary movie or the one where the HUman remembers Love? In 5D, the remote control is in your possession. Use it.

It's Less about Giving, *More* about Receiving

Keep your heart open. Let Love be your new master, but most importantly, open yourself to *receiving.* In 5D it's not just about giving anymore. If you approach this concept exclusively from a place of generosity, as a HUmanitarian act, then yes, you will definitely be helping other HUmans increase their ability to receive. Although this is a very important part of the give-and-take process, it's a place that many (sometimes, not enough) people get stuck in and trip over.

3D consciousness' *glorified* sense of martyrdom manipulated our acts of kindness and exploited our ability to feel compassion for others. We came to feel so guilty, ashamed, and undeserving of the exact HUman emotion and Love that we were sharing and making available to others.

Religion is a very big culprit in this misuse of our goodness, in part because religion was born out of a 3D level of consciousness. In general, 3D consciousness places God *outside* us, as a disembodied entity that doles out *rewards for goodness and punishments for sin.* Its core of *polarity* not only separated one group of HUmans from another but separated all HUman beings from their inner connection with their God selves.

The 3D consciousness surrounding the "Love Thy Neighbor, as Thyself" motto was a built-in reminder after a small group of self-ingratiating HUmans in Atlantis forgot this basic tenet and inadvertently erased two continents and hundreds of thousands of lives.

In 4D, you move more into spirituality and out of 3D religion, and along with that, your concepts or ideas of God broaden. 4D beliefs about God are more akin to the belief that a piece of God is within *you.*

5D is where you truly begin to wrap your awareness around the understanding that you *"are"* God. God is not something outside you. You are God in HUman form. *And . . .* so is everyone else. Then, in knowing that truth, you can only treat others with Love, dignity, and the highest of care and respect.

More importantly, this awakening leaves you with no other option but to treat *yourself* with the same reverence that you may have formerly directed to an external Godhead.

This new 5D knowing of your godliness doesn't make you grandiose, arrogant, or maniacal. It makes you kinder, more loving, and more responsible to act in the highest way possible in every interaction with self, or with others, animals, and nature.

By placing God outside of us, 3D turned God into an authority figure. This took us off the hook by making us less capable than we are and often less responsible for all our actions. We began treating God as if God was a HUman being with emotions of anger, disappointment, and unhappiness with us or regarding something we might think or feel.

Actually, emotions are attributes that we are able to experience *only* while in a body, as a HUman. Separation from our true God self within created the perfect opportunity for some of us to misuse our power and authority by controlling other people based on *"you were less versus more deserving."* This belief in an external God actually was a main foundational piece contributing to HUman separation through the posturing of both supremacy and elitism.

Initially, 5D consciousness may seem contrary to your belief system. That's why stepping fully into your 5D life often takes a while—perhaps years to lifetimes. And not because it is a higher reality, but because as you vibrationally grow into it, you will have to *unlearn* and transmute your old 3D/4D programming.

Deprogramming deep 3D imprints regarding our self-worth, "good person" syndrome and "God is keeping score" thinking feeds our fears and spins us away from respectfully owning our Light, Shadow, and Power. We learned how to feel guilt, shame, and greed about wanting, desiring, and giving to ourselves *first*. It is *now* time to retrain our understanding of *giving and receiving*. Fundamental to our new exchanges is receiving without feeling constricting, *soul*-limiting emotions.

Redistribution of Wealth and a Newfound Visibility

The worldwide pandemic created a huge crack in the old 3D duality-based system of *give and take*. For the first time, a much larger group of people in need were seen and understood. It was as if they were lit up and placed under an oversized magnifying glass. The majority were marginalized HUmans who have been scraping by for multiple generations. Many could be categorized as minorities, impoverished, homeless, or once imprisoned. In the United States, these people are often treated by the predominately White mainstream population in power as "throwaways."

In a 5D world, this is unconscionable.

When the pandemic came through, disrupting the routines and economies of industrialized countries and the lives of the *"contributing"* members of an advanced society, many of these groups were reintegrated into the mainstream as more value was placed back on them because of their work contribution during the much-needed, early stages of the pandemic. They were invisible and not seen as having value until everyone became at equal risk of exposure to the *same* virus.

The virus didn't discriminate by race, socioeconomic grouping, sexual identity, or religion. With the exception of the elderly and certain immune-compromised members of society, such as people living with cancer, there was no region or populace exempt from the contagion. It was on every continent and island. Suddenly, the 3D HUman separation that we were all sickened by, dissolved *some* of the chokehold that supremacy and elitism had on society, if only for a few stressful months. All of us were together in the same *vulnerable* pandemic boat.

And yes, the pandemic disproportionately afflicted previously *"discarded"* groups of HUmans, but those affected were already being disproportionately ignored by the mainstream long before COVID.

It cannot be stated enough, the viral pandemic was horrible. It adversely impacted many people. But if you look at the *bigger picture* of what else it brought with it, one of the silver linings in this ominous cloud was that many people got a reprieve—not the Jeff Bezos kind of reprieve—but the "average Joe" finally got some assistance. Many frontline workers and manual laborers—minimum wage earners—were forced out of their jobs. Fulltime workers whose salaries never could have lifted them out of the cycle of poverty, even working forty hours per week, were placed on state unemployment, offered federal pandemic unemployment assistance (PUA), and given food vouchers. Student loan debts were forgiven. The middle class took advantage of low interest rates to get mortgages, forgivable government loans, and tax abatements. Many others were protected by eviction moratoriums and given child tax credits. Free COVID testing, medical treatment, and vaccines, if needed or chosen, were made available to everyone.

To stave off a depression, the American government was forced into *redistributing the wealth*, which included testing a sample version of the consistently debated and often politicized, "healthcare for all" programs.

Suddenly, all the financial structures of the free world took a stunning reversal, acting in ways "contrary" to what Humans were accustomed to from many of the planet's 3D governments. Checks were actually coming into bank accounts, as opposed to many sending checks to the government. Suddenly, marginalized people became seen and honored for their service. All at once, the suppressed, invisible value of frontline workers, such as delivery people, supermarket cashiers, gas station attendants, health care personnel, factory workers in food-processing plants and toilet paper-manufacturers came to the surface. Nurses, doctors, EMTs, and other health care workers were finally acknowledged and lauded. These HUmans became our heroes. The ones who kept everyone fed, fueled up, safe, and alive until the pandemic reached a more manageable level of transmission, and it was safe for us to return to life as a more evolved, processed, and shifted 5D HUman.

All the money in the banks, possessions, and amassed savings accounts, all the things that we, as 3D/4D Humans, have been so hijacked by beyond their original purpose did not enhance the *same way,* especially during the time that we were facing a killer virus that didn't discriminate. But what the pandemic did do was to help middle class and affluent people see the HUmans on the lower end of the socioeconomic ladder in the roles they carried in a whole new Light. These were no longer "insignificant" HUmans. Possibly for the first time, their value was recognized. Even if the rest of the world chose to go back to their old 3D thinking and perspectives, at least *now* they themselves understood their value, and why they have always been a significant and integral part of a society who truly needed them. Even if it just moved the needle slightly on the dial, after 27,000 years of being in a 3D chokehold this was a victory for HUmankind.

After chasing after our 3D tails of belief about what success, money, and the pursuit of happiness should look like, the world was still terribly divided. The pandemic, in many ways, stripped us down and brought us back to the reality that underneath it all, we are all the same.

COVID brought to Light the different ways our society and our lives were out of balance. It was the first worldwide, visible sign following the 5D Ascension launch that the grossly imbalanced, 3D give-and-take paradigm was beginning to shift. COVID made us *"stop and drop."*

If you used your COVID or pandemic experience for the higher purpose that it was created, in spite of its very low real vibration, it should have reflected to you what you needed to change, shift, and reset in your everyday life. That was its invisible gift to you, as you are *now* learning to know how to identify the 5D silver lining in everything.

In 5D and above, nobody is ever seen as a subordinate being. Marginalized people are always considered high-ranking LightWorkers who have taken on some of the menial, but crucial work assignments during their incarnations on Planet Earth. Some of the poorly paying jobs are green-lit as service contracts for our ongoing 5D Ascension process out of our prior 3D/4D matrix. Some (not all) chose to come in with a contract as a homeless HUman; others as sex workers.

Remember to treat everyone with respect and honor, for you don't know who is carrying the highest God frequencies on the planet. Don't be fooled by the 3D cloaks they are wearing. They, like most of us, cannot remember who they really are or even the reason, either personal or service-related, why they are playing the roles they are in this lifetime. A lot of that information is veiled.

Everybody alive holds an important piece of the 3D to 5D puzzle, but we often cannot see the many complicated pieces of the *bigger picture* that we are a part of. Use this perspective as a basis for reflection on your own worth. You have had many roles—some purposefully hidden. Although you may not know your role on the team, it is unique. Don't be judgmental about your place in this often-crazy and convoluted Ascension process. In order to trust your value and your importance as a significant player in the *bigger picture*, you don't have to know all the details. Your assignment here might never be made clear to you, and you may never see the details in bold print. We were conditioned in our 3D paradigm to look for tangible, concrete evidence of *validation*. Let go to a higher truth and inner knowing. You wouldn't be reading this book if you didn't schedule me to remind you about all of this right about *NOW*. Jump in! Take an active part of in your own 5D transition. Receive the nudge and energetically take in the LOVE.

All *Bigger Picture* Changes Begin *"Within"*

Relationships, money imbalances, governing principles, even health issues will at some point come to the surface in your life if those are areas that you are trying to "whole" yourself around. *All* imbalances in the world are collective manifestations of our individual imbalances. These can only be transmuted when a society, a collective of people, or a mass movement wakes up, steps up, and truly understands the gold that can be mined when we take responsibility for raising our individual HUman vibration through expanded consciousness.

Profound change on the planet can only happen if profound personal shifts within are accomplished *first*. When enough of us shift individually, the collective shifts. Those are the only changes in the world that are long lasting and hardwired. That's why our 5D Ascension has taken 27,000 years to accomplish. That's why it was nothing short of a miracle.

Although our 5D HUman upgrading comes with some very new cool features, we don't just morph into advanced versions of ourselves without massive changes in our old 3D/4D HUman and its etheric body structures. We are being impacted physically, emotionally, spiritually, and mentally. Everything, including our physical DNA, emotional reactions, ways we think, and sense of *soul's* purpose will undergo their own evolution to accommodate our bodies' new 5D processors. In essence, this is a big deal, a multilevel process that singlehandedly rivals the period on the planet when apes evolved into HUmans.

Another of the *bigger picture* objectives that we managed purposefully to accomplish during the prolonged pandemic period was the restructuring of our etheric bodies from 3D to 5D. Although many throughout the world were scheduled to move in tandem into their 5D template, the deadly nature of the virus also created a mass exodus, at last count, over six and a half million HUmans. Some of those *souls* (not all) had chosen to leave the planet through the exit vehicle of the virus to serve this massive, planetary 5D transitioning process elsewhere, from a higher place. Together, the *souls* who remained here and many who left, created the final push that was needed to tip the remaining 3D energy into the 5D net.

All the behind-scenes, higher-energy shifts compounded the surrealism of life during the pandemic. It often felt, and still does, like we were spiraling out of control. As the energy fields altered, increased, and decreased on the planet, similar to tremors along a fault line during an Earthquake, they triggered and brought to the surface a lot of the *mental illness* that we are witnessing throughout society.

HUman mental health is the next *proverbial* plane waiting to taxi off the Earth's runway. Long overdue and grossly minimized, we are *now* without choice and face to face with its reality. Socially, this explains the escalation of gun violence and the horror of the extreme levels of destructive rioting. At times, it felt for many that we were facing a modern-day Armageddon. The disease of HUman separation escalated and the lines that were once drawn in the sand, which reflect personal and political differences, were being drawn indelibly, often written in HUman blood.

When the music stopped, most of us found ourselves grabbing a chair on one side or the other of the political upheaval. Mask wearing and getting vaccines were politicized, as the loud sounds of crumbling democracies played in the background din of many civilized countries around the world. A lot of families, friendships, neighbors, and business relationships didn't pass the stress test of feeling the 3D to 5D tectonic plates shifting under our feet.

The intensity of the world during the pandemic was meeting the energetic shifts that people were experiencing in kind. The world was shaken to its core and its HUmans were simultaneously disarmed from their usual *go-tos* and favorite places to hide. At that time, along with millions dying from the coronavirus, the weight of our 3D/4D belief systems about life, death, identity, safety, and survival also died. Although the residents of war-torn and developing nations are no strangers to living in *soul*-destroying conditions, the people in the upper echelon of society in industrialized nations, like countries in the European Union and the United States, never had to face anything similar. Losing financial resources along with their jobs and needing help to feed and house themselves is one of the conditions that made the pandemic so impactful in many ways, and specifically for our 5D Ascension. If the virus had just affected less affluent countries and left no real mark on countries with robust economies, then nothing of significance would have had at least the opportunity to *potentially* change.

Rightfully so, I imagine that you are probably still wondering, *"Have things really changed on the planet?"* On the physical plane, all we have to do to confirm our worst fears is to read a newspaper or watch the nightly news on TV. For the time being, we will most likely continue to experience increasing chaos and a world that resembles a post-apocalypse movie depicting the darker tendencies of HUmanity. Much of what we have and will continue to witness is the leftover Shadow pieces of our 3D creations. As hard as it is to experience, most of them are true events not TV fictions.

At the same time, changes for the better are happening. It is necessary to remember that for the 5D scale to tip ever so slightly in our favor, the invisible scaffolding that was keeping the 3D reality in place for eons had to come down and bring the hidden social imbalances to the surface. *Now* they are in plain sight for each one of us to change within ourselves—that is, if we are still not liking what we are seeing projected on the world's reality screen.

We cannot expect our HUman wounding from 3D/4D living to just go away when we Ascend. Scars, cuts, and bruises will surface. The Light reveals everything in the Shadows. Love joins in and happily makes everything that is unlike itself evident.

The Emotional Struggle Is Real

It is hard to let go of things, places, and people to which we are emotionally attached. But it is even more challenging to let go of conditioned ways of *thinking* about success, abundance, Love, and truth. These are the things we once pursued for our personal happiness, goals that are *now* up for grabs.

All concepts and beliefs are created from energy, and all energy has a consciousness. When they sense change, they dig in even harder. Wanting, needing, or desiring something is not wrong. You do not have to part with all your beliefs, or even *any* of them. You have the gift of *free will* and a plethora of choices in 5D. What created more conflict or angst than was necessary in your 3D life was not what you wanted or were attached to, but that those choices reflected an old template of who you once were. The 3D Petri dish of duality (expressed as pairs of opposites) set the stage for your subconscious mind to message you that you were facing a conundrum. You may have thought, *"If spiritual growth means having to trade off my favorite attachments, luxuries, and comforts, be they material or heartfelt, well then, thanks, but no thanks, I'll pass on growth."* Our old, dualistic, conditioned thinking wanted us to put happiness and comfort objects in a boxing ring with spiritual growth, as if only one could come out a winner.

Many shifts subtle and quantum in nature wind up feeling like either/or ultimatums. Welcome to Club HUman. Don't make yourself wrong for it. Just know when it surfaces—and it will—that it is an old, compelling 3D construct, one we will all have to transcend if we are to experience more elevated and abundant choices in 5D.

Although it might feel a little scary at first, and sound a little confusing too, as we rise into higher dimensions we will be operating under *entirely* different laws. Allow yourself the full experience of any emotions that arise in your body when you are breaking old contracts and leaving behind old beliefs and ways of living. There is no way around the initial panic, fear, or guilt reactions that you might have. As a matter of fact, *the only way out of them* is through them.

Your very HUman feelings are only reflecting an advanced *soul* going through a profound metamorphosis while both *consciously awake and emotionally sober*. There are so many moving parts involved in stepping into your Ascended self. During the transitional phase of the process, and often long after, it is common to experience loneliness and a sense of abandonment, and to question the people you Love and things you have grown accustomed to in your 3D/4D world.

Unless we are completely emotionally cut off, all of us will struggle with such feelings at one time or another. This piece of the paradigm shift has become an all too familiar "speed bump" that we encounter as we move through rises in vibration and into 5D consciousness. That's why, as long as we are on the planet and ushering in this never-done-before process, we are going to need support. Lots of it. Find your peeps, mentors, and trusted sherpas. (See the Resources section at the back of the book.)

The Physical Struggle Is Real

In physics, the definition of *chaos* is "behavior so unpredictable that it appears to be random, thus creating a dispropor-tionately sensitive reaction to a seemingly small change in a condition."[1] This passage of transcending, of moving from one dimension to another, is often a struggle for every aspect of our emotional, spiritual, and physical selves. On its surface, *change* can create what appears to be massive chaos both in our personal lives and the broader world.

When aspects of our world begin to shift, such as our perspectives of ourselves and the lives we created, a deep *grieving process* may ensue. It's much easier to recognize chaos on the more mundane level when we unexpectedly lose a job or a Loved one, experience financial hardship, or receive an unfavorable health diagnosis. But none of these tangible twists and turns of everyday life happens randomly or without concomitant factors. Personally, and collectively, every change or shift in being happens on several levels and not necessarily in equal amounts or simultaneously. This comes from our *soul* having many different levels and layers, especially when we are on Earth and in HUman form.

As we each Ascend to 5D and our duality-based reality fades, in some way we need to mourn what may feel like sudden, rapid changes. If a situation feels like it holds the intensity of life and death, you are most likely spot on with what you're doing. Our 3D selves are *dying off,* becoming more extinct. *We are awake and alive at our own funerals—*a first. Until *now,* we have never been able to slough off the identity of a prior dimension while retaining the body we were born in. This is what makes our dimensional shift Humanly unprecedented.

Our 3D physical bodies, and all they are comprised of, have to reorganize themselves to house the new energies of the 5D HUmans we are becoming. As we morph, we are activating more of our DNA than we formerly used or could scientifically ascribe a value or purpose to. Not knowing how to measure its biological functions, scientists have labeled 97-98 percent of our DNA as "junk." But in its entirety, 5D HUmans are coming to understand this as God-Consciousness DNA. The idea of "junk DNA" is a perfect example of how limited 3D conscious-ness is.

On a bioenergetic level, our bodies are slowly beginning to transition from a *carbon-based to a crystalline-based physical structure.* On a mental level, as we Ascend to 5D, our old beliefs are dying—thus, we are changing how we act and interface with Mother Earth and other HUmans. On an emotional level, we are letting go of the ways we think, feel, emote, and Love.

All aspects of duality-based perception are starting to melt away. And this will happen through no effort or fault of yours, whether or not they are things you want to move on from. So much time is erroneously spent struggling with issues of shame, remorse, guilt, and creative coverups of things like failed relationships and lack of self-worth—and everything in between. Countless hours of effort to analyze, rationalize, and assign blame for change that was going to be inevitable anyway has been wasted—because we are Ascending *now* to a much higher ground. Remember, we were full-fledged 3D HUmans for a very long time. And as HUmans, we tend to be emotional with a flair for the *dramatic*. So, when the ground beneath our feet starts shaking, we react. And as we reach out to grab something to break our fall if we stumble, it's usually our old best friend *fear*—in this case, fear of the unknown. The reason why you may be feeling a lot of fear is that we are *now* at the precipice of a massive spiritual evolutionary change for HUmanity, and there is no turning back.

As scary as the unknown seems at times, the rewards of progress are bigger than anything we can imagine. We are walking through a time when we can create, live, and be part of a quantum shift in our reality.

Hold this truth close to your heart:

On every planet, in every galaxy, in every Universe in the Multiverse, sentient and nonsentient Beings are closely watching the schoolroom of Earth and all that we HUmans are doing here. What we accomplish is not just affecting you and me, 5D consciousness, or Planet Earth. It is rippling through our solar system and affecting every planetary body in the sky.

223

On a *bigger picture* level, we have a lot of intergalactic attention and support. No one here gets to hang out on the sidelines for this Ascension. Everybody is being called to serve during this period. This is the time to open your heart, your mind, lean in and put more skin in the game. We all have an important part to play in creating this miracle. Why would anyone want to sit this one out anyway?

CHAPTER SIX

THE 5D HUMAN

How'd We Get Here?

Although the final lap of this crazy race towards 5D Ascension kicked off in 2000, we didn't approach the finish line and break the tape until twelve years later. Everything that has transpired politically from the administrations of President George W. Bush through President Joseph R. Biden, including the surfacing of some of the brightest and darkest aspects of HUmanity, was put into play between 2000 and 2020, while we were focused very intently on the 5D Ascension process. That was followed by the tumultuous *post*-Ascension years that we are still currently enmeshed in. As we finally reached the last leg of the race, those of us who had been working on Ascension for what felt like forever (many unknowingly) were relieved that we actually made it this time.

During the past few decades specifically leading up to the 2012 launch, I never for sure knew if we were going to reach Ascension, but I never felt long periods of hopelessness or doubt either. Most of us, especially teachers and other 5D Sherpas leading the way, felt the positive momentum on the planet, kept our hearts open, and never took our eyes off the prize. With no definitive 5D HUman manual in hand, we were often clueless where all this LightWork would lead. Personally, I was very blessed to have had as my teachers some of my very revered HUman-based guides along the way. Their assistance and guidance undoubtably saved my life, or at least my *sanity*.

Due to the lifetimes of blood, sweat, tears, and the incessant trusting it took to get us across the finish line, LightWorkers and

ShadowWorkers were exhausted. Many still feel that underlying fatigue today, often with no apparent reason for their chronic tiredness. All our energy in this lifetime, as well as many leading up to it was focused on achieving an Earth-based 5D Ascension by December 2012, using every aspect of our lives to reach that goal. Most of the time, we were not consciously aware of the program in play and our crucial role in making it happen.

Never in any of our incarnations as Earth HUmans were we able to assess the whole scope of the project. The undertaking was too vast, too unbelievable, and too much of a mindblowing concept for a compressed, limited 3D HUman mind to grasp.

We will continue to experience this journey in homeopathic scaled down doses. The information we are given or able to comprehend will be commensurate with our expanding levels of consciousness as we Ascend the 5D ladder. The collective information presented in this book, along with all the teachings you have been receiving through your trusted teachers, guides, and mentors, reflects how far *your* consciousness has evolved and your enhanced ability to grasp more and more of what has been unfolding around you in both the seen and unseen worlds.

We hardly gave much thought to what might transpire *after* Ascension when we didn't even know if any of our efforts would be successful or that the Earth HUmans would be able to make that quantum leap. Under those conditions, the aftermath seemed like a moot point. But it is also important to note that even if we did try to anticipate or plan for the events that unfolded, we wouldn't have been able to do so accurately. 5D consciousness on Planet Earth is rudimentary. Any outcomes we anticipated, even in earnest, would have come from a page ripped out of our old 3D notebook. You can't anticipate something that hasn't yet been created in your mind or energy field.

In 5D, real time is only in the *now,* so that is where all our ideas and creations are formed and greenlit. We no longer have the same template from our 3D linear time-space frame. In 5D, *planning* for future events is often "hit or miss" and our creations are made in new ways through the energy of the Divine Feminine, a frequency that we haven't yet fully integrated.

When we reached our 5D Ascension, many of us treated it, rightfully so, like a landmark event, a Universal accomplishment. And most of us, including myself, didn't even consider taking a victory lap. We just wanted to check it off our to-do lists and get back to leading our personal lives, hopefully *now* without the same traumas and dramas.

By 2012, many of us were exhausted from our childhoods, therapy sessions, spiritual growth classes, and participating in other higher-service, *soul*-purpose stuff. I know I was one spent LightWorker and emphatic about finally being able to get back to my simple, uneventful, "civilian" life, one that looked a lot like the simple, peaceful lives that my next-door neighbor, the grocer, and my cousin had. Like a soldier returning from the front, I sensed that my "tour of duty" had ended, and I was waiting patiently for my next assignment, if there was one coming down the pike. But I was glad to be going home.

Although I continued to work in my private practice, *and still do,* I only taught one new training program between 2012 and 2021, which was a course for a group of key planetary 5D

LightWorkers in 2015-2016. After that, as I shared in the Introduction, I stopped teaching.

Then, just when I was getting ready to rest on my laurels forever, 2016 came and all hell broke loose politically. The American populace elected President Donald J. Trump and the divide that was always there, suppressed, hidden just barely under the surface, broke through in response to his regime taking power.

Many of those who worked for lifetimes in Light and struggled through painful personal Shadow experiences to help themselves and others, were caught off guard by the election results. Others were depressed, confused, and devastated by the reality unfolding before them. Meanspirited, self-serving behavior, racism, sexism, misogyny, corruption, deceit, manipulation, and confusing lies exploded into the mainstream all at once.

Those working for the greater good felt betrayed by the Universe and duped by their own beliefs. *"How could this reality have happened only four years after the vibrationally glorious 5D Ascension launch?"* Some were able to express their doubts openly about what they once believed to be true; others, while in so much pain and disbelief, were only able to resort to expressions of rage. This was such a difficult paradox for the healers on the planet to both face, embrace and work through. It was poetic irony that many of those who struggled the most were the ones who helped the planet to its 5D Ascension. And as they did so, they also were diligently working at the same time to raise their own consciousness, frequency, and Love/Light quotient.

With the continued increase of their collective 5D Love/Light frequency, as discussed, the vibration of Love and Light will *always* bring up everything unlike itself. So, the minute we attained a much higher frequency in 2012, the leftover, impacted Shadow energy also bubbled up from the 3D world and surfaced throughout our culture and world. If we ever doubted our mission and efforts, inadvertently these unplanned repercussions tested our resolve and trust to see if we were still serious about transmuting the final vestiges of 3D miscreations into something greater. Here we are *now,* in the final stages of this deep, elongated journey of the purging of Shadow. Everywhere you look there is animus and a fight to regain control of social values. If you are honest about it, sometimes it's even hard to know which direction to take or position to hold that would move HUmanity, as well as Mother Earth through all this in a beneficial way.

If you look at everything that has transpired and will transpire over the next ten to fifteen years from both 3D and 5D perspectives, at every turn, you will see the world and everyone in it working through some of the last vestiges of 3D Shadow. The things we have been working towards and praying and hoping for will come to fruition or *not.* It all depends on the levels of consciousness, but even more importantly, the collective *actions* taken by the HUmans to uphold HUman values, rights, and evolution. Yes, as 3D continues to shake itself out, on the surface things will appear to be "spinning out of control." Some key examples have serendipitously surfaced during the time I was editing this book. News stories were exploding all over the American media, for example. In a relatively short, forty-eight-hour period, a lot has transpired.

Over the past two days, the Supreme Court of the United States ruled in favor of less restrictive gun laws, and overturned the 1973 landmark decision, Roe vs. Wade, regarding a woman's reproductive rights. But just hours before those monumental rulings took place, the U.S. Congress passed a bipartisan bill, one of the most significant in decades on gun control.

Confused? Spun around? Yup. It's the extreme ups and downs courtesy of our friends over in 4D.

Ascension Shock: We Were Shaken and Afraid

The past few decades have imposed some of the greatest psychological burdens to many of the consciously awakened *souls* on the planet. Blinded to the veiled 5D *bigger picture* and lacking understanding of their personal part in the Multiverse's plan for them and our planet, life often made no sense to many Humans, but especially the LightWorkers. All over the world, throughout every nation and language, we struggled for long stretches of time, over and over again, to comprehend what was happening in even the most mundane aspects of our everyday lives.

If even the more evolved *souls* on the planet felt that confused, is it any wonder what the impact of our 5D Ascension followed by a worldwide pandemic had on all the other 3D folks who are not awake and clueless? It was and continues to be *debilitating*. It pushed, then compounded an already difficult reality in every which direction. Whether very evolved or very content with 3D life, all of us were, although on different levels, experiencing life as if a tsunami came flooding through.

When the Ascension took place, *every* 3D, 4D, and 5D HUman was pushed forward by the wave, either into a higher gradation of the dimension they were already vibrating to or completely into the next level on the dimensional ladder.

You may have never taken a class with me or studied with any of the great 5D teachers of our era, but something led you to read this. My Spidey sense tells me that you have been doing LightWork for a *long* period of time, though perhaps not with much clarity or understanding of the *bigger picture* of the 3D–5D Ascension. Most of my students and clients have been hard at work dealing with elevating their frequencies as they faced both personal and global challenges with each lifetime's attempt at healing the planet. I believe you are just like them. Despite all the skin you have put in the game for eons, even you are feeling wrung out and overwhelmed by all the current events and their seemingly useless purpose. *You are an unsung hero.* Please don't ever forget that the Universe sees you and has never left your side. Thank you from my heart to yours for everything that you have done and experienced for which you were never acknowledged.

Now, take a moment and remember that approximately 95 percent of the world's population doesn't have a clue about what is unfolding on most days at warp speed. Many have not begun to uplevel their energy to 4D, nonetheless to 5D, simply because it is not yet their time to do so. Specifically, on and around the time the pandemic hit, most of us were thrown into survival mode as we were trying to make sense of all the deconstruction of social structures happening around us. Scared and confused, most people were either worried about getting sick or dying from an invisible enemy, panicked about losing their income, or facing eviction from their homes. Landlords and homeowners were afraid they wouldn't be able to pay the taxes and mortgages on their property without receiving those same rents or salaries on time. With no awareness or personal access to a higher conscious perspective, many HUmans retreated to what they had known to be true, their former 3D polarity roots: *"Me vs. You"* and *"Us vs. Them."* If you win, that means I lose. Polarity expanded and spread exponentially, as reflected in the vaccine, mask, and political wars.

This last example of the 3D doctrine of maintaining power and control is at the core of all racism, religious strife, sexism, and a myriad of other social conflicts. Conscious of this or not, most of us were born into this 3D/4D polarity principle and, to varying degrees have bought into it, playing it out on one side or another.

The LightWorkers stationed on the front lines of heroic efforts to overcome HUman abuse and injustice have often personally experienced a multitude of these 3D power and Shadow grabs repeatedly throughout their lives. *Being a victim of any kind of abuse is* **not** *to be mistaken as the* **reason** *why you were abused, or as a badge of spiritual honor or a justification for anyone who has abused you in any way whatsoever.* Their behavior, yes, might be part of a *soul* or Karmic contract that you share, but every HUman, especially in our *"free will"* world has the opportunity to choose higher. And those deeply painful experiences should *never* be used as the rationale for inflicting *similar* abuse on the HUmans that you believe represent those who perpetrated abuse against you. Not because they don't deserve it or need to be mercifully spared, but because we are here to stop the repetitive cycle of HUman abuse on HUman abuse.

For too many of us in this era, not understanding the multitude of *bigger picture* reasons why a situation happens in the way it does, often leaves a gaping hole in our hearts and minds that gets filled with self-hate, additional repeated cycles of abuse, and a chronic sense of victimization and joylessness.

In 2020, because things were so horrible and out of control, it was obvious that we had come to some kind of post-5D tipping point on the planet. This moment was not predetermined, and nobody was sure which way the scales would eventually tip or when, or even if, the world would regain a semblance of balance. We had arrived at an Ascension impasse. Soon it became clear that everything we were seeing play out around us had been triggered, for better or worse, by the increase of Light and Love radiating from the personal vibrational energy fields of the Earth-based LightWorkers. Spread throughout the post-5D Ascension period, the planet herself was experiencing cataclysmic quakes, flooding, and volcanic eruptions many caused by the tectonic plates shifting between the vastly different energies of 3D and 5D after 27,000 years of barely moving.

A vibrational rise in collective consciousness lifted some of the veils of our hidden social issues and society began to wake up to the existence of other realities and perspectives regarding how our HUmanity had failed us. The 3D paradigm that had formed around our ongoing fight for survival had cracked. Finally, enough people on the planet had integrated a 5D frequency in their physical bodies, so that this frequency was stable and dependable. In essence, more people had started to remember *(not necessarily consciously)* pieces of the *bigger picture* and why they incarnated to be here *now*. This was and always will be a requisite for creating a new world consciousness from our 5D Hearts.

As advanced HUmans, it is crucial that we extend to ourselves and others a lot of Love, Light, and Compassion right *now*. Compassion is necessary because, *except unconsciously*, few of us knew this tipping point was coming, and psychologically and emotionally we weren't prepared for it. On a 3D level, the pandemic involved a frightening, chaotic, and heart-wrenching series of events. On a 5D level, it provided an opportunity to consciously wake up more 3D HUmans and at the same time, help the world to reopen their hearts once again.

The timing was crucial, for we needed a cleverly disguised *"beard"* to serve as a cover for the energetic reality that was unfolding in the higher dimensions. A *bigger picture* event that would be as profound in its magnitude as the 5D Ascension itself. A red herring was needed to distract nine billion people worldwide while their 3D paradigm, holding in place everything they knew to be *true* regarding their personal survival, finances, comforts, health, as well as their country's economy and government systems, was being upgraded. Nothing short of the *whole world* going into isolation, being distracted by a medical threat, feeling disarmed by anxiety, and weakened by grief would have given us even the possibility of a successful upgrade.

If any of this remotely explains aspects of your experience during the ten years leading up to *now*, remember you are part

THE NEW 5D HUMAN

of the advanced group of the LightWorker "cavalry" sent to help HUmanity evolve.

> *"The first one who gets up in the morning is the one responsible for making the coffee. That's just the way it is."*[1]
>
> *—Mabel Katz*

As very big, unrecognizable shifts take place, our responsibility as LightWorkers is to find a path through the fog of what is presenting itself even if we are not clear on the bigger picture piece that it is serving. After we awakened, we then agreed to hold the space and illuminate the path for others to walk through as they slowly awakened too. Holding the door open for someone who is coming in behind you is one of many unspoken codes we live by. And it's still one of the kinder and more thoughtful courtesies that most of HUmanity, even in the face of extreme polarity, still abide by.

Attention All Personnel: Cleanup Needed on Aisle 3

To be crystal clear once again, 5D HUmans and the Ascension process did not cause the deadly COVID pandemic. Nobody deliberately produced a virus with the aim of killing off millions of HUmans around the world. But our wise guides and elders in the higher dimensions helped HUmanity use the miscreation for the higher good.

At a certain point on the planet, each of us will come to understand that *nothing* happens by accident and life isn't a series of random events. When this recognition fully happens, we will then have to step up individually and as a collective and take responsibility for all of our conscious and unconscious miscreations. Many of these, if not most, have contributed to the Shadow events rising to the surface to be cleaned out or transmuted back to Light and Love.

Bless the mess! It doesn't matter anymore if we caused the mess or not, we are all Earth-based volunteers who came here to participate in massive clean-up efforts. Without ascribing blame for the pandemic to any one person, faction, or country, it clearly happened for several *seen and unseen reasons,* but most probably not for the ones you might think.

And although I am not presenting an argument for the pros and cons of vaccines or mask wearing, many people felt somewhat empowered by even their remote ability to do *something,* as the virus was raging and taking many unsuspecting lives. After spending lifetimes in 3D, duality's inherent message was that most of us had no real power to alter our life's circumstances in any constructive way. Inadvertently, 3D instilled in us a learned sense of helplessness and stripped away our ability to *respond.*

The post-5D Ascension fallout, the pandemic, the dissolving of our democracy to name a few, all require HUman input for it to fully shift or evolve. The only way to untangle the *energetic* underpinning that runs a common thread through all these various Shadow circumstances is by each of us on the planet doing our *vibrational* part in it. By reducing the many accompanying beliefs, emotions, and reactions within us, even the small ones, that are inadvertently reflected back to us through these circumstances in our other world. This is what it truly means to take responsibility. It is challenging to most HUmans, evolved or not, to not deflect, deny, or defend the position that they didn't have a part in a miscreation of, something adverse or distressing in the world. For example, when we see anger or violence displayed in the world, we often judge it as bad or despicable behavior. Maybe it is or maybe it isn't, but our reaction often places us outside the problem. Taking responsibility for it is *not* the same as blaming ourselves for causing it. Responsibility gives us the opportunity to see, even if it is a microscopic version of how that unacknowledged or unprocessed anger may exist in our energy field or life, and what we can do about it to address and transmute it into more Light.

How events have unfolded in response to everything, including the world's pandemic, was actually the deliberate, predictable outcome of centuries of power struggles, greed, disregard for life, and HUman separation. It was created by HUmankind and *now* we have been impacted by our own mutual miscreation. This is meant to be a truth, not a guilt trip. It is a reason why we are here during this time period often referred to as the *"Great Awakening."* It's quite *hard* to be constantly awake, conscious, and responsible.

Our 3D conditioning soldered together *blame and responsibility* which has slowed us down individually, as well as collectively, in effectuating change. The reaction of blame is so emotionally feared and painful that we will do almost everything in our power to avoid its impact. 3D duality has weaponized it, creating a game of hot potato where no one takes any accountability for the generated miscreations in our lives or in the world.

5D adulting is not for the thin-skinned. If we are here on the planet and part of the greater whole, then there's a very good chance, in this lifetime or another, that we were at some point part of some problem, as opposed to the solution.

This is the way that we inadvertently get to contribute to the transmutation of whatever *is "out there"* that scares, offends, or enrages us. When you keep the focus on you and the ways that you might also be contributing to the coinciding 3D reality "out there," you take responsibility and accept, without reproach, that if you are here, witnessing something disturbing or unjust in the world, that somehow, you are a part of it—as we all are. Not because we are bad, horrible people, but because it fits into our *bigger picture* belief system that we are all one.

This might be a very challenging concept for many of us, especially those who work in the Light to wrap our brains around. If received with an open heart, this truth can be very empowering for those of us who consciously want to be part of the worlds "wholing," and the healing of the larger disease of HUman separation. You only have to be responsible for "your" piece, not the "world's" piece to make a profound difference. This rule of one applies to everything in your life, including disagreements, arguments, fights, miscommunications, con-flicts, and the like.

LightWorkers descended from Lemuria and Atlantis came back to take on and help transmute the various aspects of the current 3D Shadow spillover *not* for the badge of martyrdom, or even just for the *bigger picture* cause. Some of the most evolved HUmans among us, those with a Light so bright that you need sunglasses to be in their presence, were also born into their 3D incarnation to address *personal issues, wounds, and "Shadow" parts.* No one, especially the most conscious on the planet, received a pass on this one. The world and all the other HUmans outside of us were meant to be mirrors to reflect back our *soul's* "personal to-do list." Whatever external people, places, and things that we have been challenged by in our lives, from relationships to politics, all have to be healed and transmuted from within first. As we transmute the denser aspects of our old 3D experiences, beliefs, and reactions, in turn, we liberate those pieces not only on a personal level, but also the darker side of our 3D reality that we are here to transmute.

When we can separate all the distracting 3D emotions of *blame, shame, and guilt,* we can then individually look at our HUman flaws, miscreations, and errors in a responsible way. That's how we both empower ourselves and lead the world to real substantial changes in how we treat and view HUmanity, Animals, and the Planet itself.

It is the inability to weaken those old forms of control and manipulation that has delayed our stay in 3D, slowing down you and the collective from shifting sooner into a higher frequency 5D world. It was difficult enough being a 3D person trying to live in a 3D world, but *now* the challenge is even greater as most of us are trying to be a "5D HUman living in a 3D world."

The stronghold that the 3D construct once had has *now* been broken. The personal work that we have done (read: *suffered)* through the filter of our own experiences, both the good and not so good ones, has weakened 3D's matrix, which is *now* allowing these last vestiges of the 3D construct and its principles to dissolve. The pandemic was an opening for us to advance our objectives as LightWorkers.

We have been waiting for a very long time to finally have a clear path to Ascension. Try not to cloud this truth by the painful, and at times, horrific reality we still see playing out in the 3D world every single day. Unfortunately, as we bring more Light onto the planet, we will have to bear witness to this overwhelmingly difficult part of the process. Our work here is to hold the space and be the grounding force on the planet for those who are vibrationally less able to go through this meltdown.

As a multidimensional being, you are capable of holding several different realities at the same time, for all levels of consciousness and their creations coexist. It's very similar to having a split-screen feature on your computer screen or TV. The more technically advanced your processor is, the more windows you can have open at the same time. One window might be broadcasting the news of the day, while another window could be displaying excerpts of the book you are reading. Both are clearly separate entities, but you are very capable of effortlessly viewing both at the same time.

Learning to Separate *Emotional Wheat* from *Emotional Chaff*

One of the biggest challenges multidimensionally that we face as we begin living in 5D is the reprogramming of our *emotional* bodies.

During the tail end of 3D and throughout our temporary stay in 4D, our consciousness and most of our reactions were run through the filter of our *emotional body*. It also charged each significant experience or situation we had with an emotional zap and cataloged it, whether good or not, in our memory storage, which then replayed itself on a *continual* loop.

During most of our 3D existence, various outside authorities controlled our lives. We followed the dictates of institutions, such as organized religions, schools, governments, and the like. The conventions of these groups conditioned our minds, emotions, and subsequent actions and inactions. Most of the roles we played, whether the oppressed or the oppressor, were passed down from one generation to the next. With each new generation of 3D/4D consciousness, varying degrees of learned helplessness *or* learned personal power set in.

For what *now* feels like eons, our capacity to emote and express our needs freely—without social repercussions—was mostly snuffed out. Expression was rarely encouraged in a way that would threaten or diminish structures of power, status, or finance. Though creative self-expression is often the only way oppressed people have been able to rally to benefit the opposite side of the often-imbalanced equation. This power is one reason why artists, writers, and those who frequent the arts are so admired and often seem to be challenged the most.

Oppression has been around in some form within every society in history, but the tide started turning ever so slightly towards egalitarianism as we moved into the twentieth century. It may not have appeared that way to those who had very different experiences during those early years, but that's when it all started to energetically shift. Numerologically, we entered the last hundred years of the *"me era of the ones"* (1900s) and moved closer to the new vibration of the *"we age of the twos"* *(2000s)*. The earliest social murmurings of this shift stirred individuals of higher consciousness to act, some in the form of advocacy, others in the form of revolts, protests, and political unrest.

Freedom, even drops of it, can be seen in historical events of that century in the United States. Emmeline Pankhurst, a name unknown to many of us, but a LightWorker in her own right, became active in the *women's suffrage movement* back in 1880 and courageously led it forward until it disbanded in 1918. This concerted and very risky effort, especially for that period of time, led to women's right to vote in the United States in 1920.

Progress hinged on the collective awakening of the emotional body. President Roosevelt established the federal social security program in the United States in 1935, Martin Luther King, Jr., led the American civil rights movement in the 1960s. President Nelson Mandela led South Africa's anti-apartheid movement in the 1980s. These are just a few among many leaders who changed the world.

Then, as *now*, many HUmans ultimately risked their lives, financial security, and social allegiances to break from the established norms. August 16-17, 1986, LightWorkers, healers, and those who were rapidly moving into 4D consciousness synchronized a worldwide peace event known as the "Harmonic Convergence." This event *(which I fondly remember personally leading a local group in meditation in New York),* set the stage for all that spiritually transpired in the decades that followed. With each event, planetary alignment, and individual contribution of Light, Love, and raised consciousness, we were able to assemble a group of LightWorkers large enough to *risk* waking up their 4D emotional bodies simultaneously and together Light a fire under the ass of HUmanity for the sake of higher-purpose change.

After eons of 3D suppression, self-expression exploded in the 1960s. Women were fed up with trying to act like the ultimate 1950's TV mom June Cleaver. Sex, drugs, and rock and roll burst onto the scene in the counterculture of youth protesting the Vietnam War draft program. Conscious HUmans didn't want to be forced to go kill their other brother and sister HUmans in Asia. Throughout society, individuals and many groups began exploring the sensation of having a freer emotional body and using it as a conduit for creative expression, thought validation, political statements, free Love, and *critical thinking*. After a very long run in the 3D emotional dead zone, the needle on the dial moved and we stuck a toe into the 4D pool, *the* transitional *bridge over the troubled waters* on our way to 5D consciousness.

4D is where we really started waking up. We were seriously emotionally dumbed down during our many lifetimes in 3D. Similar to the feeling of having a hand or foot fall asleep, you really don't "feel" any discomfort in that state. It's when the blood and energy start moving back into the appendage, as it's beginning to *wake up* that the pins, and needles start, and it begins hurting. That's why our very overcrowded 4D of today is even more polarized, visible, and louder than ever before. Back then, when it began, it was viewed as just a small disruptive fringe of society. Although the 3D status quo was clearly threatened by it, in reality it really didn't change the ruling patriarchal world too much. But it made a great first cut and poked enough tiny holes in it that the 3D structure began to slowly leak. Drip. Drip. Drip. *Ascension.*

In theory, HUmans in 3D consciousness, as well as most levels of consciousness, had become resigned to living in their own limiting creations. Its downside consisted of an unjust world of opposites, luck, privilege, and seemingly a randomness that decided most of their HUmans' fate. The belief *"That's just the way it is"* was born out of 3D learned helplessness. It served the majority and worked very well for them for a very long time.

In 4D, all hell broke loose because the ratio of *3D people vs. 3D "sheeple"* started drastically shifting. More 3D individuals started Ascending into 4D consciousness, breaking free from 3D consciousness, and joining those who already had their sleeping consciousness roused.

Our current era is a powerful time of great turmoil, but if we use it correctly, for the sake of contributing to the highest good and in the highest way, then we can create great change. As the late Congressman and Civil Rights Activist John Lewis used to say, it's *"Good Trouble."* The Shadow side of this profound awakening into 4D is that it is stirring old dormant, compacted rage and untreated mental illness, as well as creating a lot of out-of-control aggression, violence, and fear. Societal, governmental, and familial upheavals are all a part of what we are currently witnessing *now* that we are past the initial upswing from the 5D Ascension benchmark of 2012.

Given that a very large group of people Ascended to the next level of consciousness with a never-before-seen magnitude of Ascension, a vacuum was created by the vibrational shift upward. This opened the space and magnetics that allowed the HUmans living in the dimensions behind it to also rise. As more 4D HUmans made a quantum leap into 5D, more 3D HUmans also made a quantum leap in consciousness into 4D. They arrived at the transitional 4D "weigh station" on the road to 5D, where we *now* see activism, wars, protesting, general rebelling, and an uncontrollable amount of *HUman on HUman* violence and aggression.

The scope of 4D consciousness covers a wide swath of many different HUman beliefs, ideologies, and approaches to conflict. When perspectives of 4D consciousness are positioned on the extreme ends of the continuum, the corresponding behaviors and actions ironically mimic many of the same 3D dualistic and self-righteous thinking that both 4D/5D HUmans are trying to evolve past.

All the rise in dimensional consciousness seriously rattled the usually stable and confident 3D values, mores, and power stances that existed. As we move deeply into a post-5D Ascension period, HUmans in 4D pose a "real" threat to what 3D HUmans have come to create as their 3D reality. This is where 3D oppositions escalate into 4D polarity. The 4D realm is a difficult, sometimes tumultuous purgatory that most of us lived in before making our big leap into 5D reality. It is also a very *cool* place to finally enter. It was there where we got to expand our realities, revel in choices, and find our peeps, our spiritual families, and ourselves again. Yes, 4D was just a stopover for many LightWorkers, a place to break free from the 3D rules, regulations, and controls that had oppressed us for eons. It was a place where many of us finally stopped long enough to have emotional breakdowns, go to therapy, deal with our addictions, leave abusive marriages, and begin to find *"who we are and why the hell are we even here?"* Until the 1980s, most people who had advanced to 4D consciousness did so *alone,* or without much support except possibly for that very rare friend stationed somewhere else on the planet.

The 1980s brought with it the beginnings of our 4D evolution into spirituality, which broke away as a separate entity from 3D religion. Spiritual growth, self-help books and workshops, and many of the updated twelve-step programs founded on the model of Alcoholics Anonymous flooded our world. Tools like Meditation, Yoga, Crystals, and Feng Shui Design came into play. And all reflected our newly earned collective of 4D level of consciousness. As our Earth-based LightWorker community grew, we gratefully began to find more and more of us, gathering with our long-lost family members from lifetimes in the Lemurian and Atlantean days.

When a HUman is undergoing passage through 4D, their emotional body is not only fully awakened from its 3D numb-down, but it *now* has moved to the head of the line. After eons of being emotionally asleep, our emotions and feelings rightfully got a prime seat at the table in our lives and ran the show for most of us. This was what our evolutionary process needed at the time. But remember, our old handcuffed and gagged 3D emotional bodies and our highly reactive, even hyperactive 4D emotional bodies are constructed very differently than our new 5D emotional bodies. In 5D, our emotions are calmer and less active, and our feelings have moved into a healthier level of expression. Please don't confuse this more balanced sense of calm with being in a 3D state of deep sleep or passivity. It's not by a long shot. It is a different kind of quiet, action, and creative process based in our new 5D frequency of the Divine Feminine.

The 5D matrix does not reflect or serve the 3D rules of duality, which were all built on the dominance of the masculine principle, evidenced in the creation word *man-ifestation*. 3D wasn't completely void of emotionality, but the emotions and reactions somehow became a birthright mostly ascribed to whomever the privileged group of men in power were at the time. Men got to shoot guns, have barfights, express aggression through sports, hunt, kill, and go to war, and we sadly learned to exploit their generationally learned, false sense of power. *Men were also victims of this programming.* It locked them into social roles, expectations, and limiting ideas of what masculinity is. It stifled their emotional and spiritual growth and reinforced a false sense of what we are coming to understand in 5D is *true* power. Fortunately, for HUmanity this paradigm began to alter, as it was brought out into the open at the onset of the rise in 4D consciousness. And although women led the march, over time, *after the sticker shock wears off,* men too both see and reap the benefits.

Back in the late 1970s and early 1980s, awareness of women's rights and children's rights emerged. We saw the establishment of domestic violence shelters and sexual abuse hotlines and clinics began to appear. Trained as a social worker, I began my career as a therapist working in both of those settings for many years. Those decades were a pivotal time on the planet for millions of victims of 3D violence. The #MeToo and #TimesUp movements were built on the foundation of these earlier HUman rights initiatives whose leaders often took major risks to push for what was considered very unpopular social change at the time. These individuals, the LightWorkers of their day, were also abruptly awakened by the rumblings of their own 4D Ascension. With that shift in consciousness back then came so many great opportunities and different perspectives regarding money, self-care, and the world in general that it expanded lives, but also created a lot of uncertainty, panic, instability, and personal fear.

It's 3 AM, the Lights are Flickering . . . *Last Call for Drinks*

We are *now* living in an entirely new timeline. When we are reborn into our *second incarnation* as a 5D HUman, we operate within a different matrix that has different beliefs, objectives, needs, vibrational goals, and service contracts. *What once was is no more.* Doors to the old 3D Earth are closed. Try not to be too concerned if your daily life does not feel all that terrific right *now*. We are still living with the very real remnants from the ghosts of 3D past. All the imbalances, injustices, and Shadow energy left over from the last 27,000 years must come to the surface and be faced, addressed, and transmuted into a higher level of Light. This level and depth of illumination has never existed on Earth before. If we do not fully transmute the rising Shadow energies, we will just be doing a lot of ineffective cosmetic makeovers. By not truly eliminating all the root causes of *duality,* we leave a few of its vibrational cells behind in the Petri dish to regrow once again.

As we move into this new level of consciousness, one by one, it is a bit like clearing the undergrowth in a forest. Each of us will contribute to clearing the brush for *our* path through first, and then mark the trail from 3D to 5D for others who choose to follow. And when all is said and done, nothing from our prior 3D world will be reflected in this new one that we are *now* starting to usher in. It is truly over. And although nobody really knows what lies ahead, what I do know is this: *"what was once, will be no more."* The old 3D consciousness paradigm has been deconstructed. This is what the beginning of a new stage of spiritual evolution looks like, *chaos*. This is not a fire drill or a meditator's grandiose dream. This is beautifully real. This is what we incarnated for.

As your LightWorker self steps more fully into its 5D HUman life, it's important to acknowledge that you have never had this much God power at your disposal while in HUman form! Never. What you can do *now* is a thousand times greater than ever before. Where you choose to direct your energy or which "reality show" you choose to make real will make all the difference on how fast or how slow the rest of the 5D process will take. All the old constructs that held everything in place, many running interference against the manifestation of everything that you wanted to create and believed about from your heart, have fallen away. This means we have a better opportunity *now* to create the lives we wanted and live the truths that have always guided us.

We *"Now"* Function on a Multilevel Bandwidth

Everything that transpires within and outside us has a multitude of layers, causes, reasons, and purposes, including painful experiences and the heart-wrenching realities that we see playing out every second in the wider world. But understanding and accepting that bad things have higher purposes *doesn't* give the child abuser an excuse or an abusive ex-partner a big hug and a congratulatory pat on the back for their horrific behavior. Nor does it give government policies a right to deHUmanize even the more heinous of those among us.

Although I am not promoting the random distribution of free "get out of jail" cards, I am gently reminding everyone that there is a *bigger picture* at play. Duality, along with being veiled throughout most of our 3D incarnations, has limited our ability to see the total screen and who is playing what role in any one situation. This is a challenging, but necessary perspective we need to consider when transitioning into the higher realms. How do we deal with acts upon HUmans from HUmans at different levels of consciousness? I don't know that answer. But what I do know is that there is usually a very significant unseen karmic dynamic at play.

The worlds of 3D and 4D both are real and exist side by side. This is the nature of our new multidimensional 5D *world* and capabilities. Until very recently, almost everyone has been looking at the world through their 3D/4D emotional body filters. In 5D, we begin to lose this old habit of using our "emotional body" as a sieve to help us discern, then catalog our experiences and reactions to them. Most people on the planet, including our political leaders, partners, crazy relatives, coworkers, best friends, and the homeless people begging on the street all primarily feel and react through their 3D/4D emotional body. Many will be bouncing up to 5D and back down for a while—like you and I do—and will continue to do. It's the mix of all the different emotions, belief systems, and perspectives that can turn a happy, fun Sunday family dinner into a reboot of *Animal House*. And "so it is" in our multidimensional, everyday world.

As you become more comfortable living in the multilevel bandwidth in which you *now* live, you will make it easier for others to expand their perspectives and transmute the fears and limitations that have also kept them 3D prisoners. Focus mainly on the pieces of your life that stir up *overreactions, strong emotions, anger, defensiveness, and fear*. Make issues you have *wacked-out resonance* with, or wildly vacillating feelings about, your official starting point. They are the exact things that are not only impacting you, but that you are also contributing to the situation or circumstance as it exists in the emotional field of the world's collective.

These are the issues and the big, black X mark on your life's map that your emotionally guided "dowsing rods" have brought you to. You have finally arrived at the location where all the jewels are buried! Eureka! You have just struck 5D gold!

Keep in mind, the pieces we are *blessed* to work on during this post-5D transition are not ever outside us first. All we have to do to figure out our *bigger picture* purpose is to look at the day-to-day things that we personally struggle with the most. There's nothing to study for or do except look at our own fears, challenges, worries, and things in the news, politics and the world in general that upset us the most. Your purpose is hidden in plain sight. Recognize it and you will find your piece and *peace* in the Ascension fallout.

And in turn, your *centeredness* will come from letting go to the flow and trusting something greater is trying to unfold. The more you hold space for that agenda, the more you will transcend and make an impact on the *bigger picture* that relates to everybody. You might not be having the experience of 3D, 4D, or 5D that someone else is having, but whatever is coming up for you is exactly the work you're supposed to do. Don't look past it. Don't go around it. Don't go outside of yourself too far to try to fix what's going on. **You are the Light. You are the force. You are the work. Amen.**

The more we own and then release emotions, judgments, and belief systems that are contributing to everything in our experience from the continuously morphing variants of the coronavirus to upsetting news articles, the more we contribute to dismantling the thought forms and energies that are keeping them well fed and growing. This is in a large part what many LightWorkers and ShadowWorkers came in to do.

Movin' on Up—to a 5Deluxe Apartment in the Sky . . .

So, what is the takeaway here? On some level, you already know everything I am telling you about in this book. Your *openness* is what is allowing these teachings to stir your memory and serve as a visceral reminder of what you innately trust to be true. 5D is the new "*hood*" we have all moved into recently. I'd recommend signing a long-term lease or taking out a thirty-year mortgage because we are all going to be staying here for a while. We have deservingly evolved into earthly beings able to carry and utilize more God-Light within us. We are *now* officially driving around in a hovercraft, much more advanced and updated than the old 3D Edsel we were used to schlepping around in. And like many newer car models, these come with a higher price tag, more need for maintenance, and additional operational responsibilities. But they are *sooo cool* and worth it. If you are not quite ready, then there is no real reason for you to trade in your old car for a newer model, but know it's there waiting for you . . . *once you come to your (5D) senses.*

Our new HUman bodies have more advanced skills and capabilities, as well as the ability to vibrate at a higher level of consciousness. HUmans in 5D come with a different barcode and frequency. It's preassembled, wireless, and the best part is, no batteries required! As we begin to adjust to this prime set of conditions, simultaneously, we will also need to learn how to disconnect from our old plugged-in habits of having our "power source" connected to a manmade outlet, which in 3D was always *outside* us. *Now* we generate our own power from within. Our God-Light, *soul-ar* energy source is both renewable, and in abundant supply.

5D allows us to effortlessly communicate through advanced senses, which means we are also able to pick up a broader range of thoughts and feelings, even have the capacity to perceive different realities, while also emitting and rippling out our upgraded, powerful energy field to the world around us. We have more awareness as well as reach *now.* Although our *emotions* are less intense, our *feelings* run deeper. And . . . *wait for it* . . . our need for outside validation is significantly reduced!

Remember, our higher frequency as a 5D HUman allows us to carry more torque. Akin to not knowing one's own strength, we also must get used to our new energetic range and the weight that our impact carries. Thankfully, the responsibility to operate our new machinery comes with a learning curve and a generous margin for error. Like reaching for a *sledgehammer to hit a nail*, in 5D we don't have to apply the same amount of energy as we did in 3D to get the job done, the point made or the Love felt, and so on.

And, of course *in theory,* our new vibrational abilities can also be misguided or misused for lesser reasons than the greater good of all. Even as 5D HUmans, we too live under the Universal laws of *free will*, so to a certain degree we are also capable of Shadow behaviors such as adeptly manipulating, holding sway, and negatively influencing the world around us. Given a choice, most of us are more aware of what's at stake and that we are living in a little piece of Heaven while we are down here on Earth.

The 5D higher level of consciousness doesn't abide by the same principles or paradigm inherent in 3D/4D living. We are not governed by *duality* or *polarity*—which is the filter that fear-based realities have used and continue to use to justify HUman manipulation and the need to control others. Because we abide by the more advanced perspectives of 5D *triality,* it changes the whole premise which all our actions and inactions are based on. Our newly developed abilities are part of our *soul's rights.* They come with a higher level of trust already built in for we evolved into 5D on our own accord—delivered from all the eons of hard LightWork and ShadowWork that we have done. We also won't have those old, external guardrails anymore that once controlled us but created a boundary that we were at least able to feel and react to. 5D comes with more personal responsibility and monitoring.

Shadow energies exist on *all* levels and dimensions throughout time and space, except perhaps in the highest tiers of the upper God realms. As we move up the dimensional ladder the percentage of Light energy increases and Shadow energy decreases, *but it still very much exists.* Keep in mind that our newly arrived at 5D rung is only just a stone's throw from 4D and a city block or two away from our old alma-mater, 3D. So yes, it can be misused. *Free will* is still in play and we have never been here before or even long enough to calculate how a lot of this may eventually unfold. Right *now,* most of the 5D "first settlers" are working extensively in and for the Light. Enjoy the great company of your Light peers that have gathered. You guys are *now* part of an advanced bunch of HUmans to vibrationally hang around with. Espavo!

The HUman evolution to 5D is a rarely awarded badge of honor, even with our successful Ascension in 2012. Please take this in . . . YOU earned it, and it is well deserved! It's the way the Multiverse is acknowledging you for all the difficult physical and emotional trials and tribulations you went through lifetime after lifetime, childhood after childhood all alone, believing no one was there, cared, or was watching. This is the Multiverse's way of telling you that there was nothing further from the truth. Your pain has been felt, every single thing you have gone through has been witnessed, and you have been cradled in the loving arms of your guides the entire time, as they held space for you to safely move through it all. *Try not to forget that.*

All these HUman advanced capabilities were always there— built into our HUman DNA. Most probably located in the 98 percent regions that scientists consider "junk" or uncoded molecules. As we expand into more of our God-Lightbodies, the previously described, "junk" DNA becomes activated and carries with it all our new 5D Superpowers.

It's so important to recognize that we *now* come with lots of enhanced abilities, and this is not just wishful thinking or my propensity towards the occasional *spiritual psychobabble*. Initially, you might not know your own strength in 5D or inadvertently activate these new features. Although we will all awaken this dormant DNA at a different pace, there is a general time frame recommended for those transitioning to get on board with their new 5D computer processor. That time period is not by all means set in stone, but the final lap of the race began when we entered 2000. It launched in 2012, became exalted by 2021, and will probably remain wide open as we move through the next few years. 2024 will be another time marker and check-in point as to how our post-5D Ascension is going. For those of you *slow-moving turtles* out there, you won't be able to hide out too much longer. What's the point in having these abilities anyway if we don't actively use our God-Light to create happy, healthy lives for ourselves, the planet and to assist those throughout our world?

Ascension begs the responsibility of becoming conscious HUmans, and along with this comes ownership of all the new skills we have. Keep in mind that in 5D every thought and every feeling contribute to the totality of the world's mass consciousness. Being aware of the energy we are personally projecting into the world and regulating it helps us change all that pains us "out there" by changing it at its source, *within us*. That's why it is important that we stay the course and always try to keep our frequency as high and stable as we can. Even while facing some of the darkest sides of life and HUmanity's behavior, we cannot continue to react the same, see things the same, or think the same anymore—not if we really want to contribute to real, lasting change on the planet. The onus is on us to rise above 3D polarity and hold space for the old 3D/4D world to dissolve so the new 5D world can evolve. This may seem like an impossible task, but we will never find out by *not* trying.

Having these capabilities requires us to be much more responsible about how we interact in the world because each of us is *now* a *guide* for other HUmans. In this position, no matter what we think we are actually "doing" through our actions, our real contributions will mainly come down to how we "vibrate," and the messages encoded in those ripples that we resonate to. Personal suffering, martyrdom as a badge of honor, justified violence and abuses against children, and other acts of HUman Shadow are *now nonnegotiables* and off the table in the 5D world. Operating these new vibrational values doesn't have to feel like hard work or one of the old emotionally "back-breaking" assignments that we were all traumatized by in some lifetimes. The old *3D slave-master* contracts and 4D service contracts are gone (thank God). In 5D, our contracts are *soul-contracts* centered around learning how to be a 5D HUman in a 3D world. Multidimensionality, loving ourselves, placing ourselves first, deprogramming our personal 3D conditioning, and holding the space for the *bigger picture* to unfold are all the craze in 5D living. It's all about the "vibe" and no longer about the "jive."

The Return of the Divine Feminine Energy

With resurgent feminine energy to guide us, the 5D emotional body has a more subdued field of expression. This energy has a different, less dramatic current than masculine energy. On the surface, especially in the beginning, it can be very easy to misjudge it as "weak," mainly because 3D definitions of the feminine described it as *passive, dependent, and helpless.* This was our cultural experience of it too, so although we are offended by it, we also inadvertently internalized a lot of it as *truth.* With women's natural powers being suppressed and repressed for centuries, it's been and continues to be very challenging to climb out of these set points. Both men and women alike have versions of that false narrative hardwired into their subconscious minds. But *au contraire, mon frère,* I assure you, the new feminine energy matrix has a very different storyline and a plethora of wonderful gifts for the new 5D HUman—*man* and *woman.*

A lot is unknown about the 5D emotional body, mainly because HUmans have never had one before. We are just beginning to identity some of its functions and uses, and the ways that it is very different from the 3D/4D emotional body. What we do know is that it *emotes less but perceives more.* Its vibratory field has a more refined construct but much stronger frequency than it formerly had in our 3D/4D bodies. And most importantly, it is the new upgraded frequency that we all will be using as our new foundational signal for *creating, making, and attracting money.* As 5D HUmans, we are *now* carrying more of our disembodied spirit selves, which don't use emotions as their main conduit for self-expression.

No HUman emotions are experienced in the prelife or afterlife. The spirit, our core God-Light, when it is completely out of body, doesn't get upset when a partner leaves. It doesn't feel happy when it makes more money from an exciting new promotion at work. Nope. Nada. It just doesn't happen that way in the heavens. So, it stands to reason that the more of this typically "out of body" aspect of us becomes embodied, something will have to drastically shift in its wake.

As we Ascend the dimensional ladder, specifically while we are still in body, *(3D-6D)* our need for emotions decreases. Having fewer emotions in 5D means there's more room to experience clearer, truer feelings. 5D doesn't make you less sensitive. Quite the contrary. But it might make you a lot less *sentimental*, as your perspective on everything from family to your attachments will change. In 5D, your experiences of people, places, and things are *now* filtered through an evolved sense of self-worth and inner authority. With a *bigger picture* understanding of life's events, coupled with the elimination of 3D/4D Karmic contracts, HUman processes like justifications, rationalizations, and accustomed ways of arriving at a decision also will morph over time.

The 5D emotional template, delivered through the more refined feminine energy, reshapes our ability to *respond versus react* reflexively in a split second. This distinction is an earmark of 5D consciousness. As your new emotional body starts to kick in, you may wish to pay attention to your habitual responses. Initially working with this change means remembering to *pause* before reacting to things that confront you, as you are still very much living in an often-difficult 3D/4D world with 3D/4D people. And in many instances, these 3D/4D HUmans are yourselves. Over time, pausing will become easier and feel more spontaneous. First, you pause, then you assess your feelings about a situation, *then you respond*. Remember, deciding to take no action is a valid response too.

Advanced 5D HUmans learn, over time, to engage their *feelings* more frequently as a means to express themselves to others, and more importantly, to themselves. Feelings are much harder to express because expression makes us acknowledge everything we don't want to feel from *shame* and *vulnerability* to *pain*. The shift from trusting our feelings to inform us, rather than our emotions to help express us, is an integration process that initially will take a little time.

The true test of being able to consistently sustain a 5D frequency is how well we've integrated our heightened sensitivity with the more pronounced 5D sense of *absorption*. Our new upgraded 5D HUman has many new senses, some are identified, and others, not yet. Besides the five common senses 5D shares with 3D/4D *(touch, feel, taste, seeing, hearing)*, and the sixth sense, *intuition* that is shared with 4D, 5D is the first of the HUman-based senses that carries a seventh sense, named *absorption*. Absorption gives us the ability to use the energy field around the body to "absorb" and decipher our new 5D Codex, vibrational and frequency messages. Going forward, this will be a key conduit for all the information that you will be receiving and emitting to the world around you.

CHAPTER SEVEN

GREAT POWER COMES WITH GREAT RESPONSIBILITY

Responding vs. Reacting

Separating from both our learned *3D nonresponses and our 4D emotional responses* will be a game changer for us, as where and how we direct the emotional body's resources determines our vibrational contribution to the world. The energetic makeup of an emotion encapsulates beliefs, impressions, reactions, fear, and a lot of narrative threads. We all witnessed this as the world experienced a wide range of emotions during the different stages of the pandemic with its seemingly never-ending new variant strains, but mostly throughout the polarized reactions that were aroused by the masking and vaccine turf wars. Beliefs, impressions, fear, and storylines are also similarly aroused in your life whenever you are feeling strongly about a personal issue or challenge.

It is often difficult to remember that the person, place, or situation that has been placed in front of you is *not* a random or misguided event solely designed with one purpose in mind: *to make you, your day, or your life miserable.* As you start pulling back and reacting or responding differently to what you are experiencing, you give yourself more options and choices of how to express, view, and process your "triggers," as well as how to contribute those new "triality-based" responses to the *bigger picture* 5D matrix of the world.

Going into 5D, it will take a lot of rote practice for everyone to retrain ourselves to avoid our 3D/4D emotions, stories/dramas, perspectives, and fears as much as possible. As we evolve into a higher realm of consciousness, we must adjust to not-using our emotional body in the old, *reactionary* ways from our prior dimensional use. Although in 5D, we still use our *emotions* to express our thoughts, over time this lessens as we grow more comfortable with trusting that our *feelings* rather than our *emotions* get the same job done and even better. When we do use our emotions (and feelings for that matter), it's important to note that their force and impact from a 5D level is *substantially* greater.

Initial ways to start practicing avoiding the emotional melodrama of our 3D/4D conditioning is by pausing and remembering that the situations and HUmans before you have their reasons for why they do what they do. Most of those reasons will never be made clear to you, and often, neither to them. There are so many "moving parts" to any one action in life. Often we *react* to the very top layer that is presenting itself. Although it's the most visible one, it's also the most "mundane." As a 5D HUman, we *now* have a broader range of options to choose from in how to respond to a given situation—other than coming from our emotionally skewed fields loaded with old storylines.

As powerless as you might feel at times, your ability to work and manage your feelings and emotions has been upgraded. You can *now* greatly impact and affect others as well as yourself. This capability also means that with a *slight glance or loving smile* towards a stranger, you can deeply better someone's life. But with that same glance or a frown, you can *negatively* impact someone, too. As a lovely bonus (read: *not*), the more awakened our 5D energy becomes, the more our sensitivity levels are increased and impacted also by the energy ripples that we interface with from the HUmans, environments and situations that surround us every day.

We certainly need to be mindful of how we use our energy, but equally important are the energy fields that we *expose* ourselves to. Fortunately, heightened consciousness brings with it more God-Light and this enables us to share more of the "good power" stuff, deflecting what does not serve us.

Proceed with Caution: Highly Sensitive 5DHU on Board

As long as we still have 3D/4D HUman aspects, it's tempting to get pulled in and misuse our emotions. Even if you think you can manage your responses while watching the news or reading sensationalized, emotionally charged headlines on media blogs over and over again, do you think the refiring of your emotional body can be easily discharged just by turning off the remote or deleting an article? So, then what? Do you just turn around and go cook dinner or head off to bed and it magically exits your energy field? *No, it does not.* You saw what you saw, and you heard what you heard and it completely entered your shiny new 5D matrix through your recently activated new sense: *absorption.*

Throughout 3D/4D/5D HUmans have different levels of consciousness and their absorption thresholds vary. No matter what dimensional level you resonate with, if you are a sensitive being on this planet, you are taking in copious amounts of emotional life force from other people and the collective. Stories through the media increase "absorption" levels ten-steroid-fold because of the massive amounts of thought forms and emotions attached. This is a serious stressor to your being.

After we *absorb* (our new 5D, seventh sense), unless we consciously decompress and/or take an action to "drain our *now* saturated emotional swamp," we then run the risk of passing on to others through broadcasting all the emotions that we have absorbed. They will be sent back into the world through the stories we share or retell either verbally or by the very impactful social media text or tweet. Even if we are conscious and aware enough not to actively place it all back on the assembly line for another go round, we can still inadvertently rebroadcast it through our new far-reaching 5D energy field—wherever we may go. What's even more troubling is that your new energy field and desire to vibrationally rise about the fray will be somewhat compromised.

The 5D Creative Process Filtered Through the Feminine

In prior dimensions, 3D in particular, the process of creation was primarily based on the masculine principles of doing, action, outer authority, leadership, me vs. you, etc. Our conditioning of "how you do" life overlapped another 3D favorite: a timeline that spanned a linear continuum of past, present, and future. The masculine principle dominated most cultures worldwide.

In 5D, all forms of creation are filtered through the feminine principles of being, receiving, inner authority, and intuitive guidance with less conforming, "how you do it" rules. The timeline is circular, with clock hands that only point to *Now*.

Over time, the feminine energy will be the first filter applied through most things in 5D *first*. Afterward, the masculine energy filter will be applied. As the feminine becomes more stabilized and routinely worked with, HUmanity will then be able to apply both energies at the same time, for both are equally important.. The teachings will begin for you as soon as your consciousness connects to the awareness of its existence and intuits it as a viable option to your prior way of "making things happen." Your new consciousness doesn't begin when your best friend steps into it or you hear a teacher talk about it, but rather when *you* step into it as your new way of life.

The teachings I offer, including *"The Bigger Picture"* book series, have all been designed, channeled, and created through the feminine energy to gently remind you about all that you yourself *already* know. At this point, there is really nothing new coming down the pike, just an enormous amount of deep-dive cellular remembering going on.

Do you remember back in 2006 when Pluto had a really bad day? It woke up one morning only to find out that it was downgraded to a dwarf planet. Ugh. I feel like that some days. In 3D/4D, I used to be a teacher. *Now,* I'm more like a *HUman alarm clock,* waking people up to information that they already know on a cellular, intuitive level. Hey sleepyheads, you guys up yet? Rise and shine!

The personal content that you will be transmuting represents the final vestiges of issues left over from your many 3D/4D past lives. Transmutation of old content doesn't have to be hard work in 5D, even though we got accustomed to similar 3D/4D efforts being emotionally wrenching. That is, unless you are going backwards and using outdated 3D/4D internal technology. Your 5D processor is run by the *feminine principle*, thus, creating, as well as healing, is a gentler, quicker process than what we were programmed to expect or experienced in the past.

As an example, begin by shifting your *thinking* about something you are working to heal in your life. Rather than anticipating it's going to be a difficult process even before you get started, tell yourself that your anxiety, fear, and painful memories are from the old processor. They are no longer required with your new upgraded feminine filter. Things are different *now*. You have new, super HUman abilities that will allow you to face your life, changes, and self-expression differently. You get to express and, more importantly, experience, your true feelings *now*. There is no more replaying painful memories, cleaning up your Karma, or being stuck with an emotional body that processes most things through intense emoting.

Work towards using your mental body (mind) to move your perceptions of dilemmas and situations out of 3D duality and to release the more emotionally intense filters of 4D polarity. Instead, aim to bring the situation to the highest perspective possible, 5D *triality*. This is where you take an issue out of the proverbial "boxing ring" in your head and separate the two opposing "fighters" by bringing in a neutralizing referee.

Triality is something that you will have to practice doing over and over and over. Me too. We all teach what we need to learn. I'm still teaching all this twenty-two years after I first experienced 5D consciousness because I still need to be reminded on a daily basis. I constantly check in with myself, to avoid stepping back into my old 3D thinking and 4D emotional storms. Some days I am more successful than others, but I will probably be doing this in one form or another for the rest of my incarnation here. Most of us will be.

Give yourself permission to explore *triality* and have patience with the process. You may find yourself going two steps forward followed by one step back. This is a new dance routine for all of us. Just try to stay awake throughout it all, not deflecting or hiding behind defensiveness, self-blame, or frustration. This will help you move through pieces that you feel uncomfortable to look at, not only in the world, but within your own life. Please remember also that you are a valued, contributing member of the Light team. If you can learn to lead with sensitivity, it will truly become a virtue that you can use to benefit yourself and energetically send out to others.

Take Your Time, *but Hurry Up*

Although it's very important to be patient, sensitive, and diligent when making major, unprecedented changes, don't confuse patience with having a lot of time to *drag your feet* either. Our experience of time in 3D was based on the linear paradigm of past, present, and future. The calendar was divided into years, months, and days. Hours, minutes, and seconds helped us organize our daily appointments and activities. For centuries, we used this system along with rote. Repetitiveness and conditioning mainly created what we refer to as our concepts of *truth and reality*. Our default program of what a timeframe looks like is still set by our old 3D wristwatch.

In 5D, the *construct of time* is different and for a while might feel a little disorienting. When we have a task to do or plans to make, we automatically pass them through our old 3D time sieve because that template has become so visceral for us. We are always trying to gauge "how much" time we need to do everything from catching a train to decision making. In 3D and early stages of 4D, we once had a full twenty-four-hour day to reference; but in 5D, we don't anymore, as 5D time is circular. A day in 5D has a shorter cycle because of the faster timeline. Although all time is an illusion, a *5D day* is closer in hours to a twenty-two-hour 3D day.

On some occasions, time will feel like it's moving faster or slower than the clock reflects. This is because as 5D HUmans one of our new built-in skills is the ability to play with or bend time. Without knowing how to navigate this phenomenon, it may feel challenging to delineate events—as if we're trying to discern where the sky meets the sea on the horizon. Life in 5D can seem like a blur because we are navigating multi-dimensionality and in the course of a day we could be going in and out of 4D, then to 3D, then over to 5D. So, the time zones can vary in your life in the course of a few hours. You might find yourself running chronically late or feeling like you have too much time on your hands. Your need for sleep may change or your diurnal and nocturnal polarity shifts—you could go from being a night owl to a morning dove. Many well-intended LightWorkers are very challenged by this shift and just don't do "'Earth time well."

Being that I am *now* the official self-ascribed HUman alarm clock, I don't want you to miss the powerfully constructive window of opportunity that is open right *now*. This is your time. This is our time. This is a great thing!

Stop Asking . . . Yes, You Are Different!

Most of us have bent over backward lifetime after lifetime, working on ourselves and in service of the greater good—but feeling gasLighted, misunderstood, odd, and different—like fish out of water. The 5D people I meet often say that they felt like they were adopted, didn't fit in, or were living among strangers who were their so-called family. Perhaps, like them, you were the only LightWorker or ShadowWorker in your family, school, neighborhood, or group of friends who had the advanced sense of awareness that you did. You were different and you knew it, but you didn't remember why or how this situation came to be. It was not a lot of fun to feel like you didn't belong. It was lonely, isolating and for many of us, *traumatizing*. Despite all the unpleasant and unjust things, you witnessed, experienced, and fought against, you nonetheless held on to your *vibration*. You continued vibrating, holding on tightly to the frequency of Love and Light. Light that you still have managed to carry until today.

You've been underseen, underutilized, underheard, and emotionally overworked. Most of us are ready to be done with this stage of our evolutionary development. I am so sorry that it has been such a hard climb. My heartfelt request to you is, please hang in there. The more of the veil that you pull back, the easier it will be for you to connect the pieces and find peace in the *bigger picture*. Don't give up just yet. This is your moment and because *you* are so close, we all are close too. This is the opportunity we've all been waiting for. It's just starting to get good.

GREAT POWER COMES WITH RESPONSIBILITY

Try to find it in your beautiful heart, then in your energy, to reengage with the clarion call during this intense post-5D Ascension time. Engagement does not necessarily mean going out and protesting, holding up banners, or even yelling at newspaper headlines in the privacy of your own home. If you are called to be an activist, that's different. Go do it, for it is very important work. But the personal work that you may be asked to do right *now* is likely very different than anything you have ever done before.

Right *now,* most LightWorkers have run out of zip and feel very tired, and often despondent. Fortunately, our new 5D paradigm will have a different *service contract* in it for you, perhaps even a lot softer and easier work than the lifetimes of service you've performed through the active doing of the *masculine.* You won't be doing your work anymore on a 3D or 4D platform where every challenge you address is polarized and often limited to only one or two duality-based possible "*soul*-utions."

Frustrated and heartbroken, in 3D/4D we were handcuffed by the slow, torturous drip of change that never appeared to move the needle on the dial. We usually only had only two given choices in 3D. Often a decision or action came down to choosing the lessor of two evils.

Those days are over, for *now* we have triality and we can process our internal conflicts with more neutrality. We don't have to decide between two losses or tossing everything out. In 5D, there are other "*soul*-utions" we can access in other dimensions the more we collectively raise our vibration. Because of circular time, once you energetically commit to shifting a limitation or resolving an issue, it doesn't take the same amount of time for things to settle into a harmonious form. Simply stay awake, focus on the intention with ease, and expect it to unfold effortlessly. You do not have to push or pull in circular time because *resonance* is the guiding principle rather than *3D cause and effect.* Shift your intention, driver, and energy source. That's all. Oh, and you will need a little patience and a lot of trust. Welcome to 5D.

At this level of consciousness, we are superHUman and can move through most things very quickly. As you start believing in your new abilities and function with awareness of them, you can easily command things to transmute. The trick, if you will, is learning to get out of the way of those ungodly *"hows." "But how do I control my timeline? How will this affect my day? How will all this change be possible?"* All the Universe hears is . . . "Blah, Blah, Blah and Blah, Blah." Just another 5D newbie trying to grab control of the 5D vehicle they are *already* driving.

The *art of creation* through 5D resonance is letting go of control over what the process and eventual outcome will look like. Trying to control the forces of the feminine creation is the thing that will trip you up every time. The feminine by nature is not a *do-er,* but a *be-er.*

As we cross the 4D bridge to 5D, we will have to learn to think our way around our prior mental training until, over time, we shift out of a mode of thought that is really just a bad 3D habit of thinking things are "impossible to do" or that accomplishment "takes a lot of time."

Integrated 5D Life Lessons: Integrity, Responsibility, Accountability, and Truth

As we make our way towards higher consciousness, no matter which dimensional level we identify with the most, we will initially (and maybe for most of our incarnation here) vacillate between evolving and devolving in varying degrees, depending on our circumstances, until we land on the summit of a vibrational mountain of our own making. The various gradations within each dimension that we traverse up and down vibrationally—sometimes incrementally and sometimes in one big leap—enable us to address four very important and significant life lessons running side by side along our current rise in our 5D HUman consciousness.[1]

The lessons are the same for the collective, as well as for every individual *soul*, but for those HUmans still residing primarily in 3D/4D reality, the lessons are experienced as personal, social, and collective Karma rather than 5D resonance. For those residing in 5D reality (or an even higher dimension), those lessons are *soul experiences*.

In 5D, there is no more Karma. Rather, all experiences are opportunities for furthering your growth as a HUman being and a *soul*, as well as for providing you with valuable information regarding the nature of your new 5D life mission and *soul* contracts. This will be different than it was for the service contracts and life work you were carrying out during your first incarnation in 3D/4D.

Because we are on planet Earth and HUman, throughout our lives at different times and in different ways we will all struggle with issues of *accountability, responsibility, truth,* and *integrity* (not necessarily in that order). These issues crop up courtesy of our extensive 3D "victim training." But *now,* as we are evolving, we have a lot more options available to us for how to handle our affairs. Throughout our numerous 3D incarnations, we were the energetic equivalent of a bird after its wings have been clipped, wanting nothing to do but fly. We had fewer, more limited choices and more repercussions. The reality was created by HUmans (who included all of us, by the way) whose value systems and sense of freedom were originally based on *duality* and conditioning. Our limited bandwidth greatly contributed to HUmanity's deep desire for dominance and control. In western history, for example, unless you were privileged by talent, wealth, power, maleness, or Light skin, you faced enormous restrictions. And currently, remnants of this 3D Shadow still remain powerfully active.

Our conditioning and the 3D premises it was constructed on have finally arrived at their expiration dates and are beginning to deconstruct, mainly thanks to the shift into 4D consciousness. From an evolutionary perspective this is an amazing feat that is unfolding, but from an everyday HUman perspective, it feels like an Armageddon. As LightWorkers, it's important that we don't rest on our laurels—knowing that this is just a current reality and truth and believing nothing much can be done about it.

We need to frequently revisit those four issues and draw life lessons from them to ensure we are not just "kicking the can down the road" in an effort to avoid the pain that first comes with *recognition*. The lessons confronting us are integral to our success in stabilizing 5D reality on Earth.

The most difficult part of our shift and these particular four lessons/experiences to address (according to Steve Rother in *Spiritual Psychology,* there are actually twelve life lessons) is the HUman *reactivity* factor. Each of us must ask, *"How am I reacting to all the chaos in the world and the experiences in my life? Am I using my old 4D, supercharged emotional body to process all the violence, justifications, and crazy logics that I am witnessing impact my world? Am I reacting to life with my 3D self and quietly seething?"*

Remaining calm when confronted with injustice is a big challenge for everyone, including me, who has painfully experienced multiple lifetimes in 3D in which the repercussions of "doing nothing" and "saying nothing" produced oppression, suppression, and slave programming that lasted for what seemed like eons.

Although we experienced some relief when we attained 4D consciousness, the emotional body was activated and our anger, voice, and ability to advocate openly for ourselves crossed with very significant, character-shaping values of accountability, responsibility, integrity, and truth. Because 4D is chaotic and stressful, when heightened emotions are added to the insane narratives that we have all come to witness and even experience for ourselves, things can go haywire.

As LightWorkers upleveled to 4D and our personal changes triggered massive shifts for HUmanity and the planet, new possibilities began to surface that hadn't existed one short dimension prior. A lot of the transmutation of old issues needed to be taken on.

Reentering these four life lessons *now* that you have reached 5D should not mean throwing yourself back into the depths of your old emotional work from 4D. But remember, as long as you are breathing, you will *always* have the need to both grow and evolve. It's a good idea to keep these four virtues front and center, so that if you notice yourself slipping into old habits, you can pause and make a course correction.

In 5D, it's the frequency you *vibrate* to, not what you *do,* that matters. As we become more self-accountable, we should be the first ones with a hand up asking the hard questions such as, *"Was I in integrity with that action? Did I act responsibly? Hold myself accountable? Was I in my truth?"*

Hiccups in our behavior will look different for each of us.

We are all going to have to look closely at how well we are aligned with these four values going forward because in 5D our personal energy fields are *super amplified.* Little things we used to make excuses for or try to justify, don't have the same allowance anymore.

Practicing Integrity and Responsibility

Let's look at one example of a decision that most of us would probably agree on as a clear line of delineation regarding our personal integrity. In this scenario, your friend comes over for lunch and you spend a couple of good hours together. After she leaves you notice a $20 bill on the floor beside the chair her coat was thrown over. Do you keep it or give her a call and ask if the cash is hers? Most people reading this would say, *"I'd definitely call my friend as opposed to just pocketing the bill."* They'd feel out of integrity doing anything otherwise.

But there may be some other little things that we innocently do all the time that are out of integrity because we feel that acting differently would bring up a host of other personal challenges. For example, *people pleasing* to avoid conflict.

Or how about this one? You run into someone that you know–perhaps you haven't seen them in a while–you smile, give them a kiss or a hug hello, and say, *"How have you been? It's so good to see you."* Before you know it, the conversation ends, the person walks away, and you *exhale*. The truth is you never really liked that person. Maybe the person is a gossiper, or you had a slight run in with them in the past. Deep down you know that even under the best circumstances you really wouldn't normally want to hold or kiss that individual. Feeling relieved that the unexpected encounter is over, you might not give a second thought to whether or not you stepped out of line with your integrity by doing something you really didn't want to do.

Perhaps you have told someone you Loved them when they asked, but you really didn't. Perhaps you've said, "I'm good/fine/OK," when someone asked, "How are you doing?" We all draw on rote responses such as these occasionally. Are they harmless social niceties? *Yes and no.*

When we find ourselves in one of these situations, in 3D/4D, we tend to put the needs of others *first* as a part of our old prior enslavement matrix. In 3D we often tried to *"do the right thing,"* *"avoid hurting people's feelings,"* and *"adhere to proper social etiquette."* Duality never provided many winning options for us. In 4D, we either made the other person feel more comfortable by putting them first and acting *selfless* or decided on doing what we truly wanted to do and ran the risk of being branded or feeling *selfish*. These were ingrained, learned patterns of HUman interaction. Neither right nor wrong, this was just a byproduct of social pressures and conditioning. In 5D, the stakes are a little higher mainly because our enhanced energy fields multiply everything that we experience. For instance, an innocent hug of someone you dislike can throw your sensitive energy field out of balance and more deeply impact your vibrational equilibrium or *personal integrity*.

In 3D, you might have found yourself going to a family BBQ anyway even though you knew that slimy and inappropriate uncle would be there. There was a good chance that back in your 3D days you probably had to suppress the trauma from things he did to you as a child. You literally might *not* remember why you hate being around him so much. In 4D, with your awakened emotional body, you might also decide to go to the BBQ but have some fear and anxiety about it. You may only have been able to get through it by having a few extra drinks, overeating, or scheduling an extra therapy session to help mitigate the PTSD you knew would get triggered.

So, what should you do? Ignore the person, say something that hurts their feelings, turn away from their kiss on your check, confide in a family member, or just not show up at all? All good and fair questions. The *soul*-ution lies in our new 5D matrix of *triality* and revisiting *bigger picture* ways to decide.

In 5D, all and any of those options are correct! What's more important is that when you ultimately decide, you come to that conclusion *awake*, *conscious,* and from *choice* rather than from *fear* or *avoidance*. It's a little easier perhaps to do a test run on your new "conscious" responses if your experiment is conducted away from your inner circle where the intimacy stakes are at their highest.

News reports about government-related issues is a good place to start (*maybe?*) as these typically can rile up a lot of HUmans. In 5D, you don't have to water down your political beliefs and positions on issues or apologize for your personal sense of right or wrong when you talk to anyone about them. You just must be willing to acknowledge to *yourself* that those are your beliefs, and yes, you are being very challenged by the feelings that are being triggered within you regarding other HUman perspectives. Try to express your thoughts and opinions "without adding a preexisting *emotional charge*"' from your 4D energy field to what you're saying. Express the issues or your idea of the facts to yourself and others, but do so without *misusing* it as an opportunity to validate or reinforce your longstanding thoughts and feelings about the topic or subject.

Practicing Accountability and Truth

Lack of accountability and the frustration that comes with it can be very deceptive. In 3D/4D it's easier to justify all your emotions and reactions around it, especially if a *lack* of accountability in your *family* contributed to many of your core childhood wounds. In 5D, accountability is a virtue. No one is rewarded for looking the other way or avoiding confronting other HUman misdeeds. But many of our new HUman features are so "sensitive" they can easily multiply the intensity of our feelings and reactions, sometimes triggering old 3D/4D wounds.

One of the main reasons why you have grown into 5D consciousness is that you *already* did most of the backbreaking work to heal wounds accrued during your elongated stay in what felt like 3D purgatory. Initially in 5D, intense reactions or overreactions are often more likely due to "kneejerk," default programming, coupled with a more highly porous emotional field. Its less about how much pain you are still in or your limited ability (3D/4D speaking) to be able to claim, address, and face adult responses. Many of those reactions caused massive shame, guilt, and upheaval in your 3D/4D lives. You have *now* stepped into a new realm, new frequency, and new incarnation and you are more than capable of practicing *accountability* on a much higher level.

And yes, when facing the truth about a friend or a partner, or anyone else that's close to us, it does get a little more confusing to deal with regarding *their* lack of accountability. The closer the person or situation is to us, the more likely we may be to make concessions for their actions and cut a few more corners. It's not because we "don't" want to know the truth; it's more that when we face irresponsibility head on, we can no longer peddle backward and afterward act like we don't "know." Once "truth" enters our consciousness in 5D, we know that somehow we must act either through an action or owning a clearer awareness regarding all involved. Tolerating other Humans' misdeeds or our own lack of accountability or absence of integrity is really no longer an option.

The more we follow the principles of 5D, which include self-respect, self-compassion, and self-kindness, the less likely we are to avoid facing uncomfortable things because we don't have to fear the "old repercussions" and "self-flogging" actions we learned in 3D. We start feeling better about ourselves the more we know our truth, feel pride in taking responsibility, see accountability as an act of maturity, and see integrity as something that will not take anything away from us that belongs in our newly earned 5D field of frequency. With this transition into higher consciousness, comes the willingness and desire to hold our own *feet to the fire*. It is *now* our responsibility, and we claim our sovereignty over ourselves with great pride.

As enLightened beings, we understand that if there is a lack of accountability in our personal lives, then there is a lack of accountability in the *world* around us too. Given what we are seeing in our political world today, we all must do our part and clean out the Shadow cobwebs where they may lie or be hidden in ourselves. This personal *truthing* is the only medicine for what ails us as a planet.

When HUmanity, as a group or society avoids facing the truth or deflects questions about the truth regarding its leaders, environmental challenges, disease of HUman separation, and so forth, then this collective nonaction or choice illustrates that all HUmans involved are in some manner out of integrity. The moment we separate ourselves from the issues that rile us or create distance in our thinking or allow us to extremely emotionally overreact to prove a point, then we have missed an *opportunity* to effect change.

The old reactions and feared emotional repercussions of our 3D/4D selves, along with our 3D egos, that prevent us from looking at things we do, even in teeny tiny ways, make us part of the problem rather than part of the *soul*-ution. As part of incarnating here, we agreed to use our lives and all that would pass through them as conduits to transmit the Light and transmute HUmanity's Shadow. In learning to address our own Shadows and HUman foibles without guilt, blame, shame, and self-hatred, we take responsibility for the *bigger picture* world and also, by vibrational example, make it easier for others to do the same.

With an open heart, try to take in on a very deep level, that you volunteered for this unspeakable mission while knowing that some of the work was going to be very intense. You and I both incarnated and agreed that, if we made it into 5D, we were going to be the *way-showers*, the first settlers in this pioneering territory. We were going to be the ones that looked at hard-core issues, held ourselves accountable, were responsible for our HUman lives and actions, and walked in as much truth as we could bear with integrity. If you can lead your actions with that and even just once a day catch yourself from *looking the other way, responding defensively, or acting self-righteously,* over time this new way of life will become automatic for you.

To get this integrated in a stable way, we are all going to have to do this repeatedly. I myself don't have it down, but I try to remember what is being asked of me, especially when I find myself thinking about what I can do not to over "react" when I hear the news or see a massive injustice in the world being carried out with no apparent consequences to those involved.

The Universe is a lot more patient with our learning curves than we are. When you find yourself drifting away from your 5D center, floating too far away from what you *now* know is your core work, all that you're being asked to do is to go back.

Practice returning to these four important life lessons. They will help keep you on track, aligned and reroute you back to center.

When we micro-adjust our internal GPS, we hold our vibration to a new, higher standard. Our self-corrections impact everything. They send out powerful shockwaves and weaken the strong resolve that the 3D resistance grip had on HUmanity for eons.

Resistance to looking at all our personal thought forms and taking an honest look at where truth is feared is currently up in the world and has become a very important segment for our growing 5D community. All the old programming that has clouded, controlled, and delayed HUmanity from facing its difficult truths is *now* turning a corner. Once you know this, *you can't put the toothpaste back into the tube anymore.* Once we are freed, like the toothpaste, *we are out!* We know this *now*. Holding space for this to be understood by everyone else is *now* our work.

What comes up between you doing what you want and what is true for you is the new ratio equation for 5D integrity. The rub in this lies between our efforts to unlearn the old 3D/4D behavior patterns while learning the new feeling-based patterns of 5D. Hardwired into our nervous systems are the last vestiges of our 3D/4D reactions based on a template that put everything outside us, such as others' feelings, authority, family, and God, the boss of us. We didn't even make the list— or at least not the top three items on it.

Our old emotions about things like wanting to please people or not wanting to upset or hurt others "feelings" have created a firewall between ourselves and our own integrity. The more we practice integrity, the more we will see it reflected in our politicians, institutions, relationships, and the world around us.

That conundrum might not feel like an easy fix but being in integrity doesn't have to be hard either. When you begin to consciously shift your inner drive from your emotional body to your new 5D HUman "hard drive," the upgrade automatically comes with advanced features of accountability, responsibility, integrity, and the need to stay as close to "your" truth as possible.

Although 5D comes with a generous learning curve, the more you act on and reinforce your new responses, the easier it gets and the faster it goes. And yes, that means you will have to face these dilemmas that come with massive change and upgrades. But it will only be perceived as daunting if you are choosing to look at it through the lens of your old emotional body. Your new life comes with a clearer focus and a significantly reduced traumatic charge when dealing with family, partners, friends, and life issues in *general*. It's a new dawn. It's a new day. It's a new perspective. It's the *bigger picture*.

It's a BIG Ask, but You're Up for It!

The Universe has asked us to look at how these things are still currently active in our lives. You wouldn't have been placed on the planet, at this time, to do this work, if you weren't the right *soul* for the job. If you're thinking, *"Hey, it's hard to be accountable, responsible, truthful, and in integrity all the time,"* you're damn right it is! That's why there was only a small group of us brought forward who worked in the Light to do this intense piece of work for HUmanity and Mother Earth. Our focus, knowingly or not, was first to make sure we met the very iffy deadline of 5D Ascension on December 12, 2012. The next part of the transition was to hold the space as old 3D structures dissolved piece by piece.

None of us consciously knew what this second crucial piece of our Ascension process would look like, or even if it was coming. Climate change, wars, a pandemic, democracy dissolving, HUman cruelty, disease, poverty, and food source depletion were way too much for us to understand before we stepped into transmuting them. In 5D, creation begins in the *now*. You can't anticipate or imagine it before the world creates it. Things don't happen until they *happen*.

We are so accustomed to eons of HUman behavior that taught us to plan, anticipate the next move, focus on the future, and so on, that shifting to the new 5D paradigm of being in the *now* and going with the flow can be quite disorienting at first. This mode of operation is not based on the masculine *doing* principle of creation and no longer unfolds on the continuum of past, present, and future linear timelines. We are living in the 5D time structure of *now*, creating through the Divine Feminine principle of *being*.

What we haven't yet fully absorbed is that looking at all these various pieces does not have to be a torturous ordeal. It doesn't have to be dragged out because we are not doing it from 3D/4D anymore. In 3D, in particular, if you owned that you were acting irresponsibly, it often meant you were *bad* and somehow would be punished for it. Remember, in childhood if something got broken or went awry and your parents asked you to tell them the truth about the situation? It was often followed by, *"I promise you—I won't get mad?"* *How'd that work out for ya'?*

We usually got punished for lying *and* for owning up to things. Duality set us up into the polarizing system of opposites, even when we are trying to do the right thing. If you're not being responsible, you most likely are not being "good." We never got the memo that we can occasionally act irresponsibly, screw up, and still be a "good" person.

Stepping into different truths meant that you might have to deal with uncomfortable feelings of being wrong or bad. It wasn't just that the feelings were so overwhelming that we wanted to avoid them; in 3D/4D, we also were restricted and controlled by the limiting emotional bandwidth in which we were permitted to openly have the feelings or take the actions and display pieces of self.

In the prior matrix, if you were looking at issues of integrity, responsibility, accountability, and truth, you were looking at them through a filter of 3D opposites. Deductive reasoning in 3D can only register two truths: either you're doing it right or you're doing it wrong. This judgment piggybacks on ideas about whether you're good or bad. You're either getting blamed or doing some blaming.

We stayed away from all sorts of button-pushing issues because common sense told us we don't need to touch a stove twice to know it's hot. Once the burn is experienced, we really don't want to go through the discomfort or repercussions again. 3D and parts of 4D wounded us and a lot of their principles reshaped our values and sense of self.

There's a New Sheriff in Town—and He's a *She!*

As you step further into 5D, you can retrain more of your thinking and responses simply by reminding yourself that your emotional body is not running the show anymore. Try not to back yourself into a corner with the old rules of the 3D system of opposites. Be mindful that when you are criticizing, berating, or shaming yourself, you are acting through your old 3D filter and drawing on old 3D ways of "teaching" yourself a lesson. Over time, give your mistakes and setbacks all the wiggle room, compassion, and basic kindness that 5D has to offer.

Start applying your new 5D knowledge in regard to the small things. For example, if you see a place in your life where you are struggling to address something that feels overwhelming or brings up a deep-rooted fear, you could say the following sequence of ideas to yourself:

1. "There's a new 5D sheriff in town."
2. "I accept that there are many options or *soul*-utions available outside the limited scope of my consciousness."
3. "I no longer rely on charging, inflaming, or intensifying the situation with strong emotions or reactions that block or interfere with my ability to receive and hear the guidance of my God Self and those who support, Love, and work with me here in the Light."
4. "To the best of my ability, I commit to removing my negative emotions from this situation and will hold open the sacred space needed for the powerful energy field of allowance to create, realize, or present the next step to get me through this in the *now*."

Apply these steps to most of the struggles that come up for you throughout the day and watch what shifts for you. For example, say you are having a difficult time with your finances. Being accountable or responsible *doesn't* mean you have to come up with, for starters, the fix and *soul*-utions. If you knew what to do or a new way of approaching it, most likely you would have done so by *now*. For most of us, when the not knowing what to do pressure sets in, often the avoidance, shame, and fear buddies show up. Much of this is old 3D programming and memories when we had been stymied by our past ignorance about how to resolve a dilemma. We have been deeply programmed to perceive a limited number of options that are mainly generated from only within our 3D/4D minds. To complicate matters further, if something is not "right" in our world, such as our finances, then we are also somehow deeply flawed and "wrong/bad." This thinking comes *free*—as a built-in courtesy of 3D conditioning.

The new 5D paradigm that moves us forward comes from *managing the emotions* arising around a situation that is running interference from our ability to access a wide range of higher forms and creative flow *soul*-utions, *not from coming up with the perfect choice*. Try not to get caught up in how bad, shamed, or guilty you feel about a situation. That is only a distraction, a key earmark of 3D manipulation and control tactics. Remember, *"A fish only sees the bait and not the hook behind it."* Try not to bite at the bait.

At the same time, you need to show up "awake" if you want to help move energy and get yourself and a situation back in Divine flow. Remember, the emotions you feel are leftover reactions attaching themselves to some very real current issues. Hardwired 3D reactions are often opportunistic, showing up when you are vulnerable, scared, or in a weakened state.

Many of the challenges we face in 5D are not *personal* anymore; they belong to the *collective*. Our second incarnation here in 5D, is mostly for *bigger picture soul* assignments. Technically, emotional reactions that were once based in your *personal issues* have been moved into your "rear view mirror" of your *first* incarnation here. These issues, although both present and very real, are just the remains of an old timeline running through various stages as they cycle out of your energy system.

If you recharge any issue, such as handling your finances, with recycled emotions, it just serves to delay the re-*soul*-ution of the issue. The emotions are a distraction that prevents you from receiving the wisdom about your finances or anything else that your new communication system is able to deliver to you.

By asking for wisdom from the collective mind, which is the collective God, you are not only making changes for yourself but adding to the *bigger picture* and serving HUmanity's collective ability to transition to something greater and higher. It's all tied into the unified field of the 5D *Now*.

You are not a 5D putz, a LightWorker loser, or an incompetent new HUman when you don't know the answer or have the *soul*-ution to something. There is nothing to be *ashamed* about. Focus on the truth that you are obviously someone incredibly special if you made it all the way to 5D. You are in the top one percent of the top one percent of *souls* in the world. It doesn't get much more stellar than that! *Your 5D God-*

Light is as resilient as steel and your 5D heart is as strong as Teflon! You are not the shy, scared, manipulated, and controlled person you were (and all of us were) in 3D/4D. So, go ahead and ask yourself, *"Am I being responsible, accountable, and truthful? Am I operating in integrity?"* Remember, it's a learning curve and it's our *second* incarnation job to help ourselves and the world face this shift. Use kindness and compassion, and please go easy on yourself—*but not too easy.*

Compassion vs. True Compassion

Compassion is a 3D/4D concept. Thank God, we at least had some on the planet. Although, looking around at how HUmans have treated one another, the Earth, and the Animal kingdom, you would never know it. Compassion cannot be learned. It's a natural byproduct of having an open heart, being caring and conscious, and not being afraid to use them freely. It allows us, without an agenda, to demonstrate heartfelt concern for others and their situations and struggles. It was repeatedly ingrained in us through our social and religious beliefs, but primarily expressed for "others."

In 5D, we are encouraged to relearn this key HUman value but in its more exalted form of *"true compassion."* This higher-vibrational form of Love must *now* include "you" in the equation and response. When you decide to help somebody or go to someone's aid, especially, if it's "just" emotional support, if you are not also factoring yourself in and are unaware of how that help will play out in "your" *bigger picture*, then it is no longer *true* compassion. More likely, at least some part of your response is based in your old 3D understanding of compassion, which was born out of a matrix of imbalance, opposites, and victim programming.

As a newly anointed 5D Higher Being, 3D reactions, even the good stuff like compassion, will eventually short circuit your nervous system a bit. You might get an unsuspecting call from the Universe, asking you for a "clean up on aisle 3." If you are conscious and awake, you will clearly realize when these calls come in. There is no chance you'll miss them, although at times you will wish you had. You might find yourself inadvertently pulled back into a situation repeatedly, and what eventually had started out as a good intention has *now* become stressful and burdensome. If you are truthful enough, you may even feel resentful and angry with the person for not heeding your advice or positively utilizing your Love. Often in early 5D, you will have to take a second look at how *helpful* your compassion or assistance turned out to be. When the action or reaction is out of integrity with you or has been filtered through your old vibrational filter of 3D/4D fixing or codependency, it will often come back in many creative ways to bite you. But why, if all you had were good intentions?

HUmans often filter decisions through the lens of how they see or feel about the actions they are about to take, how they will be perceived by others and what their response or impression will be. This is a very ingrained HUman phenomena. In the characteristic duality of 3D/4D, we learned that we have two basic choices for how to categorize (read: *emotionalize)* actions:

1. Acting *selfishly.*
2. Acting *selflessly.*

Both these designations come with a visceral set of immediate reactions. Selfish = stingy, not nice, cheap, self-absorbed, and so on. Selfless = kind, giving, caring, generous, good *soul*, and such.

With only those two main choices at play in 3D/4D, I know which I would prefer being identified with. *How about you?* We struggle to constantly do the right thing, give of ourselves, and stretch our hearts to be as much like Mother Teresa as possible. The good news in 5D is that *martyrdom is dead*. We don't have to throw ourselves on our own swords anymore to feel like we are good people and liked by everyone to get the big reward of eternal life at the end.

In 5D, a new choice has been added to the mix. Triality is *now* affording us a third option: *self-firstness*.

True Compassion asks you to place yourself *first*. *"Say what?"* True Compassion allows you to consider your needs *first* and *then* turn around and go help others. *It doesn't say put yourself first and the hell with everybody else.* That's 3D selfishness, not 5D self-firstness. Instead, it asks you to put yourself first, then, if you're feeling inspired to do so, to pivot to caring for another person or doing whatever the situation calls for with Love and Compassion. That's the difference between this new protocol and being selfish—where most times you're only thinking about yourself or where you're doing for others randomly, possibly out of commitment, guilt, and your prior 3D emotional training. Many of us—especially many women—have never learned how to place ourselves first, drama free.

The Universe wants you to honor the abundance of God-Light you *now* carry. Who could possibly be more deserving of your loyalty and compassion than God? And yes, everyone's God-Light is just as important as yours. But if you are offering service through the beautiful and powerful Light being that you are, then all that is being asked of you is to lead by directing it to *yourself first*. True compassion calls on that higher ordered *you-first* sequencing.

By placing yourself in the front domino position, you also place every aspect of it in correct order. Correct order brings Accountability, Responsibility and Truth, which aligns you with your core Integrity. This sacred chronology allows for the 5D advanced HUman to remove all the heavy 3D/4D resentments, regrets, manipulations, and codependent miscreations from all acts of giving and kindness.

Higher Order: *Self First*

Focus on yourself first and make sure that indirectly your *responses* are not *reactions*, that you are not somehow slighting yourself, suppressing your own needs, or holding back on your "real" thoughts and feelings. Giving for the sake of just giving, in 5D can also be an unconscious form of manipulation. Remember, our need to be Loved, liked, seen a certain way, etc., all factor into our actions. It is often painful, anxiety-provoking, and scary to witness, especially when those we Love are going through their traumas, dramas, and life lessons. Check in that you are not giving from an inner void, but instead from overspill, and that you are as aligned as possible with the *Divine Flow of Order and Love*. Only then pivot and give your compassion to another person or take the action you are called to with a clear 5D mind and heart.

And yes, at first you are going to say "no" more often, make more attempts to stay out of the drama, and engage very differently with everything and everyone than you formerly did. This shift takes a little practice. Shaking off old 3D/4D programming might at first bring up a lot of angst, fear, guilt, and shame. Our old ideas of "good person vs. bad person" may surface with a vengeance. Expect not to be clear at first on how to act or which actions to take. As we experience leaving our 3D/4D programming behind, our prior emotional body matrix will try to run interference, at times jamming up . . . as your new 5D app is just beginning to load.

As we align ourselves with a new understanding and level of responsibility, we are allowing for a higher and more spiritually aligned order for all involved. Accepting that there is a spiritual order and honoring its sequencing meets everybody's needs lovingly and equally. No one will be left behind, as Divine Order is a kind, loving, benevolent, and sacred process for all those involved, even if at a given time you cannot possibly see a Divine outcome to the exchange. Taking this new, more evolved path while awake, with consciousness, allows you to hold the space and the compassion for the highest Divine *soul*-ution to appear. This is a really great thing that you can ask or pray for with anything in your life. "I make the space for and request for the Highest Divine *soul*-ution to appear!" This is part of our LightWorker assignments to *"go first"* and hold the space for others to come along if they choose. The new 5D paradigm also includes new templates for revisiting almost everything—behaviors, interactions, and things we once had in the *"not a problem"* category. It's important to remember this, especially if you find yourself in a position where you feel deeply that saying "no" or not helping is the right thing to do but you are also conflicted about doing what you know to be your truth.

The difference between a *3D "no" and a 5D "no"* is awareness, consciousness, and True Compassion for all. This 5D principle allows you to place yourself first and then turn the actions of care over to something greater than you. In doing or not doing what is needed, that action will be in alignment with truth and integrity, and ultimately the highest good of all. The "giving" aspect then gets placed in a conducive cycle of action. Sometimes, that person or situation rights itself over time because they reached out for an intervention or assistance as a first step towards finally reaching inward for the support, they needed all along. Sometimes, a situation is brought to you, specifically, not for you to contribute to changing it directly, but rather *indirectly*. The new dynamics in 5D tend to suggest that "nothing" happens that is a mistake or a rejection, and that even your "no" was a crucial step on that person's journey to the right action.

5D comes with a broader bandwidth of consciousness, which allows you to filter life, people, and events through your new, *bigger picture* lens. Being out of the dualistic playing field that dictates a "yes" means "I help you and things get better," versus a "no," which means "I don't help you and the situation gets worse."

In 5D, a "Yes, I'll help you" that is out of integrity can be as equally disruptive as a "No, I won't help you" in 3D.

A "No, I won't help you" in 5D may be the energetic equivalent to a "Yes, I'll help you" in 3D.

Being a conscious and awake being who is no longer manipulated or hijacked by their 3D/4D emotional body will create a whole new world of untethered choices and actions for you that are aligned with the highest good for all. The other thought to contemplate is that just because something crosses your path, gets your attention, or comes to you doesn't mean that it is *yours* to act upon. When an action is balanced, even untethered, giving always comes with an exchange or an unexpected gift to the giver. You, too, might be in the throes of learning for yourself how to say "no" from a place of Love not resentment. Your soul might be working on developing boundaries, lines of delineation, and the highly valued tool of *discernment.* A person or situation that is presented to you might have nothing to do with what the "other" person needs or is asking for. There's a good chance that it might have all occurred just to assist you in redefining your new 5D HUman growth process.

Taught through the old 3D victim programming, 3D/4D compassion is mainly for the other person. By contrast, 5D's *True Compassion* can equally address the compassion/consideration for you, as well as the compassion/consideration for the other person at the same time. We don't have to choose someone else's happiness or needs over our own. It doesn't have to be either/or. That's a 3D construct. Thankfully, there is more than enough Love to go around, so feel free to spread it.

As HUmans on this planet, we are always on an unspoken mission of striving to be better and more evolved. The path of Accountability, Responsibility, Truth, and Integrity must be owned by *you first,* before others can mirror that back, not only to you, but in the world. This four-point drive is programmed deeply in your DNA. We are built to evolve and rise higher. With an internal homing device, everything we did since we took our first breath was done to move the evolution and Ascension of HUmanity to a 5D level of advanced consciousness. We've kept that intention, and the process that it took to get there, both front and center, and must continue to do so, always leading with our hearts.

All the powers that be know you were handed a *very big task*. All the galaxies in the Universe know that you are an important player. The Universal heart thanks you and often bows to you in praise. **You are not only Loved, but you are Love itself.** And in turn, you *now,* as a 5D HUman, have more of that Love to energetically radiate.

Fear Clogs the Playing Field

Do a quick check in right *now*. See if any fear or resistance is coming up. If it is, don't shame yourself, deny it, or bury it. Work with allowance and compassion to create a safe space for it to surface. Be your best friend and, without judgment, be present and attentive. Hear out your fear. *Is fear coming up for you right now about money, relationships, work, family?* Then, start with accepting that somewhere inside of you, you are asking yourself to create some space and send Love to that part of you that needs you to not resist or dismiss it. Instead, join it in an awakened space, not as its enemy, but as its friend, coming to help unfreeze or move the issue out of lockdown. Try to remember that when you feel any type of *resistance* it is most likely coming from the energy field of fear and not necessarily because of a dislike, preference, or warning. In 5D, preferences comes from choice, and not through the constriction field of resistance.

It's not always needed to discern correctly if you are having your experience from a 3D, 4D, or 5D perspective. If it is up and has cloaked itself in fear, no matter what dimension that it is generated from then it is still yours to transmute. Try not to complicate it any more than you are already burdened by it. It will only make you feel more stressed about it at a time when all you really need is some *soul-Love*. What to do about it can come later. If you are feeling afraid about something, try to remind yourself that the "fear" is really the bigger issue than the perceived challenge itself. It's not the cash flow, the relationship, or whatever. This isn't negating your fear or implying that if you stop being afraid, you will have cash flow. What I'm saying is, if you're not *feeding* the fear with horrible thoughts and electrically binding 3D/4D emotions, you might be able to approach the construct, issue, or what's presenting itself around money, and work on it through the objectivity of 5D feelings. This will give you a clearer chance to "allow" Divinity in, so that different options will appear, and a less obstructed mind will guide you.

For example, when you think: *"What are we going to eat for dinner tonight,"* if you allowed your panic to hijack that thought, it might (and probably does for many) sound something like this. *"Should I make chicken? Rice and beans? Oh, my God!! Which beans do I use? How much rice should I put in the pot? I'm so overwhelmed by this simple dish! I'm never going to figure it out. Never. I'm so depressed. I need a drink. I need chocolate. I have to schedule a session with my therapist!"*

Sometimes there are things that we perceive as problems that we don't give hysteria to, or at least we try to figure them out without having a complete meltdown or holding a dramatic 4D press conference.

Those who fear cooking might need a different example, but I'm sure you get my point.

When you remove fear from the equation, you have a clearer shot at addressing the underlying issue. It's not clouded anymore, and you can approach it with some sanity and accountability. You can look at the truth of it, act responsibly, and then do what you have to do with integrity. No matter how frightening an issue may be, integrity never comes with sweeping it under the rug or with the intention of "pulling the rug" out from under you. *There is no integrity in looking the other way, making excuses, or not showing up for what you called to you.*

If we didn't have to contend with terrifying fear or if our resistance wasn't attached to debilitating thought forms, most of us would be much more apt to look at our issues objectively and address what is needed for their resolution with calm neutrality. It's our emotion of fear from the 3D/4D conditioning that is continually replaying itself as we anticipate what we can or cannot face and resolve. All of this is based on an old version of our limited prior self. The linear 3D paradigm *creates anticipatory panic and angst.* We are conditioned to relive trauma, pain, and emotional conflicts because of the 3D timeline of past, present, and future. Our prior memory function was never allowed to just remain in the *now* experience. With that three-fold timeline construct, once we arrive at one *now,* we are quickly bumped into the next future *now*. Our 3D/4D memory stored the experience and cataloged it on its corresponding timeline. When something similar happens, or we *anticipate* (read: not in the *now* of the experience) happening—to you, your mother, your best friend, or the leading character in a movie on the Lifetime network, our brain identifies with it and pulls up the old memory attached to a similar but predictable situation or scenario. In an effort to circumvent the unpleasant feelings and protect ourselves, we avoid the issue. At one time, that may have been true but not in our 5D *now*. In this level of consciousness, crossed timelines can create backups, slowdowns, and resistance of seismic proportions.

In 3D/4D, we were led and ruled by the emotional body. It was mostly shut down in 3D and intensely overactive in 4D.

Although the *emotional body* is not the driver anymore, you might be surprised to hear that neither is the *spiritual body*. In 5D it is the *physical body* that rules. Many of us believed that as we evolved, our spiritual growth would become more and more enhanced and important. It has, and *it hasn't*. It kind of happened but with an interesting spin on reverse. A successful 5D Ascension means that we are *now* comprised of more spirit or God-Light than ever before. Awakening means "waking up" or activating more of our Lightbody, spiritual consciousness, and connection to the God self. So, in 5D, we don't need to keep reaching for or connecting to our spiritual self the same way because we already are so much more one with it in the flesh.

We don't need to study or take the same type of classes anymore—at least, not for the same reasons, which were to help us move more easily out of 3D and to assist us in becoming more familiar with our new 4D vibration and home. All our classes, teachers, and therapy sessions helped us get here. But in 5D, although those things are still very important, when you are called to them it's usually for a different set of reasons. They are no longer used primarily for raising your vibration so you can get out of your 3D/4D dramas, traumas, and Karma just in time to make your previously scheduled 5D Ascension fLight.

All those support systems were invaluable and crucial to your *bigger picture* evolutionary plans. You successfully made your fLight and have safely landed on Planet 5D. Those support systems are still invaluable, but their role and the objectives *now* are to support you in remembering your new 5D mission, helping you learn about your new HUman self, and giving you the latest "intel" on multidimensionality and the *bigger picture* plans.

We've already Ascended, and along with this cataclysmic event, a lot of the familiar rules have changed. What is going to be needed going forward is our undivided attention to the physical body. And *physicality now* covers a wide swath of issues, such as how we treat our homes and the environment, and how we respond to the needs of our new 5D bodies.

So, what kinds of food does a 5D body require? Nourishments will include clean food, good chilling, sleep adjustments, HUman touch, and upgraded sexual experiences, to name a few! Adjusting to all this newness will take a little while, but everything moves very fast in 5D, so don't dawdle too much or for that matter, *don't blink.*

CHAPTER EIGHT
THE 5D UPGRADE

Congratulations, You Graduated to 5D! So, Why Are You Feeling *Demoted?*

We are 5D children learning life skills for the first time. Confusingly, as adult-sized HUman newborns we are learning to walk before we learn to crawl. Still unlearning our hardwired 3D programming, the new ways of managing our emotions, opening our hearts and minds, and navigating the change of paradigms are not yet familiar. We are waking up to more aspects of our *souls'* original blueprints, and along with these, an understanding of our new, *multidimensional existence.* This is all going to keep us busy for a while. Very!

Our 5D Ascension transition can create a lot of stress for the physical and emotional bodies. Every aspect of your being is in the process of being reworked or rearranged. When you restructure something that has been intact, not just in one lifetime, but in hundreds of lifetimes going back to the days in Lemuria, Atlantis, and beyond, you are deconstructing aspects of your system that have survived many lifetimes of your 3D existence. That's a whole lot of upheaval, excavation, and *Feng Shuiing*!

Although this prospect may sound quite daunting, in essence every significant issue and pattern that has been left unresolved or out of balance from every 3D lifetime that you've *ever* lived was synthesized and blended into your *first* incarnation here, the one you were born into in your current body. The only reason that you were able to Ascend into 5D is because you cleaned up, brought to the Light, and transmuted everything that was most important to you and left unfinished from every lifetime that you have ever lived in a dimensional variation of 3D! And you were wondering why you always feel *tired?*

How many times did you pray, meditate, cry, or explode in an angry "chant" of *"Why do these issues keep happening to me?"* or *"Will these blips, false starts, misreads, and disappointments ever end?"* When we are in the final throes of nearly 30,000 years of cyclic, repetitive issues and all-too-familiar reality patterns—even if they are coming up for a last pass through them—it will seem like there is no end in sight. But there is. We had to unload as much *baggage* as possible before we could get a green Light for our 5D Ascension takeoff.

Can you pause for a moment and take in how much work you have done and how much you have personally and globally accomplished lifetime after lifetime? Are you tired? Worn out? Confused? Frustrated? Sometimes at your wit's end? You should be! This was nothing short of amazing, all while done not consciously remembering why. By placing one foot in front of the other as if you were traversing a desert while continually being confronted with a vibrational sandstorm, you made this possible. You are one of the unsung heroes who just kept going no matter what. All eyes have been on you. Every being in the Multiverse has been following your every move on Twitter, and still, you give yourself such a hard time and so few accolades.

Any leftover issues that appear in your life *now* from any of your 3D/4D past lives are just more aftershocks being released. All consciousness is alive, whether we view it as good or bad, or with indifference. Our old 3D life is off its respirator, gasping for its last few breaths. As you move more fully into your new 5D "thinking," letting go of your old 3D/4D needs and habits, more dross of this nature will start to break up and dissolve. If you are holding on to any unresolved pieces, there's no better time to let go of them than *Now.* Actually, there is no other time than the *now* in 5D. Left with a planet in dire need, and a HUmanity that is still very sick with the disease of HUman separation, we truly have a very small window of time to get to whatever issues remain.

Excuse Me, Does Anyone Know Where the Manual Is?

Ascension is a tricky bird. Even though we are evolved 5D HUmans, we also have to learn how to accept responsibility for our new capabilities and the impact we have on the world. The good news is that an initial grace period comes with reaching 5D. It's the least the Universe can do, given the crazy fact that as LightWorkers we are simultaneously trying to write the manual on how to fly our new 5D plane while at the same time, behind the controls and operating it. While we are figuring out how to work the fuselage, without the guidance of an experienced pilot at our side, it's not only easy to make mistakes *(read: understatement)* but downright frightening. As we continue forward as *5D LightWorker Houdinis,* please try to stay calm and centered when unexpected turbulence arises. Errors, mistakes, and a myriad of "WTF's?" along the way are only surfacing for needed *course corrections.* Although jarring, often these bumps are the results of our old 3D fears surfacing and scaring us into a moment of panic and insecurity. Our kneejerk reaction is to reach for an old 3D/4D operating manual and try to apply the outdated instructions to our new 5D HUman. Fortunately, because we are *awake now,* and not so much "sleeping at the wheel" anymore, we are more likely to do a lot less damage or cause irreparable harm. For the sake of all of us, hopefully, *I'm right about this.* LOL

Remember, in this lifetime, we are encouraged to first teach ourselves how to live from this new 5D higher perspective, and then to vibrationally model that for others. In the *bigger picture* mission that we are blessed to be a part of, by doing our assigned parts, we leave the world and HUmanity in a much more evolved state than it was when handed to us by prior generations and dimensions. Really try to revisit this 5D gem of pragmatic wisdom often, as it may help you to stop blaming, shaming, and feeling a need to make excuses for yourself about what you *should have, or could have done,* purpose-wise.

Although there was no 5D manual handed to us before we headed out on the journey, we weren't *completely* left to our own devices. We had and will continue to have "badass" spiritual guidance from a plethora of Higher Dimensions, Beings, and other really cool 5D HUmans.

Making the 5D transition is not for the thin skinned. There were and will continue to be a lot of trip ups, missteps, and occasions of "friendly fire" on our way through to higher ground. Fumbling, confusion, and fear of the unknown are parts of the learning process with anything new, especially something of this never-before-done magnitude.

Most of us are still using the operating manual that holds the 3D instructions, even though we have already spiritually stepped over into 5D. It takes time to fully wake to our new existence. We will keep hitting the snooze button repeatedly, until we are ready and able for our emotional and physical 5D selves to integrate all the many moving parts needed for a complete 5D immersion.

In many ways, 5D can be very challenging. Not necessarily because it is hard, but mainly because without a step-by-step *instruction manual,* we are having quite the time trying to figure out how to operate our brand-new, built-in, fully upgraded 5D *GPS (God-Person Satellite).* Reconstructing a new path through often rocky terrain begs the question "How can we lead without being aligned with our once familiar *old* coordinates?" Without the guardrails of 3D religion, authority, and a God that rules from outside of us policing our every move, the new 5D paradigm of higher consciousness dictates a new mandate. It is at the new vibrational summit where you become more *responsible for yourself, and your actions,* opposed to being controlled and monitored by more familiar outer authorities. For many of us, the prospect of being *accountable* for ourselves is a lot scarier than trying to evolve from spending 27,000 years in 3D hell.

So, how does one move forward and navigate 5D, when it seems like such a monumental task? You begin by making an initial commitment to staying awake and, no matter what is placed before you, reducing your 3D learned response of "hitting the snooze button," then over time, eliminating it all together. When you are willing to face what *you* have placed before you, have your feelings about it and take full responsibility for your choices regarding it, then you have placed yourself at the controls and made the decision to be present and fully live in the *now*. *That's it, folks!*

Initially, you'll be mostly working on decreasing the old, hardwired reaction that quietly signals you to look away, make excuses, avoid, sugarcoat, minimize, or placate a situation, feeling, truth, or reality. Even if at first you choose not to react or even respond, by suppressing it or erasing it all together, you inadvertently reinforce your old, outdated 3D teachings. You also give yourself the message in boldface print that on some level, you won't be able to *handle* it either emotionally or practically.

3D tenets have conflated being present with our feelings and the fear that facing them, or a situation will destroy either you, the other person, or the circumstances at hand. This core, built-in "panic button" was created on the principles of 3D duality. The 3D system of opposites continually reinforced the crystal-clear message that, in a reality based in *duality*, there can only be one winning outcome—either me or you, never us or we. Beginning to at least question some of those ingrained thoughts, messaging, and ideologies is the foundation needed to help your 3D brain prepare to release old programming and make room for some new *dendrites* to form.

As I referenced previously, the real disease that HUmanity is suffering from is separation, a fact that was lit up and magnified at the height of the COVID pandemic. But in addition, the frequency of 3D duality has literally *kept* our *souls* divided into many pieces and selves. In 4D, we spent countless hours working on our healing of the shattered 3D self; but in 5D, there is no more healing to do—just the gentler process of blending back together and *"wholing."* 5D brings more opportunities to connect aspects of our *souls,* bring ourselves back to a state of wholeness by calling back pieces of us that we may not have connected with for thousands of lifetimes.

As we have been scratching and clawing to find our way back into this moment, it is still not an anomaly for many of us to feel isolated and alone, more often than not. It's very important for all of us to be reminded that at no time throughout our journey were we ever sent into any situation or battle alone. *Never, not once.* There are so many invisible forces at work on our behalf, constantly giving us signs directing us, redirecting us, and letting us know that we are not in this alone. If your choice is awakened-ness, then know that these signs are abundant and there for the taking. If we ask for help, help will come. If we ask for Love, Love will come. If we ask for a sign, a sign will appear.

I think that's a really important message to constantly remind ourselves of. We can often feel forgotten, left to our own devices, and on a rudderless trek to nowhere. 3D living had us looking under every rock, towards our partners, friends, religion, and government officials, to name a few, to provide us with a sense of being seen and valued. 5D life comes with *Self-Love and God strength* as some of our newly built-in superpower features.

The higher our frequency goes, the closer we get to our God selves. Our vibrational levels are more refined, as they are *now* able to carry more Light than in prior dimensions. Other support systems and entities from similarly vibrating dimensions or higher can more easily communicate, impact, and guide us with our newly expanded 5D electrical grid.

THE 5D UPGRADE

There's never been a more important time on the planet. We need to work in community with our higher-level-based coworkers, not only for ourselves and future generations, but Mother Earth herself. Earth has housed us and fed us for thousands of years. *Now* more than ever, she is in dire need of our attention, support, and Love.

And I just want you to know that I know how tough it's been on your HUman aspect, for it's been both a challenging and a confusing time to be alive. When this segment of our work is done, whenever that may be, you are going to be able to look back and feel *really good* about what we have accomplished. Not all of us, but most HUmans on the planet who've been on the frontlines as LightWorkers, have had most of the details of the specifics of our *bigger picture* work kept consciously from us. Despite that, some have been so blessed and still able to do the work with more awareness and consciousness than others. But truthfully, most of the HUmans on the planet have not been able to remember what their roles are here, what they agreed to do, or even why they incarnated. Just keep this in mind as you see the conflicts play out while the 3D world as we know it begins to melt down and dissolve. There is no way around it. The *3D Shadow will rise.* Your work and knowledge places you far ahead on the learning curve.

Remember, before you incarnated, you had a clear understanding of what you were signing on for and the importance of the service contracts you had greenlit. The trick to managing it all *now* is being able to stay conscious and awake and live in the *now* as we move through this unprecedented planetary transition. Please try not to equate your *soul's* inner knowing of the task with the task being easy.

Your *soul* did know, and does know, the full scope of your assignments, *despite* how much your HUman self will struggle to make sense of all that transpires in your life and the world. *Both* experiences are true. We are multidimensional beings, juggling several realities that are all playing out at the same time.

5D Adulting

As with most experiences that were born out of the constructs of 3D duality and 4D polarization, many of our 5D responses will require tweaking and a whole lot of perspective "retooling."

The emotional aspect of our 3D/4D adult was very different from our 5D adult's counterpart. All 3D/4D adults were born into this world as babies and, unless you were a part of twin, triplet, *or one of the Octomom kids,* you came in alone. You grew up through the normal developmental stages and had years of time to be shaped, influenced, or even *screwed up* while learning about yourself and the 3D world around you. When we arrived at our current, awakened level of 5D consciousness (even though it took us 27,000 years to get here), we didn't arrive alone or as babies. The paradigm shift happened over a period of time. The raised *collective consciousness* created a global *tipping point* and triggered our Ascension. Although some children *now,* specifically those born after 2012, are being born into 4D/5D, most HUmans have arrived in 5D as adults.

The new 5D timeline happened *during* our lives, not while we were between lifetimes. Our customary process for reaching adulthood in 3D was much slower and more delineated. In addition to navigating the *deemotionalizing* of our reactions, there is no childhood, developmental stage, or adolescence in which to learn and practice being an adult 5D HUman. This learning might seem daunting at first but one of the most important features of being a 5D adult is to remember that your new HUman self comes equipped with the built-in capability to experience and handle the panoply of 5D emotions and developmental jumps in the new HUman timeline.

Because of prior conditioning, it is easy to fall back on our old beliefs and habits. We expect our feelings and reactions to play out as they did when we were 3D/4D children or adults. When we are experiencing uncomfortable feelings, often our innate reaction is to avoid, suppress, or emote (in an extreme measure) at all costs. We were conditioned growing up to believe that if we expressed, acknowledged, or even felt feelings fully, they would somehow be the end of us—or worse, the end of someone else.

Feelings in 3D were either painful, scary, or debilitating, and often led us to face a much-dreaded disappointment in ourselves, others, or God. Often associated with distress, rejection, betrayal, and loss, in 3D/4D disappointment usually punctuated a setback or indicated a blow to an expectation. Disappointments often hurt, were awkward, or put a pause, if not a full-blown end, to our plans.

No matter what dimension you experience them in, *disappointments* are a difficult part of life for adults as well as children. But as 5D adults, we can *now* choose to see ourselves as more capable, evolved beings who are able to experience all our challenging feelings from a higher perspective.

As you move into 5D, you will find a new level of confidence in your ability to look at everything more expansively from the *bigger picture* perspective. With that, the necessity to revisit many of your prior beliefs, opinions, and concepts of truth will be nonoptional. What was once true for you in your existence in prior dimensions may not necessarily be true for you as a 5D HUman. Your newly expanded 5D self is in the process of outgrowing even the aspects of your needs and desires that you once considered "right."

Any premise of "rightness" in the 3D/4D duality paradigm was anchored by a *strong belief or feeling*. Any change or shift away from it, often triggers a polarized 4D emotional or energetic charge. The 3D/4D emotional body aspect of our HUman self still holds opposition, judgments, fears, and resistance, which often leads us to make decisions that are products of our emotionally fueled, polarized reactions.

As we connect more deeply with our 5D selves, we move further away from making choices through an emotional body "sieve." 5D delivers us to a new foundational premise of triality where we begin to create choices as a response to what we need or want, not from emotionally charged resistance to an opposite choice.

3D/4D *Reaction* Choices vs. 5D *Response* Choices

We can *now* live from choice. There are three main paths and three main corresponding realities that we are *now* constantly juggling at any one time. In 3D, we choose from *duality* and *powerlessness*. In 4D, we choose from *polarity* and *emotions*. In 5D, we choose from *triality* and *feelings*.

Duality created a division in how we viewed, experienced, and decided on most things. 3D consciousness, and all the ways we used to be conditioned to perceive, ran its course and eventually turned on its own masters. Created by HUmans, it forced us to take sides about almost everything we personally valued or identified with. Singularity dictated that there were correct choices vs. incorrect choices. The 3D mind has always cataloged "right or good" choices as the ones "we" chose and the ones that "others" chose as "wrong or bad" choices.

Take your favorite or most comfortable pair of shoes as an example. If they don't fit anymore, you don't have to remind yourself that you didn't do anything wrong and aren't being punished. Your feet grew and it's time for a new pair of shoes. That's all. We don't *sit shiva* over the loss of the old shoes (*OK, maybe for our most favorite)* or reject and begrudge the new pair that *now* fits us comfortably. Hopefully, somewhere in a sane moment, we knew that it was never about the shoe, only that our feet naturally grew bigger.

Viscerally hardwired into our belief systems, duality superimposed personal truths, choices, and beliefs on our views, lifestyles, and self-expression. When any opposing view presented itself to us, our brains were programmed to experience a different choice as a foreign object, something to push back on, make wrong, or debunk. This conditioned response is at the core of most chaos we are *now* seeing in the world today. Some of the initial growing pains that 4D consciousness brings has made it nearly impossible for everyone to live in a harmonious, multifaceted, multichoice world.

As you move into 5D, it's important to challenge your "rope-a-dope" responses to your prior decisions and choices. Many spiritually evolved beings, including me, are challenged by this *bigger picture* "ask." Choices that are filtered through emotions and expressed through *reactions*, usually have grabbed their fuel from past baggage or projected expectations. Choices that are filtered through our 5D heart, mind, and feelings are presented in a more balanced form as a *response*. They have less baggage and come from inspiration and not resistance. Your feet have "just" outgrown your shoes. When you *5De-emotionalize,* all the drama morphs into just simple facts and noncharged choices. You get to the core of your truth, without all the emotional smoke and mirrors of 3D conditioning.

Getting Your 5D *Freq* On!

As beings used to identifying who we are and what we want through the strength and reactions of our various emotions, it is quite disorienting to have to readjust our lens and view life without a filter of duality. It can feel like you have lost your footing a bit as your choices of partners, sexual orientation, career goals, beliefs, and the limiting, hardwired "truths" you once possessed begin to melt away. Life starts morphing in ways that you may have never considered viable, and an abundance of newly constructed realities are yours for the taking as your prior level of vibrational consciousness evolves.

It's common, initially, to feel afraid as the newfound expansion seems like you are rapidly falling down the side of a mountain without a tree branch in sight to grab and break your fall. 3D/4D consciousness would have us believing that if a particular shift or change brings up fear, uncertainty, anger, loss, grief, or disappointment, then the change is most likely not a *good* thing or at least something to be avoided in earnest. Whatever *polarized* response you eventually land on, it doesn't change its core objective, which is in 5D to reflect your growth.

New changes (aka growth) often conjure up a lot of fear at first, but you will integrate them much more quickly when they are acknowledged and allowed rather than judged. This is a very important concept to grasp because entering the higher realms is often experienced as massive change on *steroids*. The feeling of moving up the dimensional ladder is similar to the symptoms of altitude sickness. It can be very disorienting and produce physical symptoms such as nausea and irregular breathing until you eventually adjust to the higher frequency.

Higher frequencies expand our consciousness and with this comes "change" in equal proportion. When change of any kind shows up in your life, your symptoms are just showing you *that you had a major spurt of growth*. Your responses versus reactions to growth will determine whether you will perceive it as a positive or negative phenomenon. You *now* have a plethora of multidimensional options to choose from—so, choose them all!

A shift of consciousness is often most challenging to those who are firmly identified with being on an extreme side of an issue, whether it is a personal disagreement, a political argument, or a medical ideology. From the spiritually evolved to those who think more traditionally, some of the most well-intended *souls* on the planet often fail to realize that their personal choices, *when charged by strong emotions,* are still contributing to the paradigm of 3D/4D polarity and our core wound of HUman separation. We've seen this conundrum play out in full force during the COVID pandemic in the arguments that pitched vaccinated people against unvaccinated people who felt concerned that they might lose their right to choose or choice of treatment. Most of us don't realize that even a sound choice based on preference loses its *bigger picture* impact when we *emotionalize* the choices we make in order to stand our ground. 5D responses offer another way; one that doesn't need HUmans to weaponize their feelings to validate their perspective.

The force field that polarity organically creates can only foster tension, intensity, and opposition. HUmans have not only begun turning on one another, but against the Earth and all its life-sustaining resources. *The resolution of any polarized issue can never be found on the polar end of any spectrum of belief.* But try telling someone who feels righteous about their position on vaccines, mask wearing or abortion rights that they may be *part of the problem and not the solution.* All very hard to hear, but from a distance, it's *bigger picture,* vibrationally true.

It's not necessarily in the actual making of a choice that a 3D/4D construct is reinforced, but the *intensity* in which you hold that belief and then charge it with your old emotional body that matters. When we learn not to process what we believe and want through a 3D/4D polarized lens, we can let go of the forcefields that are actually keeping our situation locked in suspended animation. Just out of reach becomes our heartfelt desire for a real *re-soul-*ution.

The degree of the emotional frequency with which we charge our beliefs, truths, and choices is what determines how flexible we can be when presented with something new or different. It's the loosening of our *emotional reactions* to issues that reduces the energy charge keeping us from growing, evolving, and healing our life-threatening disease of HUman separation.

In 5D, when the emotional body is relegated to the back seat for the next scheduled ride through time and space, our choices multiply, our views expand, and our *souls* express themselves more fully than they have ever been able to before while living in a physical body. When we shift away from our old familiar ways of making choices, we create new *soul*-utions and potential options that come from the transmutation of the energy field.

It's What You *Vibrate* to That Matters, *Not* What You *Do* Anymore

In any way you can, use your inner Light to lead the way and usher in our brand-new 5D world. In the process, you will be holding the door open for many others who are trying to find their way also through the darkness of the rising 3D Shadow.

For starters, break the debilitating 3D habit of feeling *insignificant*. Become aware of the ways you look away from truth and *feign powerlessness*. Confront stifling non-truths that tell you that you're not a higher-frequency player who carries spiritual clout or can make a difference. Look at everything squarely in its 3D face both in the wider world and in your personal life. Trust that in even the worst circumstances, something higher is trying to break through—that is, if you are brave enough to let it. Hold the space for this new world order to crystallize and become the dominant norm. This is what you came in to do. *So do it.*

You don't need to have a healing practice, a crystal ball, or the skill of Jesus to multiply loaves of bread. Know that you have everything you need within your heart for instantaneous retrieval on a cellular level. You can be a banker, computer programmer, or punch tickets for rides at an amusement park. You can be homeless, park cars in a garage, or sell hots dogs from a pushcart. You don't have to be employed, have children, or a traditional degree or title. In 5D, "it's not what you do that matters, *it's what you vibrate to!*" Resonance is the new gig.

This edict is going to come as a shock to many. Things that our egos were once very attached to in our prior dimension are going out with the 3D tide. The only thing that will be significant going forward is how you vibrate via your thoughts, beliefs, and emotions. Are you attuned to the wisdom of your sense perceptions? *If you chose to,* you wouldn't even have to speak a word in 5D to do what you are here to do you: vibrate to a higher frequency of thought, Love, and Light. Done. Mic drop.

Your vibration is composed of many things, including how open your heart is, the degree of your "True Compassion" for the HUman struggle, the amount of God-Light that you carry and your willingness to trust yourself, stay awake, and show up. The Universe will place you exactly where your vibration wants you to be. Sometimes that means you are in your car, listening to music, waiting for the Light to change when another car pulls up behind you or someone passes in front of you in the crosswalk. *That's it.* Other times, it might mean that you walk into a coffee shop and smile at the barista as you order your latte or throw your garbage out and someone walks down your street near you. *That's it.*

Often our vibration is called upon to be in an exact place at a specific moment in time—although no words or eye contact will ever be exchanged between the two parties involved or the surrounding environment. The energy field of those we pass on the street or ride in an elevator with are all influenced by our vibrational frequency, and we by theirs. Just by being in relatively close proximity *(or miles apart across the continent)* the contract is completed.

In 5D, our service contracts are often *soul contracts* and not Karmic contracts anymore. They are diverse as they are creative. Often more subtle and effortless, they can frequently appear benign. 5D will start teaching us a more powerful way of impacting and creating through the feminine energy field of *"being."*

The 5D *Inner*-Net: You Are an Advanced HUman Cell Tower!

In essence, we are starting to become like our own 5G cell towers, communicating through our frequencies without ever speaking a word or needing to be in the same room as those whom we need to connect with. We are in constant communication with those we pass on the street and in the cars driving next to us, like the UPS HUman who just dropped off a package at the front door. We don't even have to know the individuals we are communicating with or to have officially accepted the job assignment of crossing frequencies.

We also assist, teach, and guide differently *now*. It's not that you will never be called on to step in and help, but it's important to begin to apply your higher understanding of the more elevated methodology. It may take a little doing for you to fully believe that you are being even "more" effective by learning to *allow, do less, and vibrate more*. The *bigger picture* asks of your new 5D HUman to uphold the frequency of who you are, but to please include all your *idiosyncrasies* as well as the things that make sense to your choice of reality. You are an integral part of the 5D *inner-net*,[1] and like the 5D HUman morse code system that you are *now*, just by learning to *be*, you can impact all the people, places, and things that you signed off on in your updated 5D *Soul* Contracts.

As you come to understand this simple truth, it also becomes very tempting to help others see things through your new set of eyes and understanding, especially those who are really struggling with *fear*. Leading (*read: insisting, forcing, judging, conveying spiritual elitism*) people to see things your way in 5D is a misguided attempt at a spiritual directive or altruism. You are on a whole different wavelength *now,* and those who are still experiencing a 3D/4D reality (which also includes you) will not be able to absorb your version of truth in a way that will bring them some necessary relief. As a matter of fact, you might find that your take on things *spins them out emotionally even more* and may drive them further away from you and your beliefs. This is not easy to learn and understand at first because your instinct is to try to help them as you attempt to convey a *bigger picture* concept in *your* chosen familiar language. In actuality, you are speaking to them in the foreign language of 5D. They may not understand you, your motives, or your newfound awareness. Initially, this shift of consciousness will only make sense to others who speak your "language" or are just beginning to learn this new one. *Tread lightly.*

If you find yourself often engaging as a helpful person in this way, most likely you are going to feel very burned out over time. It's frustrating at best, and mainly for the sake of your own *sanity*, it would behoove you to look within and kindly remind yourself: Both *you, and a large majority of the world, are not in Kansas anymore.*

In 5D, although we are often on a continual reconnaissance mission to pick up as many survivors as possible, it can be very confusing for us at first because many of our service contracts back in 4D were agreements to *save, fix, and heal* as many HUmans as we could fit into one Ascension. We were on triple duty, to help get *ourselves, as well as many others (friends, clients, family peeps)* on the 5D lifeboat before 3D reality closed in on us once again.

In 4D, we brought the boat to others, swam out to get them, and pleaded with them to get on.

In 5D, you go out on the boat first, splashing around in the water, sunning, playing with the other adorable 5D HUmans and sea creatures—sending out to your surroundings your 5D sonic signal and you *wait*. All the while keeping a (third) eye out for the other HUmans who pick up and connect to your signal, watching for them as they follow your radar, spot you, and start swimming on over. It is at that point that you welcome them and help them join you on the boat. Ahhh . . . No more of the old service matrix of 3D/4D codependency otherwise you will short-circuit, blow a fuse, and get resentful, arrogant, and judgmental when it backfires. And it *will*.

We spent lifetimes in 3D survival, victimization, and enslavement programs. I don't have to tell you that it has been hell. And because this old agenda was "etched" into our vibration, it's *now* a little tricky to fully shake it out without feeling like we are abandoning HUmanity, Earth, and those we care about and Love. The prior mission we were on has changed. If we keep trying to act on and fulfill that old 4D agenda, it will eventually become very problematic for us and the 5D world in ways that we can't even fathom yet. It's harder to switch habits *now* and switching dimensions can sometimes feel surreal, so our thought processes will need all of our undivided attention.

Thus, my familiar 5D battle cry repeats itself once again. "It's not what you *do,* but what you *vibrate* to that matters!" With its more expanded Lightbody, 5D offers a much better reception through our newly advanced broadcasting abilities. It needs us to be in our hard-earned higher vibrations.

We Teach Through Entrainment

Our *soul* assignments can *now* include ones we consciously take on and ones that our Higher Selves assign to us. Our higher 5D frequencies are also being utilized for *entrainment*. All we need to do is casually pass by a specific person on the street, in the grocery store, or during an afternoon Starbucks run and our 5D vibration gives that individual a boost of some 5D energy or a frequency adjustment that will *trigger* their next new "ah-ha" or "oh-no" moment.

This may be why you get an occasional intuitive *ping* to take an unexpected break in your workday, go to the water cooler to "meet" someone, call your bank, and speak with a "random" customer service HUman who is able to resolve your issue quickly, or take a different route home. In 3D, such things are called *coincidences,* in 4D gut feelings or "intuitive hits." In 5D, we understand these events as *soul* contract messages, coded by frequency and direct forms of communication.

In 5D, the individual you just zapped with your vibration as you walked by didn't just pop up on your radar screen because of a random algorithm. It's more likely that sharing your frequency with them may have been one of your higher assignments scheduled for that day—or that sharing theirs with you was theirs! The interaction with a HUman may prove to be benign, helpful, or very obnoxious and rude. If that ever happens, there is a good chance that the exchange was probably from a 3D aspect of yourself or the other HUman or it was *exactly* what either or both of you needed to occur.

Whatever the exchange experience is or is not for both of you, your multidimensional being most likely will be receiving two levels from the impact of your energies crossing: a 3D-based mundane question answered (or not) and/or a 5D energy exchange in some form of a download. All our 5D experiences with 3D HUmans or our own 5D peeps are never one sided. They affect both parties even if you reside on different dimensional levels.

What matters is how awake we are and how willing or capable we or another HUman is about "looking under the hood" for the *bigger picture* story that might be presenting itself to us through that experience. The blue skies pass the dense, gray clouds of the mundane. Often in 5D, what is mainly asked of us repeatedly is to stay awake so we can show up in the "*now.*" You need to be in the *now* so that when you get that tug to call the bank or take a walk or be sad (if you are feeling sad), the awake person (within reason), heeds the call. The majority of our 5D assignments are unconscious ones. Along with our feelings, thoughts, and the signals from our newly wired "inner-net," we *now* have everything we need to navigate this "second-round" incarnation. That's how all this current incarnation stuff works.

Although all our prior 4D *intuition* skills still remain very active, as we evolve into 5D, our *Spidey sense* gets a "booster rocket" enhancement in the form of our newly awakened seventh sense: *absorption*. Absorption allows us to totally use every fiber of our being, including every cell or strand of hair, to act as a transmitter for information and data that's coming into us, and for the information and data that we are sending out.

Our 5D selves are akin to the upgraded technology inside that *next-gen* smartphone you just purchased. Initially, most of us are so excited by all its new features that we feel we have to have it. Once home, we are either clueless on how to use the more advanced apps, or we don't want to take the time to learn how to use the features that would ultimately make our lives easier and run more efficiently. *Sound familiar?* It will take time, commitment, patience, and a whole lot of rote learning to operate our new 5D HUman systems! Over time, as we continue to release the 3D brain's old limitations, more of the new operational system can be activated. This will enable us to create more of the new reality.

From what I hear, once we are up and running on all twelve cylinders, we will blow away any new iPhone, technology, or artificial intelligence out there in our world today. Your HUman self is the "I" phone, the "inner-net," and the more advanced "5" G cell towers!

5D as a *Second Language*

The paradigm of 5D is rich with symbolism, metaphors, and vibrationally coded frequencies. It uses images, events, circumstances, objects, and feelings as conduits that allows us, others, and those of the unseen world to communicate information back and forth. In 5D, most *signs* are specifically designed and coded just for *you*. Even if at first the messages aren't easy to decipher, acknowledging them will make it easier to interpret or intuit their meanings. Over time, with patience and practice, shifting from your *"surface*-based" 3D thinking, to your newer *"multilevel"* awareness of 5D perception will enhance your ability to see in the dark and navigate the density of 3D fog.

In 3D, you were conditioned to see only what was directly in front of you. And just like a plane flying through the clouds, your depth of field was severely limited. Although there might be a bright sun, blue skies, or majestic mountains on the other side of the floating powder puffs, none of them is visible to you until you are able to *see* past them. And no matter what dimension it is that you might call home, we all can agree that the clouds and sun *coexist*, even if sometimes they can't be seen simultaneously.

5D gives you a permanent set of *night vision lenses,* so you can see past the limited reality of 3D to explore other possibilities, reasons, and explanations for *why* things happened in your life—whether in your relationships, finances, or health—or appear one way versus another in the often-perplexing contemporary world. It takes us out of a very limited perception of how life works, why it isn't always fair, and why we feel deeply victimized by our past wounding and stories. It allows us not to negate our betrayals or bury our pain, but to be more compassionately awake so we may experience them from a multidimensional perspective, then release and heal from them more quickly.

Although 5D uses the very same spoken and written languages that we are accustomed to using to express ourselves in 3D/4D, those same forms of communication serve as conductors that transmit higher-frequency messages. Messages can be transmitted through words, sound, and speech *(like the words written in a book)* above and beyond our surface-level interpretation of the meanings they are designed to convey. Languages are utilized on two levels: the *familiar or mundane level,* to express a thought, concept, or action; and the *vibrational or transcendental level,* to convey a message, teaching, channeled instruction, or insight through frequency and code. The second level is a higher-level form of communication as it relays messages back and forth between your higher self, higher entities, guides, or Universal friends and you.

When one is *awake,* written words in the form of an article, street sign, billboard, movie script, or even a matchbox cover, can be interpreted with a deeper meaning. The printed material can contain personalized instructions, information, ideas, and reminders, or even shift your frequency!

As you begin to work with these new concepts, your understanding of your new HUman self will integrate more easily as you incorporate your ability to *speak and understand* the 5D vernacular. Before you get too excited, it's not going to sound very different or like the Elvish language spoken in *The Lord of the Rings*. Although its syntax is the same that you have been using in 3D/4D, it's meaning will have a broader bandwidth.

The words themselves will *now* pass through not only five of your traditional 3D senses, but at *least* another two (and counting) additional ones. Words and sentences will not only reflect a direct meaning but will be *encoded* with a vibrational frequency that is specific and germane just to you. Sort of like a dog whistle that only you can hear, certain words, images, situations, and experiences will carry information, directions, and details that are programmed by your higher selves (yes, *selves*).

As you grow into your new frequency, the more you will train yourself to stay awake to every precious moment, and the easier it will be for you to remember what you need to do to sustain this new dimension and function optimally within it. If you frighten easily, let me assure you that you won't be hearing strange voices and the *Ghosts of Christmas Past* won't show up beside your fireplace mantle to scare the "bejesus" out of you just for kicks. Your new language will most likely sound just like your own voice, thoughts, or feelings, only more so. The precursor is your advanced *awareness,* that fine tunes the clarity and focus of the messaging.

5D raises the volume on your "inner-net" connection to the unseen world.

What's important initially is *not* to dismiss your wonderful attempts with this new level of self-communication. We often take the time to listen to others, *but not to ourselves.* Making the time to connect to your thoughts, showing up in a different way, and being present for your God-Light will determine how much you will allow in and how deeply you will allow a higher self-Love to guide you.

You have one main *"soul map"* now, as the aspect of you in your mundane life merges with the many aspects of you in your transcendental life. We are moving from 3D/4D Karmic contracts to 5D *soul* contracts. Never, while still in the physical body, have we had this kind of access to our *soul's* Light, God selves, and the entire Multiverse. If honed properly, the level of interdimensional communication and personal instruction could be simply *"out of this world"!* Like any other new language or form of communication, we must first learn it through lots of rote, then reinforce and practice it *continually.* The vernacular of 5D isn't necessarily difficult; it's just brand, spanking new . . . *Nanu-Nanu.*

As higher-dimensional planetary citizens, we will be downloading trends, directional choices, and transfiguration codes for Mother Earth. The next few years will determine the course on which HUmanity sets Planet Earth. These codes are *now* able to enter our new 5D vibrational fields, for our new energy bodies can both recognize and download those codes very rapidly.

The Faster Timeline Changes *Everything*

In the next few years, we will experience big realizations, *soul-utions,* and breakthroughs, particularly developments in the field of medicine. The pace of 5D time and space constructs is faster. From the perspective of our time continuum, at first it may feel a little scary because we are used to experiencing life and functioning on the slower 3D timeline. We saw a worldwide backlash of skepticism about the efficacy of the COVID vaccine due in part to the *speed* at which it came out because people were frightened. Their conditioned thought forms said, "For a vaccine to be safe, it should take many years to develop and undergo *many* trials of its efficacy."

Whether or not this is true is not my point, but a lot of that "reaction" was from the boilerplate of our prior 3D timeline construct. We're going to see things like this happening, especially medically, in ways that seem quicker and revolutionary. The worldwide life or death crisis of COVID caused scientists—doctors, researchers, and public health administrators—to step out of their 3D conditioning, based on the dynamics of competition, and move into the extremely efficient *"hive mind"* mentality of 5D HUman cooperation.

The 5D benefit of the international community's "beehive" approach to collaboration was how it focused all experts and efforts aimed towards one common goal: creating viable vaccines. The *world* also needed medications that could serve as an initial intervention, especially during he earlier stages when many people were getting sick, being hospitalized, and dying. Why was this important to our post-5D Ascension? Because bigger than any virus, pandemic, or potential side effect, the underpinning that was festering for eons of time— long before the arrival of COVID—is and continues to be the pervasive disease of HUman separation.

Hive mentality is a byproduct of our new 5D world. And even if you do not choose to ascribe to this particular type of medicine, the move towards unifying expertise in the form of a "one mind" approach vibrationally contributed to suturing up a small area in the torn fabric of HUmanity's divisive 3D duality paradigm.

You are going to start experiencing a major quickening on the planet in the next few years. And along with healing another part of our great divide, 5D will be sending out multiple calls for *all* of us to look at how our strong reactions, one way or another, became the real culprit behind what eventually became a *brick partition* rather than just an individual "choice." There will be many more of these opportunities to revisit this HUman misstep and for us to find the good and the Light in all of God's creations and *medicines*. Although I am a big proponent and advocate of alternative treatments and holistic/vibrational medicines, many of them were also discovered during our long stay in 3D reality. Everything, be it traditional or holistic, will need to be upgraded to accommodate the 5D HUman form. Even my expertise and approach to Feng Shui design and principles had to be tweaked and updated *(5D Feng Shui)* to address the current needs of the advanced HUman and planet.

5D is the level of consciousness that touts *Triality* and *Unity*. Once everything is upgraded and transitioned, we will be confronted, very directly to look at *all* our views, opinions, and belief systems, especially regarding medicine. A combined and integrated system from all sides of the medical spectrum, including allopathy, homeopathy, and traditional and holistic medicines will all find themselves seated at the same dinner table, joining hands, breaking bread, and toasting to the God-Light in each of their individual and *now* combined greatness.

There will be a lot of medical breakthroughs and new approaches to healing devised over the next five to ten years.

At times, some of them might even be referenced as miracles! The word *miracle* is mostly associated with Jesus's actions during his relatively short, but world-changing stay on the planet. One of the most important components to anything referred to as a miracle is the "time" factor of the occurrence. Jesus is often depicted as healing someone in a moment who couldn't walk or see.

For centuries, we have equated miracles with a *rapid* outcome because many of the healings happened *instantaneously*. Jesus was a very evolved avatar, vibrating at a consciousness frequency that was higher than any other HUman who has ever walked this Earth. The higher your frequency, the faster the timeline. Jesus wasn't working from the lower 3D consciousness level that he was so brutally surrounded by. His healings took place at the speed they did because of his elevated frequency. While He was in the physical, most likely He was a 6D HUman or higher. His vibration back then planted the HUman seeds for our 5D Ascension that we have been cultivating and harvesting since the time He walked this Earth.

In 3D/4D, if someone is crippled, based on the 3D timeline structure and mentality, they might choose to find a good surgeon or possibly face a stark reality that they might never walk again. In the lower dimensions, healing has a specific protocol, and usually takes time. Those who are ill and injured are conditioned to process their experiences through the backdrop of the same dimensional timeline in which the injury or ailment was created. Our thinking, belief systems, and the speed at which we understand time influence our ability to heal and get well.

In 3D/4D, we were living in a timeframe built on an Earth year of 365 days, twenty-four hours per day, and seven days per week. We also rotate to those various time markers and have for a very long time.

In 5D, you will have to remind yourself often about the *"timeline"* change. DayLight savings time has nothing over on us! Initially things might feel like they are moving very fast, but it's not fast at all. It's just the normal timeframe in a 5D life. Try not to be so surprised, especially in your *own* life, if you feel like you are letting go of things or things are moving past and through you very quickly. This will be particularly evidenced in medicine, cures, and HUman healing.

On the old TV show, *I Love Lucy,* the characters Lucy and Ethel demonstrated what an out of control "5D conveyer belt" could look like when an enormous amount of chocolates began moving too quickly down the conveyor belt that they were stationed in front of at work. In a nanosecond, they couldn't keep up. They became overwhelmed and started eating the chocolates to try to manage the speed and the surplus. All hell broke loose as the acceleration became too much for them to handle.

5D normal is *different* than 3D/4D normal. Yes, speed is faster than in 3D, but it's a normal speed for 5D. It just feels fast because of the so many lifetimes we spent and became familiar with the 3D timeline. In 5D, time is more fluid and circular with fewer linear obstacles. With less dramas, traumas, codependency, fears, Karma and bullsh*t, things tend to move incredibly fast!

What's important to understand as you begin to *"rethink your thinking"* initially you might feel a bit thrown off and even confused as you go back and forth simultaneously living on several timelines and multiple dimensions (*3rd, 4th, 5th*). You will see this reflected in the world outside you, but you will also see this in your own day-to-day life. Relationships may develop quickly or seemingly *end* suddenly. Jobs and careers change. Relocating to other places on the planet, as you are called to be elsewhere for your *soul's* "second incarnation" work.

Our 3D/4D time programming and belief systems, still running concurrently with our new 5D selves will make it a little bit more challenging to sift through our feelings and intuition about what's right for us or what to discern as *truth*. A faster timeline means that you might feel a bit pushed at times, energetically being moved through shifts and changes more quickly, often before you even feel "ready." In our 3D/4D timeframe reference, a "successful" relationship was considered to last "till death do you part" or at least many, many years. But in 5D, you might find that everything you needed to *give and gain* from a marriage, or a particular relationship only required *five years, five months, or five days*. Sometimes the timelines move us quickly through the connection or situation, and a shorter connection only means the contract, and its objectives got completed sooner or that on the etheric level the contact was rewritten or in some instances, rerouted. It didn't need the prior dimensions elongated timeline. Imagine going back to your favorite telephone store and asking for an older model phone that is slower or to a computer store and asking for a computer with an antiquated processor to triple your wait time while downloading files. See my point?

You might find yourself moving through a lot of things rapidly. Knowing this will help you prepare for changes that might not make *any* rational sense in the moment. Even if you've yet to come anywhere near mastering it, it will reduce your 3D/4D instincts to either *"blame or shame"* yourself and others about what fell through, ended, or altogether disappeared.

Because we still have a core timeframe from 3D programming, when things start happening in a way that we perceive to be *too* fast or *too* slow, it can trigger angst, panic, frustration, and depression in us. At times, we will all think, *"How much more of this can I take? Nothing ever goes my way. My life sucks."* During those times, try to remember that the stress that feels like a deep squeeze of pressure on you is being exacerbated by your old construct of 3D thinking. *Be gentle, loving, and kind to yourself.* Take a step back and deemotionalize, and if you are really unhappy with the movie that is playing on your screen, feel around for the remote *(you are probably sitting on it)*, and switch the channel. It's all perspective and *now* you have several to choose from!

"Don't say you don't have enough time. You have exactly the same number of hours per day that were given to Helen Keller, Pasteur, Michelangelo, Mother Teresa, Leonardo da Vinci, Thomas Jefferson, and Albert Einstein."[2]

–H. Jackson Brown, Jr.

Remind yourself that phrases like *"I need time," "I need to do this slowly,"* and *"I need to start small"* are learned, fear-based 3D responses. Initially in 5D, our instincts will tell us to hit the brakes, slow the train, or when scared, abandon course. That's when a gentle reminder may be needed to help you navigate your transition. Breathe in, pause a moment, then try some 5D–talk yourself off the ledge–pep talks. Say, "Self, *the reason why everything feels too fast or unmanageable right* now *is because I have spent eons of lifetimes in 3D timelines. These circumstances are not moving faster than my 5D self can handle for I move even faster than the speed of Light* now, *I move at the speed of Love."*

5D often will ask you to trust that the Universe "always has your back." And it does. But that won't always comfort you–especially at first, when you are in the thick of it and surrounded by your worst, most paralyzing fears. During those times, often all you can do is to throw your hands straight up over your head and scream as loudly as you need to, then go binge on a bag of Fritos, *like I do!*

You will often feel like you are on a twisting, turning, massive rollercoaster ride! The 3D/4D speed at which we were accustomed to and able to *pump the brakes* and slow things down, if necessary, has *now* significantly morphed. As you adjust to your new life, you might have to frequently check that your "seatbelt" is on, secured, and comfortably tightened around your waist. You are being moved forward, although at times it might feel more like you are being *shoved*. Each micro adjustment is meant to place you into perfect alignment with your new frequency and your *bigger picture* plans. If you can look beyond all that is being presented to us on the surface you might agree that it is a powerful, blessed, and incredible time of miracles and happenings on the planet. You are absolutely *not* here by accident. You were first called (*OK, probably texted),* then *chosen.*

As we understand, embrace, and nurture our new lives and our *second* incarnations here, we will be able to embrace the world around us and the changes within us, HUmanity, and the Earth herself more swiftly and with *more Love and less fear.*

5D HUmans: The Second Coming of Christ

Those who have chosen to be here *now* and live as 5D HUmans are being referred to as the *Second Coming of Christ.* Please pause for a moment and respectfully take that in. As we evolve and connect more to our God selves and move deeper into the reverence of everything that Jesus spoke of, we are more likely to fulfill His hope that eventually HUmanity would be elevated to *resemble* Him. To be in His likeness. We have never been closer to His level of *soul* purity than we are *now*. And our HUman selves have never been closer to what is HUmanly possible than the possibilities that Jesus mirrored for us. Jesus was an Avatar, a God among men, *a highly evolved soul.* He showed us the zenith of compassion, healing, and an incredible Love for HUmankind, despite how He was seen, treated, betrayed, and crucified.

In many ways, what we are being called to do right *now* is to use our God-Light to teach HUmanity and Planet Earth to aspire to something greater. A part of HUmanity has Ascended, and with a shift of this magnitude, those very beautiful *souls* will carry with them the potential to bring Jesus's teachings and heart-based intentions forward to influence major global change.

Most of us were around back then during the time period of Jesus. Heck, my last name in this lifetime translated into English from its Italian roots means *St. Peter.* Need I say more? It's so good to connect with you all again after all these lifetimes, and by the way, *wow, you guys are looking marvelous!*

Find the *5D Courage* to Step into the Moment

Because there are a lot fewer obstacles in 5D, a lifelong search for a purpose or a path is no longer needed. As the final remaining 3D/4D Karmic programs are dissolved and released, so are many of the distractions and obstacles that we became so accustomed to slowing us down. In 5D, *all* that is being asked of you is to stay awake, and grounded, and live in the *now.* You already got the "job." It's your life.

Frustration and stress could come into play for our new HUman selves both because of our expectations for our "work" and because of our impatience with what we perceive to be delays. We are highly evolved *souls* who have forgotten that sometimes we just need to do the dishes, watch mindless TV, or go walk the dog. We struggle often, and unnecessarily, as we perceive mundane daily tasks and actions as unimportant, imagining them as things that take us away from what we "really" should be doing.

Also, the 3D/4D ego is still motivated by "doing" and status. It's a big part of who we were and at times will continue to be, as it will hang around our multidimensional self as long as we are still on the planet. Try not to make it wrong. It just needs some guidance for it functions very differently from the updated 5D brain.

In 5D, everything that you need to do, experience, or address will be placed in your path, either magnetized to you or somehow presented to you. That *doesn't* mean that you won't be expected to take any actions, initiate anything, or set yourself in a particular direction. Instead, if you can move more into a state of grace, seeing everything that is placed on your canvas as part of your purpose, the reaching for and the judging of it will over time lessen. Without your HUman self constantly leaning forward to shape and create what *does or doesn't* happen in your life, your life's "true" work plan can drop, manifest, and unfold on your path more easily.

That's what *faith* and *trust* are all about, and the only person that can reinforce their own faith is *you*. 5D dictates and reinforces that only you know what you believe and what your heart tells you to be true. You wouldn't be led this far for this many lifetimes and then accidentally sLighted or dropped onto the wrong path.

Our ideas about what the *right path* should look like leads to more wrong messaging sent by the 3D/4D brain to your 5D heart. This often gasLights the whole system into believing that your life is just *not* working out and rapidly heading down a rabbit hole.

It's challenging to give up our belief systems about what *"working out"* should look like or even means? We scripted, then pursued our beliefs and vision of what we wanted to create from the original Petri dish of our first incarnation and life this time around. We often take that vision forward into 5D life and forget that it is associated with a different premise, objectives, and Karmic contracts. If we don't switch perspectives, a perpetual cycle of believing that you are stuck, lost, and without a direction can ensue.

SPOILER ALERT:

You are exactly where you should be.
You are not lost. You can't be.

3D/4D vs. 5D Trust

In 3D, we mainly only trusted ourselves, as we were reflected through organized religious leaders, ministries, our parents, societal norms, and all aspects of *outside* authority. We didn't understand the *bigger picture* at play and how the Universe worked or even how HUmans worked!

In 4D, we had to learn to trust ourselves and our *inner* authority as well as the more benevolent and aligned higher beings once again after eons of 3D manipulation, abuse, and betrayal.

In 5D, we are learning to trust in the *process* of the greater plan that is unfolding around us for everyone's higher good. This is a little more challenging at times for the "greater good premise" also includes what we perceive to be good and correct, especially when all that is unfolding around us seems to be negative. Embracing this higher plan reality also means allowing for perceived mistakes, foibles, and things in life (as we knew it) not making much sense anymore. It requires giving up the illusion of control and judgment of what we "think" is really happening. In releasing expectations and agendas, we then trust more in our day-to-day experiences and the world's reality also. Although life may not feel perfect, we trust that the *bigger picture* plan which is unfolding is more than "meets the eye." It has a rigor and purpose and knows how to navigate itself through, even if the route through certain aspects is redirected through a dark, dangerous, and ominous neighborhood at times during its journey.

If you only knew how many millions of things and moving parts need to come into play to create just one specific moment in time, it would blow your mind. His Holiness Professor Lin Yun Rinpoche was quoted as saying: *"It takes five hundred years of prayer and meditation for two different people to cross on the same boat."* We have now clearly gathered on the same boat, crossed several oceans together, and share the *good Karma* of the words placed on these pages.

Having this information or your "ah-ha" moment means you are beginning to find your way back to your new 5D *soul* contract at this precise juncture in time. Knowing that you are not going through your 5D transition alone will hopefully make this trek a little easier. Sometimes the information can feel more overwhelming than you hoped, but for myself, I'd rather know than be clueless and scared all the time, trying to fix something that isn't at all broken in the way we perceive it to be. Although it might not be the end of the world, in our reality, *it is* the end of the 3D world.

Don't Get Caught Up in *Spiritual Elitism*

As we move into a state of higher consciousness, we will also lead more heart-centered lives. The frequency of the heart is very different from the frequency of the survival-based 3D/4D lives that we just began to transition from. It can get very frustrating at times and feel like a heavy weight when we find ourselves surrounded by people we Love and a society that has not yet evolved to the comfort level of our new 5D awareness. It's tempting to spiritually posture and inadvertently judge people or act in a condescending manner.

5D consciousness reflects merely a portion of the current population. Although technically we are *all* in 5D, not everyone has awakened to that awareness yet. But for sure, it is a level of *consciousness* that is *now* available and accessible for all to rise to as they begin to awake. Our *bigger picture* Ascension hope is that most people will seek 5D consciousness or at least aspects of it before they get ready to leave the body.

Evolution is not easily measurable. The type of measuring that our brains are most familiar with was created at the 3D/4D level of consciousness. It was based in quantitative data derived from tangible metric units from both mathematics and science. As we move into a more expansive level of consciousness, subtler senses, such as intuition, absorption, HUman frequencies, dimensions, and quantum physics, will become more common measures.

Keep in mind that evolution is a very *personal* process. It's so easy to forget this and only focus on our chosen reality and perspectives during moments of frustration. It's easy to lose patience, especially when we mainly hover over aspects of Humanity's lower level actions and consciousness. When we do, we inadvertently contribute to the exact disease we are trying to transmute: *HUman separateness.* This creates a template of beliefs that separates us from the less evolved, but even worse, means we are inadvertently contributing to creating a world where differences are not celebrated but weaponized. Although we should take some pride in and feel good about not succumbing to the 3D pressures of racism, sexism or homophobia, *spiritual elitism* is still another isolating and lonely perch to view life from. Indirectly, we often blame others for vibrating from places of consciousness that we ourselves were once at. Maybe it's not the exact same branch of other forms of division, but, for sure, from the same HUman tree.

Most of us are pretty burned out from the thousands of post Atlantis and Lemuria *"mission impossible"* lifetimes that we endured. So, when current-day life, people, media, and politics bring you to your exhausted knees, try to remember that despite all of it, none of that and worse stopped us from getting to this point of a successful 5D Ascension on the planet. *Our God-Light and invisible cavalry proved themselves to be much more powerful than all the dark realities and Shadow side that HUmanity has revealed.* We don't need most of the HUmans to arrive at a certain level of higher consciousness all at the same time. We just need an overriding percentage of the population to tip the scales for the purpose of the highest good *most of the time.*

Along with the most evolved, when there is a full-on paradigm shift, *everybody* is bumped up to a new vibrational level at every level of consciousness. Even with those we deem "unconscious," the rise in frequency, if only incremental, still impacts all of HUmanity and the collective consciousness.

In 5D, the majority doesn't factor in the same way. It is only needed proportionately in much smaller amounts. We use "other" more highly evolved forms of measurements such as *Heart-felt Vibrations, God-Light, Soul Contracts, Multi-dimensional Forces, and the Power of Love* to shift consciousness. Remember, what truly makes an impact is what you *vibrate* to because, as a 5D being, your energy field will *now* impact everything and everyone a *thousand* times more than the energy that you used to wield when you were primarily in your 3D/4D self.

Our main objective *up until now* was evolving into a HUman that can break the 3D/4D vibrational glass ceiling and blow through the 5D sound barrier frequency while still in a physical body on Planet Earth. This newfound amplification is what gave us the ability to have our successful 5D Ascension back in 12/12/12 and use higher powered consciousness, Light and Love to help HUmanity shift and climb out of its remaining 3D Shadow. We achieved this aim despite our fears and perceptions of being *outnumbered, controlled,* or at times, *hopeless.*

We're in a different place right *now.* We no longer need the majority to be with us. As 5D multidimensional beings, we can coexist with people of lower frequencies in their 3D world. The more we hone our skills and our abilities, the more we hone our new biofield. The stronger and clearer our new vibration is, the less of an impact the 3D/4D world is going to have on us. Although we may live in different vibrational fields through *harmonizing* to all the different dimensional energies, we will learn how to peacefully coexist on the planet. We do not have to live in a totally unified world, but we also don't have to stay in our *respective (perspective?) corners of the ring* just because we have frequency differences. Many of our fears and frustrations regarding *others* who have different levels of vibration and consciousness are mainly propelled by antiquated, polarized 3D/4D thinking.

To sum it up, one of the key lessons learned from our devastating outcomes in Lemuria and Atlantis (and from additional attempts in other lifetimes) is that everybody *does not* have to be both evolved and in full resonance with the *bigger picture*, for HUmanity to evolve. We were waiting back then until *everyone* was on board to Ascend. Although our patience was both, polite and altruistic, we misjudged what was needed. That concern has *now* been updated and is no longer valid.

If Needed, *Fire* Yourself!

When we view something as a mistake, problem, or fatal, we are often experiencing a *"consciousness squeeze."* Although our gut reaction is trying to figure out an action to take or something to do to resolve or fix the situation, in 5D the easiest way to get the re-*soul*-ution under way is to try to expand your *"consciousness container"* first. This will begin to relieve some of the stress, fears, or worries that are exacerbating the circumstances and/or slowing down a higher outcome.

A mundane, but to-the-point example: If you are super thirsty and your usual companion, a sixteen-ounce container of water, is just not going quench it this time, then a simple *soul*-ution would be a larger container that *now* holds thirty-three ounces of your favorite H_2O. A larger container holds more water. More water guarantees better hydration.

Sure, life would be so easy if all our *soul*-utions were that simple, but what if getting more options and assistance was as easy as "creating the space" for them to enter? Huh? We often constrict our energy fields under duress, doing the exact opposite of what is needed to resolve the situation when fear obscures the path. And it will for all of us on any level or dimension, at one time or another.

Holding this very HUman truth front and center will allow you to move towards allowance and the acceptance of feeling the stymy and, more importantly, it will remind you to let go of your responsibility for being the *only* one working on the *soul*-ution. Pivot, let go, expand your container (energy field). Trust should become your new motto. Build it and they will come. Obviously, if it was meant for you to solve a situation alone, you would have solved it already. *Instead of* leaning in, working harder, stressing, and overthinking *(read: constricting your bandwidth),* try consciously releasing the constriction in your new *highly sensitive* 5D cell tower. Breathe, stretch, walk, meditate, visualize, or go play with some Silly Putty. Think, say, or do whatever you need to yourself so that your new system in training gets the loving command *"At ease soldier,"* or if preferred, the more clinical term *"Chillax."* A larger, less constricted energy field creates more room for the situation to open up to other sources (both HUman and spiritual) that can effortlessly help—that is, if you are willing to let the situation or fear go to them.

What makes any situation a problem is that you are trying to *solve* it. Usually, identified "problems" are never yours to solve alone from their inception. Shame, guilt, and control, all Lovely byproducts of our torturous 3D/4D runs, are usually the culprits at the helm of the issues anyway.

Next time you think you have a problem, try opening the small container that you have "shrink wrapped" it in, then release the situation to someone who's more qualified to handle it than you. Specifically assign them to the task. You may find them just hanging around in the ethers, looking for a great part-time assignment and a sincere willingness to lend you a "wing."

If you are jammed up by needing an *elusive soul-ution* to the challenge or issue, then most likely the timing either is off or there are too many errant emotions and constrictions and old, 3D problem-solving ideology are fogging up the path. Oh, and one other important caveat: This new 5D approach is not a *bigger picture* pass that encourages you to not deal or participate, or to run, drink, eat, check out, and go hide under your favorite 3D blankie. 5D living and *real-soul-utions* can only happen when you show up, present and in the *now*. It requires you to be awake and a willing participant in your own life's highs and lows and all the myriad of feelings in between.

The difference between the dimensional approaches lies in their core tenets and varying principles. In 3D, we were conditioned by duality and the premise that the only two basic ways to address or resolve anything is either by *figuring it out all by yourself or having someone else—a parent, the government, or an external God—*fix it for you. In 5D, triality rules and requires your full participation but not in the old ways we were used to regarding our energetic participation. 3D was ruled by the masculine principle of *action and doing*. 5D is ruled by the divine feminine principles of *attracting and being*.

And folks, here lies the rub! You can get out of the way of the solution coming in by simply reminding yourself repeatedly:

"I only see this as a problem because I don't quite understand how it is serving me or the bigger picture plan. Just because I don't see how it will resolve itself, get better, or be transmuted, doesn't mean that a plan isn't in place.

"There are so many other beings and forces working on this with me in the seen and unseen worlds. I just haven't been made privy to all the details. My main responsibility is to do my part, stay in my own lane, and if necessary, fire my sorry ass once I try to meddle in what is a perfect real-soul-ution, the Divine Plan."

CHAPTER NINE

A SPIRITUAL EVOLUTION OF EPIC PROPORTION

You Are an Early 5D Explorer: Mindfulness, Awareness, and *Bigger Picture* Perspectives Are Your New Coordinates!

HUmans will feel an energetic squeeze of various degrees of intensity come and go at different times throughout their personal Ascension. During painful periods, you therefore may see yourself and others overidentifying with many aspects of our coexisting 3D/4D reality. It's a natural, visceral reaction to experiencing changes that are outside a familiar context. Regressing to our old default programming is often an attempt to place the unfamiliar into a category to help our brain make some initial sense of them. Do your best not to worry about always doing things right or lambasting yourself if you catch yourself still doing something the old way. Remind yourself that you are a *new settler in a foreign land* and your 5D evolution is an organic process that comes with an enormous learning curve built in. Nature is patient and God benevolent. Act in both their likenesses.

A 5D life demands a conscious, more mindful relationship with your new emotional body. Your system can *now* amplify and multiply most things much quicker because your sense of time and space have changed. What you focus on and vibrate to might bring faster results, but also move you to outgrow the outcomes more rapidly. Sometimes that occurs in the form of relationships, long-held beliefs, truths, or realities. Allow for things to unfold without intervening, but also engage and nurture yourself simultaneously, so that you grow. 5D is not asking you to completely disarm and just be a passive bystander to your own life's process. Quite the contrary! Instead, it's asking you to reconsider switching the way you get around on the planet from your old gas-guzzling "auto"-mobile to a new *"soul"*-ar powered model.

Those of us in 5D have a very different paradigm and perspective on life but, nonetheless, without a broader context, we too will often sit in 5D "shock" until something jars us out of our stupor to move forward. All the changes that are unfolding are impacting everybody, not just a few people. Try not to confuse your very blessed and precious, newly-arrived-at 5D consciousness as a special privilege that was bestowed just on you and a couple of your cool friends. Of course, feel free to sneak in a few bragging rights because you are part of that very elite group who *did* first at this never before place in our spiritual evolutionary process. But remember that the *bigger picture* objective we are here *now* to build and create is a 5D Earth for anyone who wants to or chooses to Ascend into this new consciousness. Many who have already completed this nearly impossible 27,000-year-old trek did it with the main intention of making it possible for others when they were ready to do the same.

Your Ascension was a sacred journey, and you have lifetimes of blood, sweat, and tears to prove it. You are one of the first settlers in our new world. Congratulate yourself and take a bow for a miracle accomplished. Excellent job! Well done! There are no HUmans on the planet and no unfolding processes— good, bad, or ugly—that could ever reverse or take away your

5D creation and reality. What you need to protect yourself from going forward is the debilitating impact on your sensitive 5D HUman of what will seem like a chronic, ongoing effort to postpone, delay, and redirect the miscreations of the HUmans who are still thinking and vibrating to a 3D/4D consciousness.

There will be a lot of back and forth trying for a while. The reality of 5D consciousness, as it *now* exists on Planet Earth, has not yet been stabilized. We may have landed in this new dimension, but everyone hasn't fully awakened to all its possibilities. Of course, we all hope, including me, that this seeming nightmare of our current "Earth in Peril" movie resolves itself at God's speed and that there are no sequels scheduled on the runway. How many times can anyone—no matter what dimension they resonate to—watch *Whatever happened to Baby Jane? Armageddon, Don't Look Up, the Exorcist,* or another Presidential election unfold, *and not feel hopeless, depressed, or scared out of their wits*?

Outside of the higher, divine realms and dimensions (9D and up), there will always be some Shadow that exists. If we are going to "really" heal and transmute all of HUmanity's 3D miscreations, then "dusty" aspects of the old paradigm and its belief systems will always have to *rise* to the surface and be drawn towards the Light. If these "particles" of denser energy, actions, or misdeeds are ever going to be transmuted, specifically for the individuals that carry them, then into the "Shadows" the HUmans and nonHUmans must go. The only real way out of it is through it.

The Disease of HUman Separation

As we continue to move forward, you will be able to identify with more speed and clarity the many other forms that our core planetary disease of "HUman Separation" is parading behind. Although the upset victory of the 2016 Presidential election was one of the first major signs (in the USA) that the HUman collective was teetering dangerously on a fault line of an epic divide, it took the novel coronavirus to showcase the real underlying disease as the bigger contagion on a global level. The darker side of HUmanity erupted, and its Shadow was brought forth to the surface. What goes on in the world mainly comes down to what the collective consciousness creates as a reality. Until the underlying thought forms morph, what we saw, and will continue to see, are many different variations basically on the same theme.

Most of our challenges over the next three to five years will be issues associated with *"rogue"* realities created by people who are still holding on to the old paradigms of *duality* and *polarity*. As more of us move firmly into 5D thought and the new paradigm of *triality*, we will begin moving towards more of a merge—bringing together more options and aspects of HUmanity from where we were once more separated and compartmentalized. That is if HUmanity chooses to go in that direction.

In 5D, you don't lose your HUman individuality, instead you gain a coming together, a *unity* of *souls* stronger as one mind and heart. All this wonderful, long-awaited coming back to *oneness* will not only be the medicine needed to close our

HUman separation wounds but will result in other, higher, more advanced experiences and HUman interactions.

In 5D, we start thinking with our *hearts* rather than with our *heads* only. Keep in mind, we will not be employing the old 3D/4D heart anymore that was once conditioned by emotion-based duality. Our shiny new 5D Love Heart doesn't follow the old manipulating premises of *"selfishness vs. selflessness, sacrifice as a virtue, and victimization or codependency addictions."* As each of us moves towards wholing our own personal separation from our *soul's* God-Light, we will truly begin to trust that there is no need for a hierarchy or competition. We are all aspects of God and there is *plenty* of everything to go around.

The consciousness of 5D will organically move us into a higher standard because we understand the *bigger picture* from a whole new vantage place. Thinking with our hearts becomes an exciting, creative feminine approach to a well-earned 5D life. Having the new understanding of the importance of *"leading with self,"* helps to remove the old, ingrained fears and vulnerability that come with opening up your heart. The new 5D HUman is *no longer encouraged* to do things that might hurt it in the process of trying to help others. Love in 5D is no longer used as ammunition. You can't get shot down by it anymore. Its strength and power have an automatic cut off switch that is activated when it is used for control or malevolent reasons.[1]

Polarity Strikes Again!

Back in May 2020, between some significant astrological alignments and the month's numerology (5 + 2 + 0 + 2 + 0 =

9), the vibration of the number 9 held the space for a powerful transmutational shift to occur that downloaded the energy of *completion and transformation*. There was a lot of closure in the heavens. Although hard to believe, given the current state of insanity that we are still experiencing in the world today, a main portal that fueled our 3D world for eons was sealed closed.

Although we are still in the throes of what seems like some very old, "dinosaur" thinking and behavior, and will be for a while, it's important for you to know and allow to seep into your subconscious that a lot of this 3D stuff is a wrap. What you are and will be seeing is spillover and backlash against the 5D transformation, which at times will result in major flareups, apparent setbacks, and downright losses—especially during the periods when HUmanity hits the snooze button and *dozes off again*. Hot ashes and smoldering embers that are left unattended in a forest or at home in a fireplace can easily ignite full-blown, even deadly, out-of-control fires.

We're going to be seeing a lot of vestiges of 3D's Shadow coming to the surface, spilling over, and escalating in our lives and around the planet. The most difficult parts of the Shadow will show itself through the imbalanced field of *force*, or in other words, through the *out-of-control* aspects of the masculine energy as it continues to fight ruthlessly to stay in power. *Now* is not the time to rest on our laurels or forget the *bigger picture* at play. We might be at the tail end of our 3D reality, the big fire might appear to be out, but never take your eyes off the embers that are still lit. Not for one 3D second!

We are in the throes of a spiritual evolution of epic proportion. We have made miraculous, quantum leaps, but our landing is not yet complete, nor our 5D frequency stable by any means. At times, things that you are facing or seeing in the outside world, might at first seem like it's just more of the same, like you are experiencing your own personal Groundhog Day. It's not. What is happening, though, is that as all these 3D timelines and paradigms begin to fold, you are going to find that within your own life, as well as in the *bigger picture,* most people on the planet aren't going to understand what is happening. It's too complicated, as well yet to be written. Fear and anger will be triggered and, with nowhere to direct it, initially many HUmans will more visibly act out, riot, and create a lot of social unrest.

I can't emphasize this enough. It is not going to be over for a while. We're going to feel like we're sticking our finger in one leak and another is springing open. And although we are going to feel more and more ready to get back into the game, try not to let frustration and impatience grab you by your throat and handcuff you. Make sure you take good care of your 5D heart, for it will be your heart that will help you see it through. As crazy as everything is, please trust that it is all unfolding for a reason. Our "identity" as HUmans is at stake. Try, especially during your most challenging times to commit to turning this part of the *bigger picture* process over to something Higher and allow those Light Forces who have finally been given permission to step into our planet of *free will* to assist in their part of the post-5D Ascension.

Trusting that invisible forces are currently working on our behalf through this difficult part of the planet's overall transition, might feel a little too ambiguous for your comfort, but it's a much safer bet than trusting in a very frightened HUmankind right *now.* Not because HUmans are bad, dark, or evil creatures—although perhaps a few are—but because even the Lighted ones among us are trying to find some footing as their old familiar 3D matrix is rapidly melting away. The spin of the centrifuge is bringing to the surface some deep Shadow stuff that is just trying to make its way out from 3D/4D consciousness. Many HUmans are confused, scared, and reeling from not understanding the higher plan in process. Even on a good day, most of *us* are still very much in flux, too. Nobody gets to grab a chair until the music officially stops. For me, my allegiance is with the greater plan and that's what has kept me in the game and sane (*sort of*) through all of this. Find your anchor and connect with a set of beliefs that keeps you feeling both safe but not in denial.

3D/4D Depolarization

As former 3D beings, our templates were immersed in duality reality for over thousands of thousands of years. Opposing views created everything from harmless arguments to more catastrophic world wars. "If you win, I lose" or vice versa. *Thinking* was our background in 3D/4D and the emotional body, which was often out of balance ruled. That was the only fuel we knew during those times to get our objective, point and perspective across the finish line. We still fall back on these old actions, even though, most of the time they do not solve anything equitably or at all. Everything has changed *now*. It's a new world and we have a new HUman operating system.

We have spent lifetimes in 3D duality and its watered-down version of explosive 4D polarity. Our beings, down to a cellular level, have been deeply and repeatedly conditioned by the repetition of its matrix. As we leave 3D/4D polarity, and even during the early stages of our 5D lives, we will go through a period of *"depolarization."* When that happens, initially things may start feeling and looking a little loopy. Ok, *a lot* loopy.

This is a patch of time that you will probably be going in and out of a few times, as your being is recalibrating time, space, and function. It might feel like you are in between dimensions, with periods of time that your life, as well as the familiar people around you, aren't going to seem like any of it is making much sense.

If you've been on a spiritual journey for a while, you might be thinking, *"Really, tell me something new."* But I am talking about something very different here. What's defining this lifestyle versus the old lifestyle is the new level of *awareness or consciousness* you will have about being genuinely different. You will feel at times not as much that the other person or situation is different, but more like, *"Oh, boy I'm experiencing them and how they are reacting from a different level."* Sometimes, you will feel yourself floating above your physical body or have an unfamiliar sensation of being energetically separated from it. This might present itself at various times when you are having to make a simple decision such as what to eat for lunch or it may surface during a more significant situation that is work related.

Personal exchanges such as an argument with a partner or a political discussion with a friend can quickly become confusing to your new 5D brain and emotional body. You may experience an inner feeling of wanting to respond one way versus another, but something stops you or you may not feel as strongly about your position on the matter as you once did. It may initially feel like a glitch or a system jam as your newly downgraded emotional body starts to kick in and redirect some of your reactions and subsequent responses.

Because of our 3D/4D polarity conditioning, you will want to move towards one end or one side of your reaction or opinion. This may happen on and off for a while before it settles in but, soon into your awareness of what is happening, you are going to realize that holding an ironclad old response or position *doesn't feel the same anymore*. Those days are over. We're moving towards releasing polarity, so watch for reactions that might unexpectedly come up as these polarity-based responses and situations begin to surface. We have witnessed a lot of those reactions, especially during the pandemic and the medicine choices as well decisions regarding masking or not. This is not a referendum on what to do or not do, but to remind yourself that, as genuinely as you believe your position to be true, if you find yourself on either end of the spectrum of an argument, you are contributing to HUman separation. No judgment here, just have a *willingness* to observe your unconscious part in our holding pattern.

Come up with creative ways to mentally hit a 5D pause button so you can assist your own process as your vibration resets to its new dimension and you'll make a significant contribution in helping to release the HOLD button on the *bigger picture* unfoldment as well!

Deprogramming 3D Familiarity Is Unnerving

Changing the familiar ways we function, react, and understand ourselves at the core may be disconcerting at first. The things that we hold near and dear are reflected often in our opinions and reactions. There's nothing wrong with having opinions and reactions, no matter which dimension you reside in. The challenge comes when we first enter 5D, when we will also be wavering back and forth in 3D/4D at the same time. Straddling three different planetary frequencies simultaneously is enough to give anyone dimensional "vertigo." Be prepared to feel a lot of jerky movements, as your opinions, reactions, and responses swing back and forth before you move more firmly into your new 5D perspective. Over time, you will be pulled into a more centered place that generates responses and opinions from the *bigger picture* perspective of *triality*.

Ultimately, this is a very good thing because we are trying, on a personal as well as global level, to move towards a place of *depolarizing* the intensity levels that right/wrong, good/bad posturing creates. Duality-based battle cries such as "This is my country," "Mine is the superior race," "This is my right," and "This isn't your right" are destructive byproducts of polarization.

As 5D Ascension moves us further away from HUman polarization, we are going to see many more severe outbreaks of polarizations across the planet. It sounds paradoxical, but energetically the *fear of change, status, and privilege* will have various groups and individuals throughout HUmanity wanting to go back to what they know and what is *familiar*. We will see many people in our own lives and throughout society *double and triple down* to hold their ground—digging into one side or the other—courtesy of our prior 3D/4D matrix. Eventually, the overextended rubberband of polarity will either snap back to the middle or snap apart completely, giving way to a whole new paradigm. Keep this in mind, especially when you are experiencing what might feel like intense standoffs in your own life, the political arena, HUmanity, and the world. Depolarization is a necessary part of the process as we move towards massive dimensional, quantum-level shifts, as opposed to the old cosmetic, incremental concept of change.

We are going to see a lot of this happening, as well as exacerbated, through the misuse of social media and all news outlets. The more comfortable we become with understanding the *bigger picture* process that is unfolding, the easier it will become to *not* see everything as final, permanent, or doomsday. Fully awake, we will be witnessing change in an unprecedented way. And although no one can predict where those shifts will take us, we all agreed to be here during this time to hold the space for HUmanity to move through this long-awaited, cathartic event.

This is not about something that is going to happen in the future. We are not in a rehearsal or having a fire drill. We are in it *now* and it is very real. Each day, we need to work on accepting the reality that the 3D world has closed for us.

You are *now* officially on the other side of it. Everything that you read about, studied, all the classes you have taken, and all that you have experienced throughout your many past lives were all leading up to this. To this moment's *now*.

Are You Suffering from *Ingrid Bergman* Syndrome?

Although you may be firmly grounded in your 5D matrix, waking up often happens gradually. We are not only trying to adjust to the new lay of the land, but at the same time, trying to figure out our new perspective on 3D/4D reality. As we move in and out of *several* dimensions at once, initially it can be confusing to figure out what is or isn't real. Although the perspective of truth is different for different individuals, sifting through a sea of false narratives only compounds the process.

At times, you are going to feel *gasLighted* personally and globally. Life between dimensions can create foggy thinking due to low visibility. It's HUman nature to want to understand everything that is unfolding around us, especially as we are thrown a bit while trying to adjust to our new foundation of *continually shifting sands.*

5D can create a lot of frustration and impatience for even the steadiest of hands. Some of the most helpful reality checks will come in the form of virtual Post-it notes that you creatively place all over your home constantly reminding you, "This is not going to make much sense at times. For sanity's sake, let that sh*t go!"

As You Are *Leaving*, Please Allow for *Grieving*

Your 5D rise has changed almost every aspect of who you once were along with the things you once knew to be true. You will experience many of your once-coveted beliefs, desires, money goals, and relationship choices and many of your former plans, morphing, shifting, and at times, *disappearing* altogether. No matter what dimension you identify with most, life and people will always profoundly shift and change. But the difference in 5D is that you will be experiencing those changes in a whole new way because you are *now painfully awake*. Every little bump and grind and especially *loss* will feel more magnified and exacerbated. You will have a lot less go-tos, drugs of choice, and avoidance techniques to draw upon for the journey forward. Not only because you don't need them the same way anymore, but mainly because they don't work anyway with your new 5D computer system.

Because you haven't yet fully adjusted and integrated the other supporting attributes and aspects of your 5D HUman, your newly heightened level of perception will often lead to more confusion than clarity at first. As the myriad of incremental microscopic and macroscopic frequency adjustments kick in, some of the familiar ways that you have come to navigate through your life will be completely in flux for a while. Challenged often because as you are learning to install a new way to *think*, simultaneously you are also letting go of the old way you *thought*. As you move out of 3D/4D, all your go-to coping methods and lifetimes of reliance on your well-honed skills of avoidance, denial, and blame of yourself and others will also fade away. *Blaming* was one of the greatest *perks* of our old 3D/4D consciousness. HUmans really liked doing that. *(I know I did)*. As we run out of more and more people to blame for our circumstances, feelings, and problems, it is then when we begin to take more responsibility for ourselves and actions.

When you find yourself drifting away from the familiarity of what you have come to understand as your life, along with the myriad of your usual, familiar life responses, you know then that you are well on your way to 5D wonderland. And once you start skipping down that yellow brick road, this transitional phase of your evolutionary growth will continue throughout the rest of your current Earth life's "second" incarnation.

The COVID pandemic provided the collective world with our first big, global opportunity to be *shocked* out of its usual routines. It was an important turning point that helped HUmans more quickly transition into accepting the new paradigm on the planet—without choice. The many pandemic changes on the planet are functioning like a *beard* for the Universe—disguising its operations from the masses—as it gives many HUmans somewhere to direct their confusion about their lives and their sense of reality shifts. It also is allowing for individuals, as well as the world as a collective, to move through a long-overdue *grieving process.*

A very important aspect of 5D that allows all HUmans to move forward in their lives is the ability to let go of the experiences and memories that keep them out of the *now* and tethered to the past. Tethering is a common experience in 3D/4D because the timeline is linear and based on past, present, and future. In 3D, we never really grieve properly because duality keeps us in a fearful place of being afraid to let go. Inadvertently, 3D reflected a society that was stuck in a perpetual state of adolescence, never fully emancipating into a healthy adulthood. A mature, self-actualized adult is able to express and manage adult feelings, including uncomfortable ones such as grief, disappointment, and loss. A healthy, mature adult knows how to *compromise*. They understand their significance as part of a community that both relies on their input and receives from its bounty. Our 3D attachment to both the past and the future has significantly contributed to creating everything from HUman separation, supremacy, and disease to addiction, greed, and codependency.

Because of the three-part timeline, 3D/4D HUmans have been very challenged by any effort they make in trying to live in the present. The *now* is a hard place to reside, especially if life seems random, disordered, or scary, like something you need to control. HUman behaviors, such as denial, avoidance, apathy, reactions, and survival mechanisms are not just used to cope in 3D but are often a way of life.

When we make a pact with who we once were and what we once believed, doubling down to resist change, we forfeit the peace and creativity that only comes with being in the moment, the inexplicable *"now."* In 5D, there is no other time sequence. No past nor future. Our 3D brain has a very hard time in making sense of all that which makes no "prior" sense to our old reality or conditioning.

When HUmans experience a loss of any kind, whether of a person, a beLoved pet, or a once-believed truth, they often need to go through what therapists refer to as a "cycle of grief" to process their thoughts and feelings regarding the loss. Sometimes that cycle is quick and uneventful. Other times, it can be long, painful, or immobilizing.

The late Elisabeth Kübler-Ross, M.D., was a brilliant Swiss-American psychiatrist and pioneering researcher in the field of death, dying, and grief. She created one of the first methods to help both professionals and individuals understand how to view and treat the grieving process. Her five stages of grief model—Denial, Anger, Bargaining, Depression, and Acceptance—includes many of the important aspects of moving through the HUman cycle of loss. Anxiety is clearly missing from the original list. Nonetheless, individually, and as a society, at one time or another we will be either moving through or *stuck* in one of these emotional stages. The changes that we are and will continue to experience are of such biblical proportions that the newness, along with being on a totally different timeline, is bound to trigger one or more of those stages often.

As the vibration of HUman consciousness begins to rise on the planet, so do the frequency levels of HUmankind. Before we fully acclimate to the higher, 5D frequencies, newer, less dense frequencies can feel very stressful to the physical and emotional bodies. The less one is aware of these new higher 5D levels and the evolutionary push that is happening within the body, the more likely that many of these symptoms can be misinterpreted as *angst, fear, anxiety, panic, and depression.*

The Anger Phase:
Where Most HUmans Are Currently Stuck

Many of these frequency shifts and stressors are giving way to what Planet Earth and all HUmans are beginning to experience: the *anger phase in the cycle of grief.*

So much of what we once knew to be true and all the things that we staked a firm claim in is changing. The ways that we choose to live our lives, our values (about money, our sense of what's right and wrong, our treatment of HUmans, animals, and the planet, for example), and our core principles are coming home to roost. As we start waking up to larger truths and are confronted by our Shadow aspects and challenged by what it is going to take to make *real* changes, anger will surface. Loss and changes of this magnitude will often trigger anger.

Anger is a healthy emotion that is often suppressed or overstated in the form of rage. It stands to reason that, as the world shifts, there will come a rise in violence and a surfacing of mental illness along with the releasing of lifetimes of angry emotions. Both are currently erupting across the planet and begging for HUmanity's attention, action, and Love.

The anger phase is often where HUmans try to reclaim some sense of equilibrium and power. Some use anger in a more constructive way than others, while some use the energetic force of anger to help them become mobile again.

Loss of control is often experienced as a personal threat to our 3D/4D egos. The helpless feelings that come with *"this cannot be happening"* can often trigger a fight-or-fLight response. Eventually, as you start feeling more familiar with 5D and ultimately safer, you will be able to let go and move more easily into *acceptance*.

Keep in mind, this model is not linear. Watch for the various stages of grief to unfold at different times. You don't have to go from *denial to anger or from bargaining to depression then acceptance*. You could experience some or possibly all of the stages. Or you might experience none. Your response to your Ascension versus somebody else's response to theirs may cause one of you to accept changes more easily, while others to have a more difficult time with the new. Or the opposite. Allow for different pockets of mourning to come in waves, curves, or tail-chasing circles.

Because you are aware of the possibility that these stages will be both coming and going, you *now* have a head's up when you find yourself feeling stuck, angry, depressed, and so forth. Knowing that you are not going through this alone and it's just a part of our growing and releasing process will also help you tremendously through some of the rough patches. Either way, experiencing these symptoms for more than a couple of weeks here and there, might be an indicator that you can use some help, support, and *relief*. Please don't isolate, and especially *don't assume* that suffering for an extended period, is par for the course on the road to and through your 5D Ascension. Depression is depression, anger is anger and grief is grief—no matter what dimension you are on or headed towards. Reach out for support, guidance, counseling, therapy, and medical intervention from a place of Self-Love and True-Compassion. It's the new 5D way.

Pivoting:
The New Olympic 5D Sport

Please give yourself permission to go through all your emotions. Allow for your feelings, including the meltdowns. Don't be afraid to have periods of negativity, as you will. Just work towards not staying in them too long or letting them take over and become your new reality. What you want to be mindful of is not getting stuck in any stage, or not sitting in one of them for an *extended* period. A well-connected 5D timeline will help you get to that ultimate place of acceptance easier, as well as faster. It is there where you can begin to fully move into and start enjoying the new circumstances.

When a period of "stuckness" finds you, gently remember to *pivot* back to your center so you can move more rapidly out of this period of vibrational turbulence. If you learn to work your 5D rudder properly, it will help you to navigate away from the often choppy 3D waters, making your transitioning easier.

THE 5D PIVOT PRAYER: FOR WHEN YOU HAVE LOST YOUR WAY

Yes, this change is happening. Yes, this doesn't feel good. Yes, I'm scared. Yes, I don't know what's coming or how this will turn out. But whatever I am experiencing is happening only for my Highest Good, with a Higher Purpose. I have no clue as to how this will turn out. This is a Universal truth, for, at this stage of the unfoldment, it was never meant for me to know. That aspect of my creation was not on my conscious watch. I have already passed the baton on to the next being in my higher "chain of command." The why, when, and how of this situation are now with very capable souls, as the responsibility for these next steps lie firmly with my divine other selves.

Change Only Means You Have *Outgrown* Your Present Circumstances

Cutting out the "awfulizing" and getting to the feelings and facts will allow you to be in real time with your real feelings, and not in your distracting and overwhelming 3D emotional body. We can choose to look at the *change, loss,* or *situation* only through the lens of the Shadow aspect and allow it to continue to scare the hell out of ourselves or we can *choose* to let go and trust what we as 5D HUmans deeply know—there is always a greater plan or *bigger picture* at play—and the Universe always has our backs, as God is always Loving and benevolent, not malevolent.

It's OK to have your feelings and doubts too, but then go back to what you know to be true in your heart. There is going to be a little (*OK, a lot of*) turbulence along the way through, especially during this current elongated, post-5D Ascension stretch. The fLight's trajectory is still relatively unaffected despite a few of its passengers may be starting to panic a bit. The real concern arrives when you see the fLight attendants, copilot, or especially the pilot panicking. At that point, the turbulence becomes the *least* of your problems.

It's imperative that you start owning your 5D place on the planet which you so rightfully earned by claiming your God-self. The Universe is not going to try to trip you up or throw anything at you that you wouldn't be able to transmute or handle. Yes, you'll be faced with choices and changes, but remember that nothing, not even a hair on your head, is ever sLightly moved without you on some higher level, signing off on it. You have a say in it all even if, at the time, it might not feel that way. Don't assume things happen out of the blue, as they really don't. Your consciousness may have gotten the memo *last,* but everything that you have ever done led you to that current moment, shift, or goodbye.

As a 5D being, you are amazingly powerful right *now.* What you choose to focus on is going to multiply in ways that your present understanding cannot fathom as of yet. Be welcoming and grateful, and approach it all from an intention of peace and balance. You are *now* ready to step into something new.

Own the grace. Own the moment.

Overthinking Is *Older* Thinking

Try not to overthink your transitioning process into 5D too much. Your new reality perspectives will never make much sense or satisfy your old 3D/4D thinking or mind's programming anyway. Our mental body had a very big function in our 3D lives. We ascribed a lot of power and deferred to it as our primary go-to and final decision maker. Its lead position was an integral part of 3D life, and it served us well and honorably. *It's how we thought we think*. It was responsible for the development of our intellect and the storage house that held all our memories.

The 3D mind Loves to distract you, run interference, and even sometimes scare you just enough for you to *not* move forward and evolve from your once familiar life. It doesn't do it to harm you or control you anymore than you have conditioned it to do. It can only engage you in the exact manner that reflects your old leftover truths and beliefs about how to keep yourself safe, protected, and managed. Our 3D thinking reflected some of our misguided ideas that were based in duality. It's inherent system of *opposites* often lulled us into believing either we are in control of everything that happens in our lives (as well as everything that we have cleverly managed to avoid) *or* have absolutely no control of most things because of outside influences and authorities, specifically God. The 3D brain spent countless lifetimes trying to figure out how things are going to turn out and what we can do to steer it all in a favorable direction. It kept us out of the moment and focused on the *elusive future* of its three-part timeline. Energetically speaking, using the mind this way in 5D is a colossal waste of yours, mine, HUmans', and God's time. On our current 5D Earth plane, that specific piece of the action to overthink is not in our job description anymore. Thankfully it is not listed anywhere in the "edicts," "bylaws," or "fine print" of our upgraded 5D *bigger picture soul* contracts either.

Your 5D Memory Keeps Most of What You Need Stored in the *Clouds*

One of the things that is profoundly changing in relation to our 3D mind is the prior function of our 3D memory. We are moving to a nonlinear timeline that's going to feel very accelerated initially. Things are going to appear to happen faster, suddenly, and often with *no* prior notice. Our old 3D brain and memory function is going to feel *short-circuited* and possibly a little overwhelmed from processing life at different speeds of comprehension. Your new 5D self at first will try to store everything it can into its memory bank. As we evolve more expansively, we come to understand that most of what we jammed into our brain for future recall, is useless in 5D. The past rarely serves us because on this new timeline we are constantly creating, but from the *now* and not from yesterday's news.

Most things we expect to happen *usually* don't. Not in the way that we expected them to happen anyway. Our 5D bandwidth is more expansive *now* with better Wi-Fi and *"inner-net"* connections. There is a lot more information that we can receive as well as send out at any given time. There are too many additional twists, turns, and frequency redirects occurring for our prior memory function to process accurately. We will find that because "technically" all that there really is or really matters in 5D is the *now*—holding on to certain past bits of information, details, memories and most importantly, *emotions* truly don't serve us anymore. In 3D/4D, repetitive thoughts, reenactments and a constant retelling of our storyline allowed us a way of to keep them fresh in our minds and crosshairs so they didn't get buried too far down that our psyches would forget what we came into this life to work on. But in 5D, because we are always in the process of creating new, the memory aspect is more functionally used to store information such as where you had parked your car, left your keys, the time scheduled for your next appointment or your partner's *first name*. This last feature will come in very handy—especially if you would really like to remain in that relationship.

Although we have just barely scratched the surface regarding our understanding of the new 5D memory and its uses, it's important for us to at least acknowledge that the familiarity of its old functioning is under major reconstruction. As we move through this very significant functionality shift, without this recognition, we might misinterpret some of the in-between periods, moments, and memory-related experiences before all our morphing becomes more stabilized as *anxiety, fear, or a negative-boding event*. As our overall 5D HUman downloads and then upgrades, our nervous systems, language interpretation skills, and responses need to follow along.

Most of your changes will be unnoticeable until after the fact, when you will consciously realize that you are not having the same *emotional responses* you once had to familiar emotional triggers or that insignificant data. Much of your memory will still be retrievable if needed, but it will not be taking up the same gigabytes of space in your being as before.

All is shifting to accommodate your upgraded 5D HUman, as you *now* require a state-of-the art construct that will serve your 5D life, body and newly acquired *soul* contracts.

Maybe you don't yet know how to use your 5D features or even exactly what they are. Even so, they were included with the standard "package" that came with your 5D upgrade. Over time, you will be able to identify their purpose and understand how and when to utilize them. In 3D, our memories were clouded with unimportant details that produced polarized reactions.

By comparison, 5D memory is not clouded. It is "cloud based," so it doesn't clutter up your synaptic pathways. It doesn't hoard lifetimes of moments, situations, and Karmic events. It doesn't hold on to an annoying verse of a popular song that keeps repeating itself at random moments in your head. Everything that is ever needed is stored where you can pull it down when you want or need it. Life will be a lot less emotionally exhausting, as 5D is like a poultice for *releasing old emotional experiences instead of recycling them.* This will free you up to *create* happiness, peace, and a Lighter HUman life filled with more of what feeds your *soul*.

Our Engrams Have Been Depolarized!

On a physical level, the brain is responsible for memory. It stores and receives learned information in the short-term and over prolonged periods of time. Specific neurons in the brain, *engrams,* are charged and activated, allowing for various events and experiences to be encoded, categorized, and then retrieved through the psychological process of what we refer to as memory.

The physiological way that we encode memory is basically the same for all HUmans. But the types of memories we store, their quality, and our acuity in recalling them varies person by person. Everything from our diets and emotional balances to our conditioned responses and personal levels of awareness impact how our memories will imprint *engrams*. The strength of the synaptic pathway that provides the *electrical signal between engrams* plays a very big part in how we capture our memories.

In 3D/4D, the brain stores experiences and events that were filtered through and based on duality and polarity. In 5D, memory is upgraded. We moved out of 3D duality, 4D polarity, and officially moved into 5D triality. We've been *depolarized*. We do not have the same DNA helix to reinforce or support our old, polarized thinking anymore.

Our 3D/4D selves effortlessly imprinted memories that were first processed through the filter of polarity. Both the *negative experiences* of polarity, such as unresolved childhood traumas or hurt feelings, and the *positive experiences*, like loving moments in a relationship or that super-fun birthday you had on a cruise ship were stored. Sometimes these things might seem benign or insignificant to someone else but, to you, your 3D/4D memory deemed it worthy to "photograph" and store.

As a function, 3D/4D memory doesn't discriminate which memories to catalogue because 3D living is based on a system of *opposites*. Both 3D/4D negative and positive memories carry biochemical, electromagnetic charges. It could be a bad memory or a great memory, but for you to truly imprint, store, and catalog it, it has to have an "electromagnetic" charge. That charge, whether good or bad, came from the emotional component of your nervous system, as well as your heart.

Our 3D memories are mainly old, recycled experiences, thoughts, and ideas. Approximately *90 percent* of our thoughts on any given day are not new! Most things that we perseverate on, overthink, or obsess about, although charged once when they initially occur, are recharged again in the engram and synaptic pathways *each time* we revisit the original events or corresponding emotions in our head. Without consciously working on *minimizing, reducing, or reframing* their impact in our psyche and nervous system, these charges remain in our energy field until they are *transmuted, released, or discharged.* Not until then will we be able to stop recreating that vibrational blip that duplicates itself from relationship to relationship, fear to fear, situation to situation.

In this way, aspects of 3D memory basically held us captive on a never-ending hamster wheel to nowhere, lifetime after lifetime. With remaining emotional body charges and imprints eventually transferring over to our next incarnation, or others after that, we really didn't get to move on or significantly create any new stuff—just many different variations on the same theme.

The more consciousness we had, the more we were able to act outside of the box, take growth risks, scratch out a few changes, and so forth. Mostly we were able to break off little pieces here and there, albeit slowly during our elongated 3D run of the specific memory pattern and repetition of the dynamic. In essence, this is the definition of *Karma*. For the

Karmic wheel of *cause and effect* even to exist it has to be fueled by a slower-moving timeline based in the linear thoughts of past, present, and future. That's why, in part, Karma is mainly a byproduct of 3D/4D thought and experiences.

This repetitive dynamic has made trying to leave a *Karmic* relationship, moving past an inherited socioeconomic level, or rising above a fear or circumstance nearly impossible. In 3D, because of our learned understanding of time and space, everything is *programmed* and *thought* to take a long time to change. Social, educational, and cultural beliefs, and so forth, created the collective 3D reality that took Earth HUmans close to 27,000 years to revise.

During our current lives, simple experiences, such as going to grade school for eight years and high school and college for four years apiece, are examples of how time and space shaped our choices, decisions, and opportunities. All these HUmanmade events represent expressions of beliefs associated with the 3D consciousness timeline. Energetically speaking, linear thinking is flat. It conditions us into believing that most things must be created in tiny little steps. Although that is only one way in which the creation process can manifest. From a time and space perspective, there are a multitude of timelines, especially through quantum physics, that we are *now* able to access and create through.

5*De*-Emotionalizing

As you move into 5D, you will begin to learn how to have more *objective* experiences based on both the situation and the facts, for they will not be electrically charged the same way by your overreactive 3D/4D emotional body and nervous system.

Our limited 3D duality perspective was a hardwired template that most of the time gave us two options at best to process what was happening. The two-option choice was a *chronic trigger* for the emotional body to respond to the situation from a no-win, trapped, mistake-fearing, scared perspective.

Example: You were in a relationship that you were not happy in, but the thought of leaving was so overwhelming that it did not even feel like a real possibility. Most likely you found yourself preoccupied in a game of mental ping-pong, spending copious amount of time volleying between the two options of *staying or leaving*. Going back and forth, thinking, planning, fearing, and awfulizing all your prospects, you exhausted yourself and couldn't make a decision. The "3D shuffle" duped your psyche into believing that you were actually *doing* something about the situation by worrying. But your 3D duality-based brain had inadvertently set up the two opposite choices that *either way* would scare you the most and keep you running on the neverending "road to nowhere" hamster wheel.

The overwhelmingly frightening thought that you might make a wrong decision is often why we stay in relationships, jobs and keep old milk containers in the fridge long after they have passed their expiration date. Staying in a relationship or leaving it are both definitively real options, but only *two* among infinite possibilities.

In 5D, the multitude of "other" possible outcomes that reside alongside the two polar options that the 3D brain tends to perseverate between are available to us. In 5D, our experiences, *soul*-utions, options, and choices are based in *triality*. They become available to us as we consciously step into, and not a minute before, the truth that other realities exist outside of the ones that the mind is showing us. Creations in 5D happen in the *now*, not in the past, which 3D/4D memory is based on, or in the future, which is based on projections, speculations, and a lot of missing data.

The 5De-emotionalizing of your experiences, along with the opening to the unknown options in your new 5D triality reality, takes a little doing at first, and truthfully, for a while thereafter. Many of the imprinted parts of our *auric field* are still responding from the 3D HUman of our recently existing past. This is common and will take some time.

You will come to understand that in 5D you do not need to have or attach an *emotional* charge to your reactions to categorize and catalog them on your experience timeline. As you learn to neutralize your *reactions* and transmute them into *responses*, you will experience having your truer, heartfelt *feelings* more often than espousing just emotional reactions that often skew the frequency of the 5D experience. Blurring the lens of the moment takes us out of seeing and understanding the *bigger picture* of that situation, why it is happening, and what gifts, information, or opportunity it has brought with it.

You have *now* moved into a faster timeline that will more rapidly create almost everything that you will be experiencing. It is a very exciting prospect knowing that we can begin to create anything we want, but we also must be mindful that our more familiar 3D perspectives, patterns, and memories are still very much in play. Our old habits will still fight for control at times and attempt to lead with how we *used to* create in 3D/4D, through perseveration, rote, and the *masculine* doer energy.

Often, we thought to create what we wanted based on what we *didn't* have. We would, for example, try to create by focusing on the void or the negative ideas like *"I want a large house because I never had my own bedroom as a kid."* Or from a totally opposite approach, through recycling old experiences that were pleasant or positive memories. We would try to recreate things in our lives that were perceived as good, thinking *"I lived in a big house as a child and would like to have a large house just like I did then."*

None of these ways of creating wants, intentions and reality are wrong. They are properly based on the construct of 3D duality, a system of opposites, and a 3D timeline of past, present, and future.

In 3D, we spend most everyday recycling thoughts from yesterday, last week, last year and from what we have been conditioned to be true or real from society, culture, religion, media influencers or from our childhoods. Very few of our thoughts, wants, and desires are original, fresh, or even our own. Ironically, many of our repetitive thoughts often do not manifest because our creativity process over time becomes numb to them. The 3D timeline is more drawn out, and so more space and time passes between our thoughts and their manifestations. The void in between allows for many ambient thought forms, emotional fears, and fantasies to attach themselves to the creation process that often kept us on a hamster wheel of fear, worry, and incessant longing. Easily sandwiched between blaming bad experiences ourselves for not being *deserving enough* to attract what we want and resenting others for getting more without much effort, we struggle and suffer.

A SPIRITUAL EVOLUTION

In 5D, as you engage in your new way of life, the only thing it really asks of you is to show up *awake* and ready to live and respond in the present. Becoming more aligned with your *now*, you cocreate from the moment or experience in front of you through inspiration, intuition, heart math, absorption, and Love. Inspiration is a spark of spontaneity that can only be derived through accepting, allowing, and remaining an open conduit for the higher mind, self, spirit, and all the *fly* guides that you personally hired for your journey here.

Life that is lived in the *now* can only be created in the *now*. You really can't plan too far ahead. You can try, but just be ready to pivot at a moment's notice and remember to enter most appointments in your calendar with an *eraser-tipped pencil*. While our prior 3D, linear thinking has limits and is finite, our 5D, circular, *bigger picture* thinking is limitless and infinite. Thinking "out of the box" in 5D means accessing the mind of your broader God self to think, process, and create.

Not to worry, for as your new memory begins to shift, it will take with it some of the very handy options from your prior 3D brain. Tried and true functions, such as cataloging, and the repetition of tasks like *"It's three PM–time to pick the kids up from school"* or my personal favorite, *"Isn't it time to eat* now?*"* for example, will remain but sharpen. For many of us, those old 3D features didn't work so well anyway, especially after a long, stressful day or a couple of sippy cups of *mommy juice*.

To completely shift over to using 5D memory and inspiration, your brain will go through a period of *decompression*. After millennia of handing over your creation abilities to nonexistent realities of both *past* and *future* events, you will go through several periods of time, during the switchover when you feel foggy, confused, and have difficulty with your memory *(nothing unfamiliar here)*. Energetically, you're going to find it harder at times to retrieve the right words or recall certain experiences, especially as you start extinguishing and 5DE-emotion-alizing the charges that were attached to your polarized memories, thinking, and cataloging.

You might feel a bit unsettled by your forgetfulness, especially when your *old childhood issues don't seem as intense or even as important for you to recall in the same way.* It's not that they aren't significant anymore but that they were created and "impacted" you during your prior incarnation in 3D/4D and don't hold the same regard in your new incarnation and 5D life.

At first, you may feel guilty or imagine that you are betraying yourself by moving on from those memories, their importance, or the pain the experiences have caused you. Remind yourself that the only reason why you were able to evolve into 5D consciousness was because of *all* the work you did during your 3D/4D life around all those *exact* memories in question. You thoroughly processed the events (experienced the Karma) and/or completed the *soul* contracts that you had regarding the specifics, lessons, and HUmans involved.

We may have done our work, but often hold on to the circumstances because moving on from them, feels like we are giving the offending parent or party a "pass," and letting them off the hook, especially when they haven't taken responsibility for their part in the contract and wounding. Challenging as this is to our 3D/4D hearts, nothing is further from the truth. As a cocreator, LightWorker, and *now* ShadowWorker, in 5D you've come to understand the concepts of multidimensionality and the *bigger picture* of every exchange and relationship.

This does not condone any abuse or wounding *ever*. But it should help remind you that there are other realities playing out here and in the unseen world, and although you may never be made privy to them while in the physical, trust that Spiritual Law is just. Use that knowing as a Light cushion between your advanced 5D self and your old 3D/4D self. Then, reclaim your life, your new level of understanding, and move peacefully into the *now*.

In 5D, there is no real benefit in enumerating or repeatedly striking an old chord or vibration with your new processor. One important caveat of your new upgraded system—it does not discriminate, *nor can it always tell the difference* between an old 3D/4D memory replaying itself from a new, 5D creation. What it will do, though, is recreate and multiply whatever you spend an enormous time projecting on your life screen. 5D, although advanced, still functions under the Universal law of *"free will."* It works similarly to your computer. Everything that you feed it from your keyboard or voice commands gets projected on your monitor, including the typos! Even though you are *now* a 5D HUman, if you constantly (not occasionally) regurgitate old 3D/4D habits, emotional reactions, and limitations, that's exactly what your 5D HUman life will print out. *Junk in, junk out.*

5D Memory Has a New Master: The Physical Body

As discussed, 5D memory serves us very differently than we once needed it to as we are no longer holding on to excessive amounts of emotionally charged experiences. The emotional body has stepped aside in 5D. Although it is still very much in the picture, it is no longer front and center. Most things in 5D are *now* centered around the *physical* body because we are *now* carrying a lot more of our own, high-octane God-Light.

Our prior 3D/4D bodies were only able to physically contain our *soul* Light in a subdued, separated, and refracted manner as reflected through the divided centers of the chakra energy system. Our solid vibration of unified God-Light had to be separated from its original wholeness and divided up into the corresponding seven colors of the rainbow. Incarnations on 3D/4D Earth had to be in a lower density HUman body that vibrated to a significant reduction in frequency. *Our bodies are to our soul, as a lamp shade is to a bright bulb, both help soften the Light's intensity.* And most lamps come with a warning notice: "Do not use with a bulb that exceeds a specific wattage, as danger of an electrical fire can occur." We too, as physically based *souls,* need the correct body frequency that can carry our Light's electrical currency and not implode.

As your physical vessel upgrades, your body's DNA will morph—from a 3D carbon-based constitution (part of the cycle of decay) to a 5D crystalline-based constitution (part of the cycle of regeneration). Since our Ascended 5D HUman outgrew its prior 3D/4D body, a newer, biophysical 5D model had to evolve to support all the higher frequency changes. Our

5D HUman has gone through personal transformations, as well as a major evolutionary shift. Because these changes are so vast, our old emotional reactions will often distort, if not at least blur, our *now-based* 5D experiences.

As you practice 5De-emotionalizing, over time, your reactions and recategorizing them into feelings and responses will become easier and more fluent. Catching yourself directly and indirectly identifying experiences and events in your life as *good or bad* will help enormously. Perhaps it will be a little strange at the beginning, but it's going to be very important to have the awareness of no longer needing old memories to serve as a catalyst to create new things in our lives.

In 5D, we are bona fide creators. We *now* have more God in us than ever. We are amplified. We are Lighter and more conscious. We are more capable superHUmans.

Allow for the *New* That Can Only Unfold in the *Now*

When we begin to reduce our learned 3D/4D habits of creating life from the old memories and experiences, our lives begin to shift and change *drastically*. For millennia, we found familiarity and safety in our ability to recycle our ideas, fears, pain, and tears. Through our 3D/4D memory function, we not only recycled past "snapshots" of our lives, but with each round of revisiting, we lulled ourselves into believing that we were taking more control of their narrative.

Learning to live in the 5D *now* throws us headfirst into living a more spontaneous life. Spontaneous living is synonymous with learning to say an exuberant "yes" to the moment, then *allowing* for what it brings.

The slower, preparatory timeline of 3D/4D did not encourage living life in the moment, or the trusting of a higher outcome even when you tried. Allowing for all the new that can only unfold in the *now* and saying "yes" to having new experiences can leave us feeling vulnerable and, at times, unprepared. Dropping our kneejerk reactions, defensiveness, blame, shame, or seeing everything through the lens of right and wrong is disorienting at first (and second, and so on). Life in 5D starts appearing in ways that look like nothing we may have ever considered or wanted to consider! *How could we even visualize specific future outcomes if they haven't been created yet?* Learning how to say a *5D "yes"* opens us not just to what we thought we wanted, but to a myriad of brand-new experiences that the benevolent Universe has cocreated for *and* with us.

New, unrecycled options and realities can't draw on old fears or storylines from your 3D/4D emotional file cabinet. New realities often can't vibrationally identify with emotions based in 3D duality. Besides the denser emotions like worry or fear, your new creations also are not able to fully resonate to some of the Lighter 3D/4D responses, like *"Wow, I'm excited"* or *"This makes me so happy!"*

Take a breath. It's not that you won't experience joy, happiness, or a much desired inner peace in 5D. Actually, quite the opposite *(pun intended)*. You will find more often that your range for having all these emotions exponentially increases the more you remove 3D/4D templates from your experiences.

Things that brought us those feelings in 3D/4D were based on lifetimes of limited beliefs, societal conditioning, and duality-/polarity-based options. Old, recycled memories, emotions, and experiences are life force depleting, whether they're perceived as negative or positive! Old templates and outgrown desires can really hijack or at least slow the new paths being outlined for us by forces from a much higher paygrade then ours. We must learn to adapt to living in the *now,* emotionalizing less, being in allowance, and making the space for a multitude of dimensions and realities to coexist. It will take a while to acclimate, assimilate, and understand how and when to apply these 5D principles, but you will get there. We all will.

Our 3D Physical Body Carried a Lot of Weight and Density

The 3D/4D physical body is very dense compared to spirit. Spirit, before and after incarnation, is etheric, weightless. To anchor even a smidgen of its totality away from its free-floating existence it needs to be encased in an Earth-based, physical body that has a significant amount of material density.

Although our bones and muscles supply a lot of the needed poundage, our *emotional body* can also carry an excessive amount of stored weight and density. The degree of its *heaviness* varies based on how much "emotional weight" one is *carrying.* If any or all parts of a traumatic or impactful experience were left unprocessed, the emotional body will store it as energetic weight, an energy imprint or tuck it away for a later retrieval in our cellular memory. Outside of a physiological component, excessive weight gain often comes from these various, hidden, and intangible sources.

One of the biggest challenges that HUmans have on Earth are the painstaking attempts at trying to manage their physical weight. The emotional component to our deficient or excessive weight issues are often not addressed from the vibrational or energetic point of view. *Pound for pound, emotional weight and memories take up a lot of physical bandwidth.*

As you become more engaged with living a 5D life, neutralizing your emotions, and the subsequent ways your memories are stored, your new biosuit will begin to lose more of its once-needed density and anchoring weight. 5D will bring with it a lot fewer glances in the mirror wondering, *Does this Shadow make me look fat?*

As you drop the old emotionally based reactions, the new Lighter HUman biosuit will allow you to feel and openly Love even more. Being energetically closer to your core God-Self, you will be closer to your truer 5D feelings versus your 3D/4D emotional buffering.

It was our *emotions*, not our feelings that managed to cross our wires and blur the lenses we saw through, confusing and distracting us for so many lifetimes. The spin often left even the best among us not knowing if we were coming or going or making correct or flawed decisions because our emotionally scrambled fields weren't able to pick up clear signals anymore.

Your physical body that housed all the 3G networking, let's just say, *dropped a lot of "inner-net" calls.*

Your transition into 5D asks you to be more mindful of working towards getting more comfortable with *reacting less* and *responding more*. This is going to help train your 5D

HUman and allow your physical body to release more density, and all that depressing physical weight that many of the HUmans have been carrying around! Our 5D bodies, minus all the 3D/4D emotional weight, has more room in its energy field for carrying more of your spirit and your God-Light. We need to support it *now,* as the temple that houses our *soul* and the new freedom that comes with it. Our physical bodies rule in 5D. Take good care of it. Love it, feed it well, exercise it and treat it like the *golden chario*t that it is.

You're Having a Really Big Change of *Heart*

In 3D, the emotional heart was virtually silenced. Most HUmans capitulated to that truth as 3D consciousness assigned complete authority and veto power over to the mental body and its logical-based mind. Our 3D mind, based in duality and on an external value system, decided for us what we held on to, what we considered a great memory, experience, opportunity, and so on. Even our heart-based choices got filtered through the mind, which shaped and finalized them through its *nonheart-based* sieve.

Over millennia, what was meant to be a true gift—our practical, resourceful, scientific mind—became overactive, dominant, and out of balance with the rest of our valued HUman systems. Inadvertently, our emotional and spiritual bodies were contained, diminished, and only able to experience limited growth. Although 4D polarity created a level of consciousness that was spiritually elevated over the 3D consciousness of duality, its highly charged emotional reactions needed to be reworked to reflect our new 5D heart.

THE NEW 5D HUMAN

The 5D higher frequency has *now* bumped the 3D mind out of the lead position and placed our *heart* forefront as the new authority and final decision maker. With it, our 5D heart promoted our *feelings* to a higher significance, relieving our 3D/4D emotional body from its prior use as the main form of HUman expression. As we move forward into these next few years and decades of 5D living, we will be letting go of defining experiences in good or bad, dualistic, or polarized terms. Sometimes, it will be a relief. Other times, you might feel quite lost or emotionally impotent.

We have spent lifetimes defining our values, opinions, politics, and selves through our emotional reactions. You might even feel at times that you are losing your sense of compassion, cut off from caring, because you will be responding to life and all its day-to-day events less frequently from anger, frustration, self-righteousness, and a once-valued, limited 3D/4D perspective. As you evolve, so does how you see the world, the multitude of dimensions that surround us, and other peoples' perspectives.

CHAPTER TEN

STAYING IN COMMAND OF YOUR 5D REALITY

Learning to Hold Your 5D Frequency

There are things you can start doing immediately to retain your 5D frequency until our new paradigm takes shape and makes sense. Start by practicing to stay awake—even for the small stuff. Your *how-do-I-do-this* prayers have been heard. Answers are coming from our Light being counterparts throughout the Multiverse. As you work on keeping your vibration lighter, clearer, and less emotionally dense than it once was, consciously decide to surround yourself with likeminded people, places, and things that you believe will support your 5D frequency. Just start somewhere. Hang out with one friend, take one class, or read one book, and subscribe to 5D newsletters and websites (see Resources). If you begin spending time with 5D peeps *now,* eventually you will have a whole 5D community around you.

This will be a very important step, especially during the early stages of your Ascension. These simple acts of connectedness will help you sustain and stabilize your new higher frequency. Peeps who gravitate to those same places, for the same reasons you sought them out, will enable you to anchor the new higher frequency more deeply into your energy matrix.

Especially during the transitional period, your sensitive 5D self may be extra vulnerable to the insanity caused by the escalating 3D Shadow around you. There could be a lot of challenges for you and those around you who have resonant frequencies as everybody will be trying to recalibrate and get their footing as 5D HUmans living in a 3D world. You are certainly not alone in your unprecedented, evolutionary balancing act, as the world has collectively reached a 5D tipping point.

Personal aspects of who we once were, including our false identities, masculine energy-based drives for success, and outdated beliefs and values will rapidly reveal themselves to us. Our inner *3D Shadow* will show up in spades, not as a punishment, but so we can kiss it goodbye and send it on its merry way.

We've waited lifetimes to arrive here—fantasizing, visualizing, and praying that the day would come when the gates of 5D would open, and we would be free to leave the "Land of Nos." What a difficult 3D/4D crossing we had! The amount of stress caused by waiting for anything worthwhile to significantly shift demanded so much patience from us that more often than not it felt torturous.

Try your best to release any of your residual 3D programs related to the control mechanism of scarcity, survival, and fear. As your 3D being senses change occurring, it would not be unexpected for all your deepest, darkest, polarized beliefs (which kept you on a very short "freedom leash") to get exacerbated. Yes, the new freedom is going to feel very scary at times, but the more you understand what is unfolding on various dimensional levels, the less likelihood there will be of you letting such fears dupe you into shutting down your transition process. Old fears that masquerade in your subconscious psyche as truth are the exact 3D illusions that most of us need to come to the surface to be transmuted. Let them. Embrace them. See them for what they really are: old versions of your prior realities. Nothing more.

Before *now,* we said "no" so often to things we wanted due to our filter of *fear.* We clung for dear life to all sorts of unfulfilling relationships, warped principles, and stubborn thoughts. We were attached to them because of our old rogue friend, *fear.* This reality was limited at best because illusions in 3D were presented as *truth.* We never confidently learned that just feeling frightened doesn't always mean we are in danger or that fear's assessment is even correct. Limits on what was possible were created by the establishment of *emotional firewalls* and mental set points in us. We were always encouraged to take safe, little baby steps to reach our goals instead of going after the big outcome we would have really loved. This dichotomy created many lifetimes of fear-based 3D madness and an inability to see past only one potential reality at a time—the one we thought would bring us happiness, safety, and security or the one that was destined to take it all away.

A 5D world is going to be a real game changer. We are finally awake—sleepy eyed but aware of our surroundings. It's much harder to dupe someone who is conscious than someone who is sleeping. If you hold strong to your 5D understanding of what is *now* possible for you and the world, your life will begin to change and make progress in ways that you could not even fathom.

In 5D, we are *"erasing"* and *"reversing."* Our upgraded energy field comes equipped with an automatic setting for a new *Karmic neutralizer* feature. This really cool option organically moves towards turning everything back to a *right side up order* again. Although we seriously get that at first things are going to feel a little bit crazy, our practice every single day is to try, even a little bit, to withdraw our emotional reactions from the overall construct.

Practice Alchemy. Spin your fears into a Golden Key that opens the 3D gates and frees you. Try to make fear your friend, *not your story or your commanding officer.*

Pain Is Sometimes a Given, but Suffering Is a *Choice*

For lifetimes, our 3D selves have been conditioned to accept a lot of our limitations, behavior patterns, and reactivity as "hardwired" truths about HUman nature and mainly inevitable because of our familiarity with them. As you begin to create more daylight between these old ideas and your new ideas, try to remember that although this conditioning will attempt to draw you back to doing the familiar, it doesn't mean you are not free to *roam.*

Remind yourself that we all tend to stay close to things that are familiar to us, even if those things limit our choices and reduce our capacity to experience the happiness, joy, and peace we truly seek. Moment by moment, make the conscious choice "not to suffer or tolerate suffering." The 3D victim mentality is deeply evident in our confusion, frustration, and hopelessness about making changes in general. These states were an integral part of our 3D experience. *We learned to suffer very well.* The more we bought into ideas of duality, the institutional rules of religions and other authority figures, the deeper down the rabbit hole we went.

As you move into and stabilize your energy in 5D, take a long, deep, overdue breath of knowing that you don't have to collude with personal suffering or the perpetration of suffering on *others* anymore! Although there is much struggle and pain in our present world, you can make a conscious decision to hold "compassionate space" for the *energy* that holds 3D/4D *suffering* in place. Doing this will help to transmute it without adding a new charge to the strong 3D/4D emotions that helped create it, such as *hopelessness, shame, guilt, anger, and fear*. These old 3D/4D reactions are core constructs that will only serve to create more suffering for you and others.

With every opportunity that comes your way, do your best to consciously practice the new habit of *not-suffering*, especially in regard to your health, relationships, finances, or any other area in your life that you experience as *wounded or hurt*. Challenge the underlying storylines that continue to fuel the existence of your old reactions. Over time, as you hold firmly to your new choices, you will be able to take back power from all the old 3D habits that you worked so hard to end and evolve beyond.

Gracefully, with all the Love in your heart, *let go* of your 3D program of suffering. Thankfully, you won't be needing it anymore.

If you find yourself feeling stuck or frozen, think back on the five stages of grief outlined by Dr. Kübler-Ross: denial, anger, bargaining, depression, and acceptance. Check if you are feeling jammed by some unprocessed emotions as you are dying off aspects of your 3D self, reality, and life.

Managing Disappointments and Frustration

Disappointment is going to be an important feeling for you to learn to navigate *now*. Because you have shifted from a slower 3D timeline to a faster 5D timeline, initially, you may experience frustration and loss more often and with less warning. Your 5D lifestyle, with its new *autobahn* speed, allows you to create the things you clearly desire and envision much faster, and it can also move you *through* those creations a lot faster. You might often feel like the ground beneath you is slipping away, like when the wet sand unpredictably shifts under your feet as the tide comes in.

Jobs, careers, relationships, ideas, creations, and inspirations come and go more rapidly, and what we create may not appear to last as long as it did in 3D/4D. For example, a relationship that lasted forty years in 3D/4D might only last ten or fifteen years in 5D. A career direction may suddenly shift, or a business idea will quickly fizzle out. As a first "reaction," it won't be uncommon for you to feel disappointed or that you did something wrong or didn't do enough, or to feel ashamed that your great idea or opportunity tanked. Our 3D/4D Karmic contracts—whether social, genetic, or personal—and their lessons, had us running in place for millennia. But in 5D, we are moving through life without carrying the weight of our old Karma. The pace of every experience is simply faster.

Another adjustment in 5D living is that we are *now multidimensional* beings. We might not experience our creations in the same tangible, physical ways that we formerly did in our 3D lives. Sometimes, *just* by having a thought, image, or desire, you will vibrationally extract and download everything you need from that creation into your 5D mind or emotional body without requiring it to manifest on the physical plane.

The world around you benefits from your *absorbability*, too, as you radiate the lessons you learn to the environment around you. Remember, absorption is one of our new 5D senses. *As multidimensional beings, we can also simultaneously contribute our thoughts and creations to beings who need them in other dimensions, even if we don't exist physically in that dimension.*

Without understanding the faster-moving paradigm of 5D and some of the nonphysical variations in how our 5D creations can manifest, you could easily feel disappointed and frustrated every time something doesn't turn out as you had hoped. Your old 3D "friends," the feelings of shame, low self-esteem, and ineptitude, can quickly consume your emotional field and pull you down into a 3D/4D rabbit hole personalized with your custom narrative about what "didn't happen" and why.

In the prior 3D belief system, which, as discussed, is based in duality, if things you wanted to happen did happen in the physical plane, then they were considered *good*. If things you didn't want to happen did happen in the physical plane, then they were considered *bad*. Duality created conflict. There really was nowhere else to go mentally and emotionally other than to feel chronically disappointed, not good enough, and blame ourselves or others because we lived in a state of extreme scarcity and deprivation.

Our old understanding of life didn't include the *bigger picture* variables that the Multiverse does. This worldview didn't account for *multidimensionality, vibrational downloads, nonphysical manifestations, or triality* as viable explanations for why things did or didn't turn out the way we planned, intended, or hoped.

Driving on our new 5D "high speed highway" of life, we create faster and move through our creations faster. Some will manifest in our physical world. Others will manifest in alternate dimensions. Some will manifest in our emotional body or a spiritual realm, where we can download them from our "cloud" as needed at a later date. Retraining our thinking and perceptions to understand these new possibilities related to our constructs will help offset a lot of chronic frustration, blaming, and disappointment.

Take Loving Ownership of Your Energy Field: If You Don't, Someone or Something Else *Will*

We get to make a *"yes" or "no"* decision regarding our second incarnation in every single moment. If you don't take control of the wheel of your existence–meaning, if you don't allow yourself to live in the state associated with your chosen frequency of consciousness–then, over time, that lack of alignment will create vibrational *loopholes. Not claiming your life as your own will leave you vulnerable to something or someone energetically deciding for you the direction and shape that your life will take.* And there are a plethora of variables, good and *not so good* actors who would happily step up to oblige.

It's really not a choice anymore to allow yourself to be entrained by the outer world. For, in actuality, you already committed to upleveling your vibration and consciousness long before you stepped into your new 5D life. It came with the "waking up" part. That's why you are here right *now,* "reading descriptions of the agreements you signed off on in your new 5D *soul* contracts." Many of us who were with you in Lemuria and Atlantis "signed" many of the same contracts.

Post-Traumatic Stress

We know what happened the first time we tried to Ascend the planet to 5D, and we *now* know some of the players who were also involved. Some of the players, in fact, were *us.*

In world events today, we can see evidence of many cycles repeating themselves. We are witnessing the often painful reality of aspects of HUmankind's decaying levels of consciousness.

We've come to understand that the Shadow side of HUmanity, like it or not, will have to rise. If you are a conscious HUman, awake and present for all of this initial chaos, *how could you not be scared?* I am, often. As the energies continue to tumble and ricochet, so do our psyches. Many of us are experiencing lots of flashbacks of those final months in Lemuria and Atlantis. Subconscious memories and feelings have triggered many of our *current-day post-traumatic stress symptoms,* such as fear, anxiety, apocalypse, and a pending sense of doom.

Although many HUmans have struggled from PTSD for eons, this phase of the experience is not "personal" anymore; *now* our trauma is collective and global. The coronavirus and the threat of nuclear war are triggering our memories of the evacuation, loss of family, friends, HUman separation, betrayal, anger, fear, and, for me, the radiation poisoning at the end of our stay in Lemuria and Atlantis. Back then, it may have been the crystal energy grids that exploded and volcanic eruptions that led to tsunamis, drowning, fires, and flooding, but today, we have many of the same trauma triggers and fear happening just on a more sophisticated level.

I want you to think about *yourself* right *now*. All the traumas you are struggling with in your life today are very real, but they are also being presented to you as an opportunity to resolve your Karmic PTSD and process the part you played during our original *failure to Ascend* and its traumatic aftermath. This is a gold-framed doorway for you on a personal level to release seemingly unrelated anxiety, grief, sadness, hopelessness, and some illnesses. The fact that you are here in this era, dealing with *The L&A "Take Two" Show*, means that you have the willingness to be part of the world's reset and launch.

You've carried post-traumatic Karma for almost 30,000 years. *Now*, you are finally in a place where your *power* is not contingent on what happens around you. Because you are multidimensional, you can deal with several complex factors at once. You can deal with what's going on for you. You can deal with what's going on in the world. You can deal with the dual consciousness of the 3D world. You can deal with emotional chaos of the 4D world. You can deal with the speed at which the 5D world moves and creates! You can deal with any of the content on all the frequency channels of your vibratory cable box.

So don't act like you can't. Because *now* you can. It's a choice. This is a time to rise. This is your time. Don't waste it. Don't get lost in the shuffle. Don't get pulled in and caught up into the polarized emotions and succumb to them. Everything is an *illusion* playing itself out. Don't waste this moment in time for *anything or anyone.*

Creating Your Reality

Why only fantasize about it when you know *now* that you can create it? You have a 5D biofield. Explore it. It comes with new capabilities, options, and a raised level of consciousness. At some point, you will have to start testing all this out—why not start *now?* Pick whatever is up for you and apply your 5D skills to the process of navigating it.

If this suggestion brings you *any hesitancy (aka resistance),* just do it as an experiment. Your reality truly can reflect what you want. Not due to the familiar positive thinking model or a set of affirmations you might have encountered in a 4D training program. It's more than just a different way of thinking. It's creation *5D style.* This important stage of our 5D Ascension process asks us not only to start creating in a new way, it also encourages us to allow those creations into the day-to-day reality of our current lives.

As we become more comfortable with 5De-emotionalizing our reactions and creations, over time the process of creating will happen more quickly and without draining our emotional resources. The 3D/4D system of creating by attaching either positive or negative emotions to the visualization is still a very viable way to "bake the pie," but this mode of creativity is still based in 4D polarity and 3D repetitive thought. Although it's far from wrong or ineffective, you are awake enough to begin to explore other avenues and more evolved ways of working the dashboard.

Taking dominion over your creations without adhering to the familiar instruction that you "have to" charge them through your electrified emotional field for a desired outcome to occur should bring you some welcome ease and relief. You have stepped into a place in your 5D life where a primary rule of encouragement is that you "take ownership over your reality." *You'll create through the energy of your thoughts, words, feelings, and deeds but with the fuel and vibrational resonance of the Divine Feminine.* Use all of who you are, both your Light and your Shadow, to declare that your life is *completely* your own.

As you transition to higher realities, as a multidimensional being, you will still witness a lot of injustices in the world and many despicable *HUman on HUman* behaviors. Understandably, you will feel offended or upset by a lot of it. At the end of the day, however, if it showed up on your life's *teleprompter,* there is probably an opportunity for you lurking in the Shadow of it all—that is, if you know how to shine some 5D Light on it. The lesson is that we can also channel our abilities, focus on our truths, and create the realities we want to experience, whatever they may be, in and out of the Light. Don't waste anything.

We are *now* becoming more fluid with pushing back on alternate realities that we aren't in resonance with but still can learn from. We don't have to go full throttle into a strong emotional reaction in order to erect an internal guardrail against the perceived threat. If we shift just one iota of the same energy that we give to our emotions and thoughts and redirect it to shifting our reality to 5D responses and thinking, our lives will change on a dime.

The main obstacle is often that we were trained to identify what we believe, think, or feel through the filter of an outside authority or stimulus. In turn, we were trained to create our lives based on what we bounce off of or what we react to, rather than creating from what we truthfully perceive within. That is the way the *masculine energy* taught us to create. We *now* have a different vibrational bandwidth to experience our new HUman on, the *Divine Feminine* being the new *top dog*.

Now that all sorts of constructs, institutions, and old masculine-based realities are crumbling before our eyes, it's starting to feel pretty intense out there. Just know, if you're feeling wobbly or a bit woozy (and *you haven't been drinking or using drugs*) with all this upleveling, you are not alone. Your inner state of "*WTF?*" will eventually stabilize as you gain more familiarity over time with your 5D self.

Keep in mind that as we move more into 5D, everything holds less of an emotional charge, and you will have less desire to react verses respond. *Truth is transcendent now.* There is no real "rule of law," except for the one we each hold as truth in our hearts. It will be both unnerving and mindblowing not to take an emotionally charged position *for or against things* as we had learned from the opposition of 3D/4D polarity.

3D/4D *Rule of Law* Is Unmooring

To many of us HUmans, what made us feel safe in the world was having aspects of the *rule of law* in place represented through various governmental institutions, such as the police and military. It had lulled us into believing there was some kind of hierarchy, order, and controls in place. All of these protective institutions were created in 3D. Although our societies are still very much in need of their services, especially now, as we are being faced with a seemingly out of control rise in 3D/4D Shadow, they too need to be reworked and upgraded out of their old masculine premise. As we move into 5D consciousness, we have to responsibly consider that all current *rules of law* are based on the duality principles of *right versus wrong.* With as many as we have in place, they are not an effective enough dam to curtail the onslaught of HUman-on-HUman carnage, increased gun violence and escalation in untreated mental illness. *Our challenge lies in the fact that it is not Spiritual Law but 3D HUman Law that is imperfect, inconsistent, and derived from the now rapidly dissolving masculine energy.* As 3D melts away, this *little* caveat has come back to the surface to bite HUmanity in the . . . *hypocrisy.* The increase of the higher Light stemming from our new 5D consciousness has brought to the surface and triggered what we already knew for decades. Our world has been carrying an *excessive* amount of well-hidden 3D Shadow energy.

What we didn't expect to so blatantly be confronted with was that some of the same HUmans we placed in charge to uphold or reinforce these rules have been behind the scenes flagrantly violating and breaking the exact laws they were hired to protect and reinforce. We witnessed this unfolding as the backdrop to the past four to five years—as everyone, in professions from *policing to politics,* also had their own personal 3D Shadow drawn to the surface during our *bigger picture* post Ascension process. We witnessed this with police officers who tragically participated in murdering George Floyd, with President Donald Trump aiding and abetting the January 6, 2021, insurrection at the U.S. Capitol, and with the extreme federal and state court rulings in 2022 suppressing the right to vote and women's reproductive rights. As painful, disgusting, and disturbing as it is to witness all these events, trust that no one gets a *pass* during our planet's unprecedented 5D Ascension process, even if on the surface it may appear that some HUmans are above the *rule of law.*

Our post-5D Ascension period has created an energetic vacuum that is syphoning out all the hidden Shadow pieces left over from our stay in 3D duality and 4D polarity. The more we consciously do everything in our *soul's* power to keep moving HUmanity forward and towards the higher Light, the more we will have to expect this kind of radical Shadow purging.

As all this muck surfaces, it will become our *souls'* work *now* to *hold the space* for HUman darkness to transmute through this part of the Ascension process. Hold as many other hands as you can until this segue eventually completes itself. As we move further away from 3D/4D and create a different dimensional focus, it will be a strange time and involve a massive undertaking.

In essence, you are being asked to stand strong and not overreact, being *fully awake* and watching as the *world burns down.* Yes, it's that *surreal!* Please make sure while you are reaching out to hold someone's trembling hand that your free hand is also reaching out to allow another HUman to hold *yours*.

The root of the word *authority* is *author*. You want to be the author of your own life's story. This means, you need to step in and exercise your authority over the reality you choose to create. The one caveat is that your new reality should not be based on old beliefs about what's *right and wrong*. It cannot be based on judgments, either positive or negative. Those beliefs are often trip switches that limit what we can create.

Subconsciously and consciously, we all have beliefs about *what we can and cannot do*. We have many built in "set-points," delineating boundary lines and transparent glass ceilings. It can feel very scary to exceed those limitations. Acknowledge that . . . then go exceed them anyway!

A lot of these internal "stop signs" are actually spillovers of old 3D/4D formulas embedded in our prior training in "creation skills 101." Trying to apply the "how-to" instructions from our old HUman textbook will slow us down considerably or downright prevent us from growing into our newly minted 5D life. From our upgraded 5D core we *now* get to radiate the highest frequencies of Love and Light, be our own "gods," and move from being "servants" to being "masters" of our own destinies. Everyone likes how all that sounds when we talk about it. *But in order for us to function like this idea of gods, we first have to blow the lid off all our limitations and the way we once perceived reality.*

The expansion that 5D brings is where all HUmans will be headed eventually. We will give ourselves permission to step out of our prior limitations safely, without feeling out of control or wronged by the expansion of our desires. I don't know how the next year or decade is going to play out, and by the way, *no one does.* But if we are going to take this game of life to the next level, we have to stay calm, remain awake and engaged, and take 100 percent responsible for everything in our lives. *We need to want 100 percent peace, and more importantly, be willing to stay the course.* Once we are, then we can let go of all our resistance and surrender to that truth and whatever comes with it. Everything will fall into place if each of us stays in our *own lane,* holding front and center, our own life's mission of 100 percent responsibility.

Lemurians knew that whatever they *thought* would eventually become their truth and creation. They knew to take responsibility for their thinking, actions, and responses. Because of their understanding of their place in creation, they were able to change many things instantaneously. They knew that, if they came from a certain space and place in their heart, their manifestations rooted in Love would come to fruition. They understood that all acts of creation affected everyone else in tandem. If they could sense something using any of their available *sixteen* HUman senses, then it was immediately placed into play as a new, accessible version of reality. All because it was what they had created.

Higher beings, as well as many Earth-based HUmans who carry the consciousness of the Lemurians within themselves, *hold the secrets* of this ancient sacred knowledge of creation. Some of these secrets are *now* in our consciousness, but most of them are still in our subconscious. With each incremental sleep that we gradually awaken from, the information we so cleverly stored within our *souls'* DNA becomes active and conscious. Although it took us a long time to get here, we had to first be able to face the imprints of lifetimes of trauma still stored in our subconscious memory bank.

For some of us, remembering can be terribly upsetting. Most of us agreed that if we actually had a successful 5D Ascension launch, that we would self-correct the final glitches during *post*. We also knew that the plan was always to use our *current world's* events to trigger a massive "experience" recall for HUmanity's final push towards an overall healing. Just as a homeopathic remedy is sometimes a tiny "poison" that initiates an ultimate cure, this version of events is a cyclic repeat of our Karmic past. *Not to repeat it, but to finally release it for good.* In many ways, we have recreated a pattern so mindblowingly precise that nothing short of an all-hands-on deck "miracle" could have pieced it together.

The purpose of spiritual life on Earth, especially for LightWorkers and ShadowWorkers with the *bigger picture* assignment of raising the frequency of HUmanity's collective consciousness, can be difficult to grasp. Some of our work here is to also make peace with our HUman Shadow creations and those of *others*. The collective of what we witness on a daily basis and often *detest,* is only reflecting the untransmuted Shadow energies of each individual.

This horrifically unpleasant period in history is designed to deliver us to a much higher-level consciousness, if we let it take us there.

An Awakening or Inner Knowing?

We've all been called here *now* to be an integral part of the 5D Ascension process and what's turning out to be *one hell of a post-Ascension* period! There's no resting. So don't disappoint yourself by waiting for it to come. Not right *now* anyway. What there is and what you should strive for is *peace*. Peace in knowing that we are not doing this alone. Peace in knowing that we're not crazy. Peace in knowing that there's a *bigger picture* at play. And that in the Multiverse, we are clearing up Karmas and righting wrongs along the way as we are Ascending. We are doing some magical, phenomenal, kick-ass stuff!

Don't let your lower HUman emotions make Ascension a *win-lose* situation. **This is a sacred process, and you are one of its unsung heroes.** You do not yet have a scintilla of feedback or evidence to know deeply how much good you have done for HUmanity. Don't slow down yet. Keep going higher in frequency. Take what you know and use it to grow who you know *now* is at your core, *your God Self.* Embracing that truth will be a very significant accomplishment.

We're rising, and when we rise, everybody else rises too. When everybody in a community or nation rises, the world rises. When the world rises, the Universe rises. When the Universe rises, *all* the Universes rise. The rising energy spreads throughout the Multiverse in every dimension and to every being of energy, as their *hearts* are watching every effort we make. And from what my inside sources are telling me . . . we're doing an unbelievably great job, even on our *worst days.*

As we move forward, we will continue for a while to feel like one day we are riding the bull, and another day, the rollercoaster. Just as one transition passes, the next wave of change will come through. And yes, there will be a lot more fallout up ahead as our post-5D Ascension period is far from over. There will be a lot of last-ditch efforts to retain the current power structure, especially as we move into the next few national election cycles in the USA, taking place before and during 2022 and 2024. The European Nations will shift and change as the British Monarchy, for the first time in seventy years, will have a new leader: King Charles. President Zelenskyy and the Ukraine are currently still at war with Russia and Vladimir Putin, and rogue leaders such as Kim Jong-un are all still wild cards. Which direction HUmanity will take is totally in the hands of HUmanity. We will not know, *until we know.*

In 5D consciousness, we are no longer held victim to old Karmic repetitions, patterns, or predetermined destinies. We are free to choose or not choose. Anticipate that some challenges up ahead will be lost, others revisited, and some transmuted back to higher Light. We will witness many of the same unpredictable upending of masculine-based power structures as the world too will be shaken up and destabilized at various times across the planet. The 3D, 4D and 5D pendulums will aggressively sway back and forth, first to the left, then to the right, and then all over again, in a vibrational effort to try to find some core homeostasis.

Many of the big 3D players around the world, including the Putin and Xi Administrations in Russia and China will make attempts to reassert control, but really, the old 3D and 4D power structures and brokers are running out of gas. And the

United States, with many of its shortcomings, is still the leader of the free world and has some of the best bones of any nation to lead the planet through the post-5D Ascension. This is part of its divine grace and higher calling for it has the largest footprint of "collective Light and HUman hutzpah" on the planet to trigger change for the better on an enormous scale, in supersonic time.

Why is this important to recognize and support? Because we have a *relatively small window of time* available for us to push this epic HUman evolutionary transition past the finish line. The *now* is calling.

Just send the world Light and Love. This is not a winner takes all process. This is a choice to Ascend or Descend. Hold the space and do the job you said you would do. I'm holding you to it. You hold me to it. Let's together hold the space for this next miracle to unfold.

There's a lot of Karma being resolved and transmuted every second that we shine LOVE on to something. The *worse* something appears on the surface, the most it *will be impacted* by redirecting our Love back to it.

We talked about multidimensionality and how many HUmans are working through Karmic residue from their 3D incarnations. Maybe you haven't fully dealt with all of your own Karmic issues? Maybe things haven't gone the way you wanted them to go in your current life? Maybe you spent decades dealing with abuses, addictions, disappointments, hurts, and injuries while earnestly trying to clean up your own Shadowy messes? I know I have. But if you haven't completely finished and you'd like to "*readdress the mess,*" then go do it *now*. Just this time coming from Light and traveling through it all at the *speed of Love.* Make peace with the truth of probably never *consciously* knowing, during this embodied lifetime anyway, why every crazy, painful moment went down the way it did.

Everyone has the *right* to clean up the mess they made and often it first begins with the *recreation of a version of it* that we can work off of. All HUmans on the planet are responsible for cleaning up the mess they made in whatever lifetime it occurred. The dissolution of old Karma has moved us through to our current state of our successful 5D Ascension. And yes, it has moved us through it at such a ridiculously warped speed– that our HUman eyes, mind, and hearts have a very difficult time detecting any motion at all. *Let me reiterate this, we are moving so fast it feels like we aren't moving at all.* Try to revel in that reality for a second and then wrap your arms around the world and where we all are right *now.*

As mentioned, the ancients in Lemuria had an inner wisdom and an inner spirituality that was never discussed or argued about. There was only *absolute empowerment* or *Love* in their civilization, without all the power struggles that we see around us and also participate in today. The core beliefs of Lemuria were based in the innate power of Love and respect for one another and the Earth herself. Those truths are the closest to what Lemurians and a lot of Atlanteans considered a religion. There was a knowing within every HUman being at that time that all of life was harmoniously connected through the unified language of the heart, rather than the separate compartments of mind and body. Their most important values were based in unity, comMUnity, awareness, centeredness, respect, Love of others, and unconditional Love.

The main transformational force in Lemuria was Love of Self, which went hand in hand with being able to let go of many of the unawakened emotions like fear, greed, possessiveness, and jealousy, among others. Lemurians knew that we create our own world, and if a reality exists outside of us it also exists inside of us somewhere, too.

As your Lemurian memory is activated within you, it will simply take the form of your own *inner wisdom*. Sometimes it will come in stages, other times in moments, but these are the backbone of your *5D Ascension*.

We All Had a Part in Creating the 3D Paradigm

Many significant Humans back then in Lemuria and Atlantis contributed to the final outcome, which was the failure of our attempt at a 5D Ascension and, ultimately, the destruction of our beloved civilization. My personal recall and part of my *bigger picture* Karmic work has been to specifically remember certain parts played during that profound period by the *souls* at that time, some being William Barr and Donald Trump from today. I obviously carried some intense Karma associated with that time period, as I am sure I do here, *now,* in this place and time. I accept that knowing and understand deeply that this book was as much for my own Lemurian healing and my alter-ego *Jonathan III of Aveidon,* as it was for all of you.

In life, if you know where to look, everything becomes an opportunity to learn, unlearn, and grow. I had a part in what happened *or* didn't happen at the end in Lemuria. I may have acted too slowly, addressed the rise of the HUman Shadow over in Atlantis too late, or was myopic in my views of what HUmanity would ultimately be capable of. I truly don't know all the details of what actually transpired, and frankly, I am very grateful I don't. But what I do know for sure is that without having awakened to the *bigger picture* concepts and understanding about my multidimensional self and world, I might have had a much longer stay in the energetic abyss of lifetimes of remorse. Although I do not take responsibility for the direction HUmankind veered off in, I do take responsibility for whatever intentional or unintentional part that I may have contributed, both then and *now*.

No matter what side of the aisle, perspective, or puffery we may choose to be on, none of us alive lives without some responsibility for releasing these remaining pieces of our current world's Shadow Karma. We are all experiencing the day-to-day effects of the Shadow's Shadow, otherwise we wouldn't be here *now*. It's really not a complicated equation nor one that aims to shame, blame, or indirectly manipulate. It just *is*.

And yes, there are many different levels of culpability and Light/Shadow consciousness at play, at any given time. Some blatant and obvious, but a lot of it sometimes is *not* so obvious. It is so tempting for HUmans, especially out of their strong sense of *Light* and *wrong* to get caught up in ascribing blame to the perceived guilty person or parties. But keep in mind, even those of Lemurian descent serving here on the planet, also incarnated with Karmic ties to past event, actions and specifically *inactions*. Many HUMUs are personally here to learn how to address, speak up for, and own their complete Light force as God's very powerful creative beings.

Many back then didn't speak up and erroneously believed that as beings of the Light, they were somehow exempt from taking more masculine-based, physical actions that may possibly have resulted in another direction or outcome.

In the higher spiritual realms, *passivity and complacency* are sometimes considered a "dereliction of duty," an unconscious act of omission. As we spiritually and vibrationally Ascend, we also need to engage our new consciousness and Light capabilities towards the resolution of all divisions in our world that we currently perceive to contributing to the underlying illness of "HUman separation." As minimal as some of these pieces initially seem, when we turn a blind eye and allow ambient Shadow energy to grow within ourselves, families, cultures, religions, and societies, we inadvertently contribute to its proliferation. This is what we did in Lemuria, throughout our lives, and often do *now*.

The Spirituality of Politics

At one time on the planet politics represented policy, how we choose our federal monies to be spent, the *rule of law* reinforced and the upholding of the constitution, etc. But now politics are part of the new mosaic of 5D HUman spirituality. In our world today, **VOTING** is the single, most powerful thing you can actively do to make your *voice* and *vibration* count. The democratic election process and the genre of politics are *now* an integral part of our new "*5D Spiritual Currency.*" Intrinsically tied to a *bigger picture* set of outcomes and consequences that span the Multiverse, we can no longer distance ourselves or conveniently feign ignorance to the impact that our "one solitary vote" has. Our work *now* is to steady the rudders, hold the vibrational space for the highest outcome, and *5De-emotionalize* through the upset that often comes with setbacks initially interpreted as tragic and/or permanent.

Elections Have Consequences

In this pivotal time during all this planetary noise and chaos, we often forget, especially as things seem to be spinning incessantly with no end in sight, that we are still led by the very powerful rule of Spiritual Law, *free will*. As discussed throughout this book, *free will* gives us the inherent power to act out of *free choice*. Although HUmans aspire to this exalted state of complete ownership over their lives and the decisions that they make, most often, even when given the legal right to make and choose, they tend to default on that *right*.

When someone doesn't vote in an election and are not limited by law or circumstances (*illness, accessibility, fears about being arrested or killed if they go, or impacted by voter suppression laws, and the like*), they knowingly or unknowingly divest themselves not only on a personal level, but on a spiritual level, of their contribution to the greater whole. Because in any dimension the "collective consciousness'" creates the groups' chosen reality, which its members then live in and experience. Each dimension, 3D, 4D, and even 5D, is constantly recreating new percentages of its Light and Shadow quotients.

Over the next two to six years, I believe we're going to see a lot of evidence of how HUmanity's consciousness has shifted, whether it has evolved or devolved. As to which direction it will take, only time, actions, and the greater participation of our ***"Heart Light"*** will tell.

The world's priorities will have to change if we are still interested in leading with the things that *truly* matter. Anything short of an unwavering focus of unified God-Light that seriously benefits HUmanity, the Planet, Animals, and the *"Soul Rights"* of the Earth-based HUmans will throw us more and more off course. We are at a time *now* where our window of opportunity can either narrow and close or expand and burst open.

Economies are important, but they will be shifting and changing significantly worldwide over the next decade or so. They will continue to morph, ebb and sway until we arrive at a system that is *fair* and works for every incarnated *soul* on the planet, no matter who is in charge or elected. "Fair" doesn't necessarily imply socialism, capitalism, communism, or the like. As a 5D society we haven't yet created an economic system(s) that will restore HUman dignity and lead us into a 6D Ascension. *(Yes, I said 6D, not 5D)* But from whatever dimensional or multidimensional perch we choose to observe HUman life from, we will never be able to serve any aspect of the *bigger picture* agenda without first meeting HUmanity's basic survival needs, like food, water, and healthcare.

Anything that is currently unfolding is unfolding in exactly the way it is supposed to. *Most* of the time, the more evolved part of me believes this to be true. Even on the days when this insane world and the darker side of HUmanity can bring me to my knees, I still *try* to return to this perspective. It's the best way for my *heart* to recenter itself.

What I do know is that it is our *collective agreement* to be here *now*, in an often-confusing world with many flaws as well as color-rich sunsets, sparkling oceans, and limitless beauty. We all have, in the *"name of the Light,"* gathered back together to work through, rethink, reconfigure, laugh, Love, and find peace as we ultimately Ascend to a higher frequency—mainly and foremost for our personal *souls'* growth and collectively for the evolution of HUmankind. We are helping to create "kind-HUmans."

One of our greatest Karmic lessons is one that has been repeated over and over again throughout many of our lifetimes, especially from our incarnations in Lemuria and Atlantis. Back then, we tirelessly worked on expanding our *Lightbodies*. We erroneously believed that the Shadow side of HUmanity mostly existed in others and outside of us. Throughout our very long reign in 3D, a lot of our work along the way placed emphasis on helping others transmute *their* Shadow energies. Albeit we left our own HUman Shadow parts unacknowledged and often unintended. This may have been a form of *spiritual elitism* that we were collectively blindsided by.

Back then, and even *now* many former Lemurians believed that the Shadow, as an energy mostly existed outside of the Light, and didn't completely understand it's totality as an actual fractal of our God-Light. The Shadow is also a gift, a teaching aspect of our God-Self that also needed and needs to be Loved, embraced, integrated, and transmuted. In part, I believe that our misconceptions in regards to the Light/Shadow aspects of HUman consciousness *and beyond*, multiplied and contributed greatly to the heartbreaking repercussions and dire ending of that time.

Having Shadow or Light aspects doesn't make anybody all good or bad, just *HUman*. Having awareness does not make one HUman *better* than anyone else. Consciousness just reflects different depths of understanding and awakened-ness.

Our biggest challenge going forward will be moving through these, hopefully last few vestiges of 3D/4D Shadow in the HUman consciousness. HUmanity, comprised of both the evolved and the not-so-evolved, needs to take a *closer* look inside, that is if we are brave enough and willing to live and vibrate from LOVE. Then, with great courage, clarity, and accountability, we must choose either to bring those pieces back into Light or reseed them again for continued growth.

If you're walking this path, it is imperative that you open your mind and your beautiful heart to the truth of the *bigger picture*. Accept that Spiritual Law is in play in our world right *now* as unfathomable as that sometimes appears to be. Nothing that is currently happening was not set up perfectly for a relay to the next thing that is meant to move us closer to the complete consciousness of God-Love. Everything on Earth has an inherent inner drive moving it constantly towards the frequency of Light and Love. That doesn't mean Love, in its totality is here today, but it also doesn't mean that it isn't here today. either. During the rougher times, force yourself to get an ice-cream, watch a sunset or roll around the floor with your dog or cat. Find the life forces that raise your chi, open your heart, and remind you that it's not all terrible here. It's not a hell, even though there are times that it is hellish.

Even as 5D HUmans, we are still very much veiled from most of what is "really" happening at any given time in both our lives and the outer world around us. Speaking for myself, most days I am focused on how I can assist HUmans who have been placed in my care and in turn, the *bigger picture* where all HUmanity resides. I do my utmost to keep my personal energy and consciousness as elevated and in a Loving state as much as possible. I am a *bigger-picture* person. (read: *not* a bigger person) I am here and walking the same path you are on. I am challenged often, and on certain days it feels like I am trying to swim upstream. *But I swim anyway.*

For me and my old self, Jonathan III of Aveidon—and most likely, if you've come this far, *for you too*—following my *heart* was always the only *choice*.

CHAPTER ELEVEN

FINAL THOUGHTS

> "A mind that is stretched by a new experience can never go back to its old dimensions."
> —Oliver Wendell Holmes

Life as we know it is changing. We are moving into a vastly different way of experiencing our lives and the HUmans in them. We are at a completion point, which means that multiple lifetimes in 3D are coming to an end all at once. Each successive cleanup on *aisle three* that you have undertaken has substantially reduced the mess, angst, and chaos left behind. Closure of 3D altogether is expedited every time we choose to live as a higher version of ourselves in any context, relationship, or interaction. And because enough of us have cleaned up our *Shadow side* by *now*, the world itself is making an incredible, quantum transition into the higher dimension of 5D conscious-ness. We've done it!

There are very few times in life when someone gets the spiritual opportunity to be one of the first HUmans to walk a path, especially when the new path only emerges as it is being walked. Today everything going forward in this world is created for the path we are laying out for those who choose to follow.

Lead with the profound knowing that you matter and what you have contributed for the last hundreds of thousands of years has made an incredible difference in God's *bigger picture* plan. YOU are never ever alone, never not seen and always Loved.

More importantly, with each breath you take, lead with your *heart*, and always, always come from LOVE.

428

ACKNOWLEDGMENTS

Dr. Heather Anne Harder, Karen Bishop, Lynn Grabhorn, Barbara Rother, Patrice Fields, Psy.D., Morrnah Nalamaku Simeona, Maureen St. Germain, Mabel Katz, Lauren Gorgo, Stephanie Azaria, and Kamau Kokayi, M.D., with deep gratitude for all your lifetimes of incredible Guidance and Service. Thank you so much for having the courage to walk the path *first,* so I and many others could follow.

Sheila Bachmeier (DoLiv Publishing), your high-vibrational infusion while editing the class transcripts, along with all the support and encouragement you gave me during the early stages of this project made all this possible. Thank you, my magical friend.

A heartfelt thanks to my *"Directional Beacons,"* Daniella Tome-Whitaker, Michelle Ackhar (Brazil/Portuguese), Vivian Reynolds (Bolivia/Spanish), Ilaria Bochicchio (Italy/Italian), Patsy Balacchi (Graphic Design), and Diane Hoffmann

(Meticulous Editing). Without your major contributions of Love, Light, and Awesome Skills there would be no book or worldwide access to its guidance.

Stephanie Gunning, my incredible Editor/Alchemist on both *Feng Shui & Health* and *now The new 5D Human*, you've taken a *vibrationally* complicated manuscript and spun it into 5D gold—way beyond *its written words*. With heartfelt gratitude, thank you.

Orin the Great! I hope your stay on Jupiter is everything that you said it would be. Thank you for all of your help and reminders with my writing. I love you and miss you very much.

Julian Wolfe whose beautiful light has held the "sacred space" for me to become more of who I am. With great Love and Thanks for everything.

Greer Jonas, *"God's HUman Paintbrush."* With each channeled painting she makes this world a more beautiful place to be. So much gratitude for lifetimes of friendship and unconditional Love.

San J Pan Wan G. HUmanity doesn't know how blessed they are. Thank you for all your help during the pandemic. *I am a dreamer, too.*

His Holiness, Grand Master Thomas Lin Yun Rinpoche, thank you for having never left my side, even in the afterlife. Your Love and Guidance continues to HUmble me.

Steve Rother and *the Group,* my 5D Mentor for the past twenty-five years and my *Dad* in other Lives. You and Barbara have led an international community of LightWorkers to and through the 12/12/12 5D Ascension with much Love, Kindness, and Integrity, modeling by example what the best of a 5D HUman can ascribe to. I love you.

ACKNOWLEDGMENTS

To all my Clients, Students, Friends, former Lemurians and Atlanteans, especially those who had participated in the thirteen *"Bigger Picture"* webinar classes that became the foundation for this book, thank you for all your Lifetimes of LightWorker Service, for *you* all are the unsung heroes of our new 5D World! My heart is full of gratitude that you found me again and walked the path you said you would eons ago. *Espavo!*

NOTES

Chapter 1: Living in a Multidimensional Reality

1. Steve Rother and the Group, https://espavo.org.

Chapter 2: From Lemuria to Atlantis

1. Susan Miller-McCormick, my key Captain in Aveidon, Lemuria, provided the correct spelling of Aveidon during my classes in New York City.

Some of the Lemuria information was influenced by Shirley Andrews, author of *Lemuria and Atlantis: Studying the Past to Survive the Future* and *Atlantis: Insights from a Lost Civilization*. Other sources include:
- International group of researchers: http://thegreater picture.com/atlantis.php

- Fractal Enlightenment: https://fractalenlightenment.com
- Ascended Vibrations History of Lemuria: https://www.ascendedvibrations.love
- In 5D, "Team Earth," https://in5d.com/really-happened-lemuria-atlantis

Chapter 3: From Atlantis to Atlanta

1. Steve Rother and the Group. Planet Eargo was introduced in a class in fall 2019.
2. Stephanie Azaria, 5D Astrologer, reviewed Donald Trump's astrological chart in 2020.
3. Claire Kinsella Holtje coined the phrase *Atlantis to Atlanta*.

Chapter 4: A Pandemic Enters the Fray

1. Charles Osgood. "Everybody, Somebody, Anybody, and Nobody," Condensed version, SweatYourAssets.com (accessed August 19, 2022).
2. Patrice Fields, Psy.D., https://www.spirit-evolving.com.

Chapter 5: The New 5D Codex

1. Definition of chaos. Lexico.com (accessed August 19, 2022), available at https://www.lexico.com/en/definition/chaos.

Chapter 6: The 5D HUman

1. Mabel Katz. remark made during an online Ho'oponopono class 2016.

NOTES

Chapter 7: Great Power Comes with Great Responsibility

1. Steve Rother, *Spiritual Psychology: The Twelve Primary Life Lessons* (Las Vegas, NV.: Lightworker Publications, 2004).

Chapter 8: The 5D Upgrade

1. *Inner-net* is a term coined by Wendy Adams Mendenhall in the early 2000s.
2. H. Jackson Brown, Jr. *The Complete Life's Little Instruction Book* (Nashville, TN.: Thomas Nelson, 2000), item 322.

Chapter 9: A Spiritual Evolution of Epic Proportion

1. Lauren Gorgo's Think With Your Heart monthly news reports over the past decade inspired parts of Chapter 9 and other areas of this book. She is an amazing guide for the 5D Ascension and the Earth HUmans. To learn more about her work, visit www.NewEarthInstitute.love.

5D HUMAN RESOURCES

Experts and Services

Andie SantoPietro: 5D TransDimensional Healer, Therapist, Ascension Guide, Spiritual Teacher, and Author. *5D Psychotherapy, "Soul Talk" Sessions, Frequency Upgrades, 5D Feng Shui Consultations, and The Bigger Picture Series Webinars. www.AndieSantoPietro.com*

Steve Rother: Spiritual Teacher, Channeler of "The Group," Empowerment Specialist, and Author of 8 books (18 languages), including Re-member: A Handbook for Human Evolution and Spiritual Psychology: The Twelve Primary Life Lessons, *and 5D Webinars.* www.Espavo.org

Stephanie Azaria: 5D Cosmic Consciousness Astrologer, and Spiritual Teacher. *Highly Intuitive Master of Interpreting Advanced 5D Astrology Charts, Cosmic Consciousness for the Golden Age, Webinars, Creator of the www.TheCosmicPath.Love*

Kamau Kokayi, MD Holistic Medical Specialist in Primary Care: *Chinese Medicine, Homeopathy, Acupuncture, Applied Kinesiology, Biogeometry, Nutritional and Metaphysical Medicine. President of NY Homeopathic Medical Society. Offices in New York City and Los Angeles, California www.HealingHealthServices.com*

Patsy Balacchi, 5D Graphic Design, Visual Branding, and Vibrational Artistry: *Unique blend of Graphic Design, Feng Shui, and Biophilic Services for the Conscious Business Owner and Spiritually Evolving HUman. www.Zenotica.com*

Greer Jonas, 5D Inspirational Artist & Healer: *"God's HUman Paintbrush," Sculptor, Teacher, and Lemuria Prints and Notecards, New York City. www.GreerJonas.com*

ABOUT THE AUTHOR

Andie SantoPietro is a 5D Trans-Dimensional HUman. For over thirty-five years, s/he has been in service as a healer of both *Soul* and *Space,* guiding students and clients worldwide through the challenges of being a 5D HUman Living in a 3D World.

An International Lecturer and Best-selling Author of *Feng Shui: Harmony by Design* and *Feng Shui and Health: The Anatomy of a Home,* s/he currently offers 5D Soul-Talk Counseling, Frequency Upgrades, 5D Feng Shui Consultations, and *"The Bigger Picture"* webinars. *The Bigger Picture Series* Vol. 2 is due to be released in summer 2023.

Andie lives on the Beach in a *5th* floor apartment located on the *3rd Rock from the Sun.*

www.ingramcontent.com/pod-product-compliance
Lightning Source LLC
Chambersburg PA
CBHW062321120626
46553CB00015B/40